THE UNIT DEVELOPMENT OFFICER'S HANDBOOK

F. A. Hilenski, Editor

CASE

© 2002 by the Council for Advancement and Support of Education

ISBN 0-89964-369-8
Printed in the United States of America

The Council for Advancement and Support of Education is the largest
international association of education institutions, serving more than
3,200 universities, colleges, schools, and related organizations in 45
countries. CASE is the leading resource for professional development,
information, and standards in the fields of education fund
raising, communications, and alumni relations.

Editor: Theodore Fischer
Art Director: Angela A. Carpenter
Design: Barbara A. Shaw
Research: Laurie Calhoun

COUNCIL FOR ADVANCEMENT
AND SUPPORT OF EDUCATION®

1307 New York Avenue NW
Suite 1000
Washington DC 20005-4701
www.case.org/books

TABLE OF CONTENTS

Foreword v

Preface vii

Introduction: The Role of the Fund Raiser in the University College 1
       F. A. Hilenski

I. BACKGROUND

1   The Distinctive Role of the Unit Development Officer 31
    F. A. Hilenski

2   Evolution of the Unit Development Officer 39
    Margarete Rooney Hall

3   Characteristics of the Successful Unit Development Officer 49
    James W. Asp II

II. ESTABLISHING AND MAINTAINING KEY INSTITUTIONAL RELATIONSHIPS

4   The Unit Development Officer's Key Relationships
    Within the Campus 65
    John C. Halton III

5   The Unit Development Officer's Key Relationships
    with the Central Advancement Office 75
    Bayley Mason

6   The Unit Development Officer's Key Relationships
    with Disciplines and Institutions 87
    Molly Ford Croft

7   The Unit Development Officer's Key Relationships
    Outside the Campus 97
    Amy Doonan Cronin

8   Hiring, Training, and Supervising the Unit Development Officer 103
    Marta Garcia

9   The Durham Integrated Income Generation Model for Fund Raising 117
    Scott Hayter and *Peter Slee*

III. HANDLING THE COMPLEXITY OF UNIT DEVELOPMENT

10 Starting a Unit Development Office 129
Pamela Cook and *Dwain N. Fullerton*

11 Managing a Unit Development Office 139
John W. Crowe

12 Unit-Based Campaigning 153
Scott Nichols

13 Directing a Unit-Based Foundation 161
Paul Gardner

IV. MAKING THE CASE FOR UNIT DEVELOPMENT

14 Defining the Constituencies of the Unit Development Office 171
Dottie O'Carroll and *Harry Vann*

15 Making the Case for Development in the Academic Unit 185
James C. Schroeder

16 Making the Case for Development in Academic Support Units 199
Timothy L. Seiler

17 Making the Case for Development in Dedicated Research
and Service Units 207
Lawrance Bailey

V. UNIT DEVELOPMENT IN CANADA AND THE UNITED KINGDOM

18 Unit Development: A Canadian Perspective 221
Guy Mallabone

19 Unit Development in the United Kingdom 229
Tania Jane Rawlinson

Conclusion: Charting the Future of Unit Development 239
F. A. Hilenski

Bibliography 257

Contributors 261

Index 271

FOREWORD

Unit development officers (UDOs) are the people who handle fund raising for particular divisions of their institutions—academic colleges, professional schools, museums, theaters, research institutes, and foundations, among other types of units. Although UDOs represent the fastest-growing area of the advancement profession, their story so far has gone largely untold. Margarete Rooney Hall's *The Dean's Role in Fund Raising* (1993) was the first book to focus on the activities of collegiate development officers; the onset of unit development officers; and the evolution of centralized, decentralized, and hybrid academic fund raising. *The Unit Development Officer's Handbook,* edited by F. A. Hilenski, offers a far more comprehensive view of unit development. It traces the evolution of the profession, outlines the role of today's UDOs in various disciplines and settings, offers field-tested advice for effective performance, and charts a course for the continuing evolution of the position.

Although unit development now represents the cutting edge of contemporary academic fund raising, it boasts a long and storied past. The earliest efforts to link the academy to potential donors were made by medieval "benefaction-chasers" on behalf of the individual university colleges of Oxford and Cambridge, with centralized fund raising catching on only with the ascendance of the German research university model in the early 20th century. The UDO position itself emerged in the middle of the last century, often casually or accidentally as development officers on temporary assignment to conduct campaigns for a particular college remained permanently with the unit. In fact, the rise of present-day unit development offices represents a full-circle return to the roots of academic fund raising. As Hilenski notes in the Introduction, "the decentralized or distributed model for unit development that emerged in the 1950s and 1960s and came to predominate the university in the 1980s and 1990s stemmed from the seemingly spontaneous and unrelated decisions by individual deans to acquire their own development officers, either by hiring them outright or by browbeating the central office into assigning them. In so doing, they collectively and intuitively were—are—reclaiming a decanal function dating back to the founding of university colleges in the 11th and 12th centuries."

The Unit Development Officer's Handbook contains the original contributions of 22 authors working in advancement all over the United States as well as in the United Kingdom and Canada. Representing public and private institutions large and small, their units range in type from academic colleges and professional schools to affiliated institutes and foundations. This diversity of backgrounds notwithstanding, the writings address certain common themes and concerns, including the crucial importance of the personal and professional relationship between UDOs and their deans; the persistent challenge of delineating central office prospects from unit office prospects; the tightrope UDOs must walk to promote the whole institution while they make the case for their particular units; the inherent friction between UDOs with central development officers and, often, with the faculty of their units; the differences and similarities in the ways UDOs and central development officers go about their business; and the requisite personality traits and professional credentials of successful UDOs.

The Unit Development Officer's Handbook is an original and important work that has much to offer everyone who works in the development field. UDOs will receive a vivid depiction of the context of their position and specific advice for improving performance. Central development people and university administrators will gain perspective on what UDOs do and how they do it. What they will all learn are ways to put forth a coordinated effort to maximize fund raising for the institution—the ultimate goal of all development.

Vance T. Peterson
President, Council for Advancement and Support of Education
June 2002

PREFACE

Whenever the author or editor of a work attempts to describe the terra firma of a new discipline or field such as this one, questions of nomenclature inevitably occur. In my case, the question I asked myself repeatedly during the preparation of this book was, What should I call the position of the fund-raising officer who serves the colleges, schools, institutes, centers, laboratories, programs, libraries, museums, galleries, concert or performance halls, hospitals and clinics, and student services and housing offices of a university, both in the United States and, increasingly, in Canada and the United Kingdom?

In her landmark study, *The Dean's Role in Fund Raising* (1993), Margarete Rooney Hall coined the term "academic development officer" (ADO) to describe the position. But inasmuch as her work focused exclusively on officers who report to deans—that is, collegiate development officers—by the time I began to survey the field, almost ten years after her data were drawn, I thought the label was already too restrictive to describe the variety of units such officers were presently serving and certainly not indicative of the direction the position was heading.

So, in place of the word *academic* I substituted the word *unit* because I believe that most of what can be said about the experience of collegiate officers applies just as well to the experience of officers serving in other sub-units of the university (and vice versa), academic or not. I also thought the more generic term was appropriate because I believe the growth in this field is toward clearly nonacademic units like student services, housing, outreach services such as economic development offices or agricultural extension services, and other similar units of the ever-expanding multiversity model both here and abroad.

A second issue I had regarding Hall's label for the position concerned the word *development*. In fact, up until the point where almost all of chapters of this book had been assembled, the operative term in use was *unit advancement officer*. My rationale was rather narrowly based on my own career experience, in that the position description for three of my four appointments as a unit officer actually included responsibilities for communications and alumni relations as well as development. However, in reading the chapters submitted by my colleagues, many of whom had had careers as long and varied as mine, it became clear to me that I was somewhat unusual in having the full advancement "package" on my plate. Most of my authors, as do most of my readers, I believe, clearly see themselves as fund raisers or development officers first and foremost, even if in their day-to-day routines they also have to edit the newsletter or plan the homecoming reception. Such versatility is all just part and parcel of the complexity of the position. So ultimately, I decided on the term *unit development officer* (UDO) as the appropriate title for this role.

Once the material for the book was assembled, an unanticipated debate arose regarding the title of the book. Two issues in particular caused me grief, the first concerning the term *handbook*. The standard definition of a handbook describes it as "a manual or small reference book providing specific information or instruction about a subject, activity, place, or the like," which certainly described what I had in mind throughout the writing phase of the book. Looking at the assembled chapters as a whole, however, I wondered if that definition still fit the true nature of the work. Nietzsche had noted that there are basically just two forms of knowledge in the world: the knowledge one gets from books and theories, which he called *wissen*, and the knowledge one gets from personal experience, which is *erfahrung*. At the end of the day, which kind of knowledge did this book actually represent?

Certainly it had begun as *erfahrung*. After serving five different deans in four different colleges in three different universities over a 22-year advancement career—in every case being the first full-time officer to fill the UDO position—I was convinced I was seeing patterns of experience repeat themselves in my professional practice, regardless of the unit or institution I was serving, that were not described in the professional literature or even discussed at professional meetings. So as to generalize and confirm these patterns, I asked several current and former UDOs to share their experience-based insights—their *erfahrung*—on the work that they do. Despite their diversity in terms of geography, gender, genus of institution, and gestation in office, these authors displayed a remarkable consensus that seemed to confirm the parameters and dynamics of the position I saw. Still, I was uncertain about what kind of book we collectively had wrought.

The opinions of those from whom I sought advice were evenly divided on the matter. Those who said the book was not a handbook—the *wissen* school—thought such a term trivialized the new ground the material breaks regarding the origin of the position and undervalued the arguments made as to the true status of the position in the context of the academy. Those who said it was a handbook—the *erfahrung* school—emphasized the depth and breadth of the collective experience the book mines and the extraordinary delineation of the lessons learned from this experience captured in the "Recommendations for Best Practice." I suffered several weeks' more author's angst than perhaps was warranted over this issue until the new editor at CASE Books, Terry Fischer—who, like all good editors, is of the school of common sense—observed simply that development officers as a breed are highly practical people, so calling it a handbook would probably appeal to them. That argument tipped the scales for me; thus, *Handbook* remains in the title—although I still have my doubts.

This decision also helped to clarify the other concern I had regarding the title—for whom was this book written? When I began this work, my most ambitious hope was that it would mark the coming of age, as it were, of the UDO position, that it would delineate the role so definitively that the post could take its place alongside that of the annual giving officer, the major gifts officer, the corporate officer, the foundations officer, and the planned gifts officer as one of the recognized subspecialties of educational fund raising. Toward this end, I felt strongly that the dynamics of the position needed to be better understood not only by all of the various types of development officers, but also by the many relevant administrative positions with whom UDOs interact—alumni directors, public relations heads, development vice presidents, university presidents, and, most certainly, deans, department heads, and directors of the various sub-units of the university. Strong as this ambition was and important as these audiences were, clarifying the title and thus the purpose of the book helped me to maintain the focus on the primary audience of this book—the individual UDO currently serving in the field.

Located often in offices where their immediate co-workers could care less about their work (although they may care a great deal about the outcomes of their work), isolated frequently both by space and circumstance from the day-to-day interplay, dialogue, and peer support of their professional colleagues, UDOs are the lonely long-distance runners among university fund raisers. Indeed, I believe these officers do the single most challenging job in all of development and are perhaps the least recognized for their effort. Moreover, they are *my* colleagues, and I am proud to consider myself one of their number. Thus, among other things, this book is an attempt both to define and honor their—our—unique professionalism.

And especially to the UDOs who contributed their knowledge and expertise to this book—thank you. I am forever indebted to each and every one of you not only for your thoughtfulness and insight but also for your exceptional patience and uniform good spirits during a prolonged period of publication.

In closing, I must say a word about the giants upon whose shoulders my colleagues and I stand. Personally, I see myself as working in a tradition of nascent scholarship in this "minor profession" of ours, to employ Nathan Galzer's useful terminology. In this regard, this book would have been inconceivable without Hall's seminal work, *The Dean's Role in Fund Raising* (1993), a must read for every UDO. Not only was she the first to define the field, but also she placed it in the context of university decentralization that provides the perspective necessary to see the position in its true light.

The first half of the decade of the 1990s produced several other works that also contributed enormously to our understanding of the field. *The Campus Green: Fund Raising in Higher Education* (1990), by Barbara E. Brittingham and Thomas R. Pezzullo, provided the first thoughtful overview of the origins, practice, issues, and research relevant to the growing importance of college and university development. *The Development Officer in Higher Education: Toward an Understanding of the Role* (1994), by Michael J. Worth and James W. Asp II, was the first work to characterize the generic role of the development officer within the university setting. I am especially grateful to Peg Hall and Jim Asp for updating their models and applying their insights to the particular situation of the contemporary UDO.

In addition, the demi-decade of the 1990s also saw the publication of *Educational Fund Raising: Principles and Practice* (1993), edited by Michael J. Worth. Besides being the first work to make a conscious attempt to define this emerging profession, this book also captured in print for the first time the comprehensive systemic template of perhaps the most original and influential thinker in educational development today—David Dunlop. His chapter, "Major Gift Programs," is timeless. Which leads us finally to Dunlop's idol and mentor, who is in fact the source and foundation of all serious writing about professional fund raising, and that is Harold J. Seymour. His *Designs for Fund-Raising: Principles, Patterns, Techniques* (1966/1992) is, of course, the great classic of the field; but one should not overlook Seymour's lesser-known first book on the subject of fund raising, *Design for Giving: The Story of the National War Fund, Inc. 1943–47* (1947). This work not only describes the operations of the profession during a vital period of its pre-history, as it were, but it also provides insight into Seymour's "middle-thinking" on fund raising that grounded his later writings, making it all the more fertile for my own.

In the Preface to the first edition of *Designs for Fund-Raising*, Seymour wrote of his hope that, as a result of his book, "it will be better understood that if [the] vineyards [of philanthropy] are to thrive and bear their best fruit, they must always have first-class attention." The scholars and thinkers I have named herein certainly have provided the quality and kind of attention Seymour enjoined, as well as the standard the present work seeks to emulate.

INTRODUCTION

The Role of the Fund Raiser in the University College

F. A. Hilenski

Director of Development and Communication,
Ivan Allen College, Georgia Institute of Technology

THOSE WHO REPEAT THE PAST ARE CONDEMNED TO FORGET IT.
—F. A. Hilenski, satirically rephrasing George Santayana

In 1993, I was fortunate to receive a so-called CASE Fulbright Fellowship to study university fund raising in the United Kingdom. During a visit that year to the development office for Balliol College, Oxford, I was graciously afforded the hospitality of the Master's Guest House. Its understated decor impressed me—as it was no doubt designed to—with both the history and eminence of the ancient university college and its unpretentious but obvious wealth.

In my bedroom there that evening, just before dropping off, I found myself idly perusing *Balliol College, A History: 1263–1939*, Professor John Jones's (1988) award-winning chronicle of an institution that, along with University and Merton Colleges, Oxford, can lay claim to being the oldest extant university college in the English-speaking world. Skimming through the initial chapters, I remember still how surprised I was to find myself in intellectual territory that—despite vast differences in time and locale—seemed oddly familiar. As I read on, it became increasingly clear that the reason I found this material so familiar was because much of Jones's history consists of accounts of the patronage, or "benefaction," afforded Balliol over the course of its almost 750 years of existence. With a growing sense of discovery, I stayed up most of the night poring over Jones's descriptions of the lives of the college's many donors, what they gave, how they gave it, and how the college ultimately disposed of both donors and gifts—that is, the stuff of the contact reports that I, as a university development officer, read daily.

A History Lesson from Oxford

As a development officer who had spent essentially his entire career advancing various colleges within several universities, I was especially edified to read the exploits of Balliol's great "benefaction-chasers"—deans or masters of the ancient college who were especially adept at encouraging the generosity of donors. They above all seemed to have understood that, as Jones wryly observed, "the character and fortunes of a college are determined . . . as much by its members as its money, provided of course that there is enough of the latter" (1988, 134). Jones, who is a tutor of physics at Balliol, concluded his history by noting with all seriousness that the college, as "it looks forward to the next century . . . [must] not forget its long history, *nor its benefactors, without whom there would be no future to contemplate*" (279, italics mine).

He ended the book by quoting in full an ancient Balliol Bidding Prayer, in which "We render most humble and hardy thanks unto Thee, O Eternal and Heavenly Father, for all Thy gifts and graces most bountifully and mercifully bestowed upon us; and namely, *for Thy benefits, or Exhibitions and maintenance . . . by the liberality of [our benefactors]*" (279–280, italics mine), each of whom is then cited by name. Lying that night among the abundant physical and intellectual luxuries of the college, I could not help but be impressed—as a development officer—by the correlation between the length and quality of that prayerful listing and the obvious results of those prayers surrounding me.

At High Table the next day, I was fortunate enough to encounter Professor Jones himself. Over coffee, I asked him why nearly the entire first half of his 280-page book, which covered the first 300 or so years of Balliol history, described little other than the business of "securing the benefactions." His answer was as straightforward as it was illuminating: "Because that is the documentation contained in the college archives."

Startled by the implications of his response, I pressed. "Are you saying that the bulk of the papers that have managed to survive from the college's earliest history are those that pertain to what today we would call 'development' or 'fund raising'?"

He took a sip of his coffee and replied, "That is essentially correct. But actually, it's more deliberate than that. It's not a matter of these documents accidentally surviving. Rather, *these are the documents the college chose to keep and preserve*."

I relate the minute details of this visit, and especially of this conversation, because those words in the context of that moment constituted what could be described only as a professional epiphany. In that instant, I understood with crystalline clarity both the ancient and essential role of fund raising in the university college and my role as a functionary within the institution. Only then did I realize just how profound a product of philanthropy Balliol was, and that the record of its benefactions constituted both its most vital and valuable institutional memory and its fundamental identity as a college. The implications were clear: Inasmuch as Balliol's existence had been and always would be dependent on "chasing benefactions," the task of fund raising had been and always would be an essential and integral a part of college life. To the extent that all American colleges and universities stem from the English university model, I also realized that fund raising must be therefore an essential and integral part of these institutions as well.

This realization provided powerful insight into my role as a college (or unit) development (or advancement) officer. It enabled me to understand my job in a new light and to perform my professional duties with a renewed sense of purpose and pride. Specifically, it gave me a clearly defined place and authority within the academy. Previously, I had simply assumed along with my colleagues and faculty that university fund raising was a relatively recent phenomenon, distinctly if not uniquely characteristic of the American university in the modern era. I had also assumed that the role of the academic development officer derived from fund-raising professionals who flourished in the for-profit consulting world beyond the academy. Concomitantly, I had acknowledged and learned to live with the fund raiser's humble status as an auxiliary to the academy at best, a necessary evil at worst, and an interloper in any case. After Oxford, I realized that none of these assumptions were true. As the history of Balliol makes abundantly clear, universities have always engaged in fund raising. Even if fund-raising or development officers are new to the scene, the academy has always had individuals—presidents, deans, bursars, or faculty members—who functioned as fund raisers.

In addition, modern university development officers in general and certainly university college development officers in particular—together with presidents, deans, and others who raise money for their institutions—are vested with a special authority by the academy. Adhering to the tradition of historic academic fund raisers, they possess the distinct if not unique authority to negotiate the terms and conditions of the gifts that will create and sustain the identity of the institution. As Abrams, a fund-raising consultant, and Travers, an English professor and former development officer, explained, ". . . asking for a major gift is really negotiating a contract. In exchange for the gift, the institution will perform a series of specific acts that [the institutional fund raiser] and the donor have negotiated" (2000, 8). The institutional fund raiser's role is to instruct donors that the terms and conditions that constitute their individual contracts with the institution further constitute an implicit social contract by which the constituent community (as represented collectively by its donors) agrees to provide for the institution's continued support.

With this renewed sense of purpose, I found myself taking increased pride not only in my tradecraft as a fund raiser but also in my office within the university. But I continued to wonder what exactly were the historical links between my role as a collegiate development officer and that of those benefaction chasers of old? I quickly realized that the history of university fund raising was usually hidden from direct view, and, even where exposed, hard to see clearly. For the most part, it is as if the almost eight centuries of university fund raising history did not exist or was deemed irrelevant to today's fund-raising enterprises. On the rare occasions when this history is acknowledged, it is often marginalized or treated as a quaint embarrassment, like the discovery of a humble or disreputable ancestor in an otherwise distinguished family lineage. After Oxford, I realized that such perceptions of historic university fund raising stemmed from intellectual blinders put in place by modern professional fund raising itself.

Whenever "non-cumulative developmental episodes" in a given discipline or field become "incompatible" with the old, a new paradigm ensues (see Kuhn 1970, 92–94, 97–98). All new paradigms are revolutionary, inasmuch as it is the nature of revolutions to break radically with the past by ignoring or obliterating history altogether. As it evolved over the first half of the 20th century, modern professional fund raising comprises just such a paradigm and thus a revolution, inasmuch as the new ideology—philanthropy—that drives it is usually incompatible with past notions of charity and charitable practice.

Today, charity usually connotes providing relief or serving the poor by means of direct appeal or begging. Philanthropy "takes a more impersonal and dispassionate approach to bettering the human condition by institutionalizing giving," focusing on the root causes of human problems and systematic reform rather than the immediate condition of people, and "recognizing a responsibility to the public interest . . . to effect social change" (cited in Brittingham and Pezzullo 1990, 6). Modern professional fund raising, as it developed during this period, deliberately ignored or obliterated its humble if lengthy previous history, the better to invent itself anew in light of the progressive social ethos of the time. When, during the latter half of this timeframe, universities began accepting the agents and agency of modern professional fund raising to fuel their own progressive social transformations, they also admitted the new fund-raising paradigm and its attendant disregard for history. As a consequence, both the lineage and the success of modern university fund raisers are typically traced solely to the nonacademic fund raisers whose practices they employ. "The role of the college or university development officer . . . originated in the for-profit consulting world," and the "legacy of this history may account, at least in part, for why there continues to be a perceived cultural gap between [development officers] and members of the academic community" (Worth and Asp 1994, 9).

But if the role of the modern college or university development officer originated in the for-profit consulting world, its function did not. Rather, I would argue that the function of the present-day college or university development officer is, as Hall (1993) noted in her landmark study, *The Dean's Role in Fund Raising*, ". . . as old as higher education in America" (30). Indeed, as the history of Balliol illustrates, it is as old as higher education in Western Civilization itself. If university development officers allow themselves to be defined solely in terms of their professional practice, they ignore their historic role as educators and negotiators of the social contract that defines the societal relevance of universities. Rather than interlopers in the academic community, the role of the fund raiser thus dates from the very onset of the institution and is at the heart of the academic enterprise.

Before they can expect others to perceive their historic roles and attendant responsibilities, development officers must begin to recognize and recover their history. No one else will do it for them. As Hall noted,

> The battle to bring the development function into the mainstream of higher education management was hard fought and only recently won. The establishment of central development offices headed by vice presidents signaled that universities had accepted development as a full partner in managing higher education. [The establishment of advancement offices within units] is perceived by many academic leaders and advancement officers as a retreat from the commitment to development's role as one of the key functions of high-level university leadership. (1993, 30)

Certainly, the university's central development office may find it difficult to see the relevance of this history. But in the university college, where fund raising is bound up with the mundane business of academic life and the unit development officer depends as much on maintaining an extraordinary range of relationships and managing complexity as on tradecraft, the relevance of history receives daily confirmation and affirmation. If we unit development officers are to become better fund-raising practitioners, we must become better students of our office. This Handbook therefore begins with a review of the historic origins of fund raising and the role of the fund raiser in the American university.

Fund Raising in Early American Colleges

As Brittingham and Pezzuillo (1990) noted in an excellent chapter on the history of university fund raising, "American philanthropy as we know it is a European import, developed from European traditions and institutions and often, in colonial times, nurtured with contributions from European donors" (5). But, like most American traditions and institutions, philanthropy was entirely reconceived and reborn in the New World by "men and women who crossed the Atlantic to establish communities that would be better than, instead or like or different from, the ones they had known at home" (Bremner 1960, 7). From the start, these people viewed the American college as one of these improved institutions. Thus, between the founding of Harvard College in 1636 and the U.S. centennial in 1876, colonists and later citizens transformed the British university college into a discreet and unique institution ideally suited to perform functions of settlement and nation building.

In the beginning, fund raising per se was not a designated role in American colleges, but rather an integral function of everyday college life, as it was in British universities. Patterning themselves after the university colleges of Oxford and Cambridge, early colonial colleges adopted their methods and manner of obtaining financial support (see Hofstadter and Wilson 1961, 2). For the most part, fund raising fell to the college president, as was the case with the English college master or dean. Along with recruiting the students, establishing the curricula, and even teaching classes, colonial college presidents industriously sought funding. They solicited local governments for financial support, set up giving circles, and wrote endless begging letters to sympathetic constituents and alumni for modest contributions, which often came in the form of produce or labor. At times, desperation drove them to try more dubious means, such as lotteries, which "Fair Harvard" pioneered, tendering no less than four such offerings between 1775 and 1806 (see Cutlip 1965, 5).

But whereas the fund raising done by the master or dean of an English university college could build on the concentrated wealth and influence of an established church and aristocracy, the fund raising conducted by the president of an American college had no such basis in colonial society. Fund raising for colonial colleges, therefore, almost invariably included a trip to the motherland, beginning with the famous Weld-Peter "begging mission" on behalf of Harvard in 1642 (see Cutlip 1965, 3–4). There, they sought and found (the Harvard solicitors subscribed more than £500 in commitments) support among the wealthy of Great Britain who were both familiar with the traditional role of patron and sympathetic to the vision and promise of the New World (see Rudolph 1962, 178).

Then as now, colonial college presidents played the key roles in obtaining truly historic benefactions. As Hall notes (Chapter 2, this volume), "their tasks then were similar to those of presidents today: They traveled, gave speeches, and invited potential donors to campus. They also built personal and professional friendships with potential donors based on shared interests in the content or the process of higher education—friendships that often resulted in philanthropic support." In so doing, these early presidents relied on Old World precedents to guide their actions.

Thus, when Nathaniel Eaton took up his duties as the first master of the college founded at Newtowne by the Massachusetts Bay Colony, he also assumed the implicit task of fund raising. He did not, however, have to invent a revolutionary new way of funding his school. A graduate of Cambridge who doubtless understood his new role in the context of a Cambridge college master or dean, Eaton simply followed the example of those at Cambridge who had been soliciting benefactions for more than 400 years. Thus, in bringing the Reverend John Harvard, a fellow Cambridge graduate, to visit the new school, he was employing a practice that had proven successful in similar situations throughout the history of English universities (see Hall 1993, 31). And in responding to Eaton's solicitations, the Reverend Harvard, a prosperous Puritan clergyman recently arrived in New England, conscientiously followed the lead of other wealthy Cambridge alumni and patrons by leaving a benefence in his will that, upon his death in 1638, effectively instituted a new university college, if not for his British alma mater then for one modeled closely on it.

Although the organization and operation of early American colleges and universities closely resembled those of their counterparts and predecessors in England and Scotland, their institutional origins, and thus their social raison d'être, were entirely different. Although both Old World and New World institutions were founded by pilgrims who sought religious freedom, Oxford and Cambridge had been established by migrating communities of professional scholars, whereas Harvard, William and Mary, Yale, and others were started by settlements of nonacademic laypeople. The English university college was and is essentially self-governed by its faculty, with only a lay "board of visitors" to help adjudicate decisions the faculty cannot or will not decide for itself. In stark contrast, the American college was and still is usually governed by community leaders outside of the academy. Harvard College was created by an official act of the General Court of the Massachusetts Bay Colony, headed by the governor. It is governed to this day by a Board of Overseers—note the nomenclature—which initially consisted of six magistrates and six ministers of the colony and pointedly excluded members of either the faculty or the administration (see Hofstadter and Wilson 1961, 3, 14–15).

In the colonial era, these lay communities were usually sectarian, and so their early promotional tracts touted the contributions colleges were making toward fulfilling a sectarian vision of community. For example, "New England's First Fruits" (1643)—often described as the first university case statement—addressed the predilections of a mostly Puritan donor pool by emphasizing the efforts the Massachusetts Bay Colony's college toward educating clergy and converting the "heathen Indian." Many more tracts and trips were to follow, all designed to interest one segment or another of English donors. In 1753, Thomas Clap made the definitive case for the sectarian American college by asserting the moral if not legal obligation of such institutions to observe and keep trust with the original intent of their donor constituents, who were almost invariably "Church-Men"—an argument that may constitute the first statement of donor rights in American history (see Hofstadter and Wilson 1961, 6–7, 91–95, 111–116).

But changes in the demographics and the aspirations of host constituencies necessarily brought about changes in the case for support as well. As the colonies approached independence, college presidents, instead of lauding comparisons with their English prototypes, began to draw sharper distinctions between British and American institutions. Principal among the differences commonly cited was the superiority of American colleges in the formation of moral character, a claim that proved especially popular among the American sectarian communities to which colleges increasingly had to turn for donors.

Because these communities were always looking for ways to demonstrate their spiritual superiority over those their members had left behind, American colleges throughout the colonial and early national periods were widely promoted as instruments of Christian evangelicalism, essential to the progress of civilization in the New World (see Hoftstadter and Smith 1961, 115–117, 140–141). During the Great Awakening, an American religious revival that peaked during the 1740s, the brilliant English evangelist George Whitfield, over the course of his seven visits to the colonies, hailed the good work of Harvard, Dartmouth, Princeton, the University of Pennsylvania, and many other Protestant American colleges in steering young men into the ways of righteousness. He routinely took up collections of books and money for their support. "If no single institution can be regarded as his monument, the reason is partly that he helped so many" (Bremner 1960, 23), although Whitfield's largess was a matter of some controversy (see also Hofstadter and Wilson 1961, 62–74).

Whitfield's success in raising such funds led presidents of American colleges for the next century and a half to deploy a small army of itinerant clergymen as agent-solicitors to canvass sectarian American communities for gifts for their institutions (see Cutlip

1965, 5, Rudolph 1962, 182–183). Indeed, until after the Civil War, "The American college was an expression of Christian charity, both in the assistance that it gave to needy young men and in the assistance that it received from affluent old men" (Rudolph 1962, 178).

Be that as it may, as the forces of sectarianism throughout the colonies began to dissipate in the growing tide of nationalism, the constituent communities governing even sectarian American colleges grew more secular and democratic. The charters of late colonial colleges such as Columbia, Princeton, and Brown, although factional, nonetheless made liberal allowance for the inclusion of individuals of all Christian denominations. This policy of inclusion covered not only their respective student bodies but also their faculties and boards of trustees, enabling them to broaden their base of support as well as to moderate their stridency (see Hofstadter and Wilson 1961, 99–103, 134, 145–146).

An important factor mitigating such sectarianism was the direct monetary support many early American colleges also received from local communities. This support often came directly out of governmental treasuries, with no notice whatsoever taken of what historian Rudolph called "the romantic regard" later generations paid to distinctions between the "public" or "private" nature of these institutions. In fact, state legislatures began terminating direct financial subsidies to private institutions only in the early 1800s, when the sheer number of newly established colleges began to drain their treasuries, and the practice did not entirely end until after the Civil War. Even now, both the state and federal governments assert some control over private institutions, directly through the regulation of grants and contracts and indirectly through the granting of tax-exempt status, a subsidy "of incalculable and uncalculated value" (see Rudolph 1962, 184–190). In order to gain valuable start-up funding and maintain a base of financial support, private as well as public colleges of the era therefore had to serve the civic needs and aspirations of the young republic.

And, too, the birth of the new nation at the end of the 18th century saw the advent of state universities as pure expressions of secular American nationalism and democracy. The trend began with the University of Georgia (1785), the University of North Carolina (1789), and the University of Tennessee (1797), and it culminated in Jefferson's University of Virginia (1825). Routine support through annual state appropriations did not come until later, though, with the University of South Carolina becoming in 1833 the first state institution to receive an annual appropriation from the state legislature. The establishment of a political rather than sectarian community as the primary constituency of a university, however, signaled a revolutionary departure from the English university college model, wherein the influence of Scottish educators and universities and later German research universities were to have an indelible impact. Rudolph wrote:

In the decades after the Civil War . . . the American people turned to the state universities . . . as institutions that were attempting to generalize what had once been the proper education for an English gentleman, attempting to democratize it, to transfer it from the exclusive domain of a particular religious-social purpose and group to the people at large. To this purpose were added a deep sense of public service and a commitment, however difficult to support, to the ideals that were embedded in the [emergent modern American university]. (1962, 286)

Given these circumstances, the health of the relationship between a college or university and its constituent community was of vital and ongoing concern to the early college president—as it is to college presidents today. The well-being, if not the very existence, of the institution depended on the perception of its relevance to the core needs and aspirations of its host community. At the same time, the early college president was still the general factotum of his institutional community. He admitted and registered students, dealt with housing and disciplining students, hired and supervised faculty, and oversaw everyday operations of the school—everything from ordering books for the library to setting the menus for meals—all while teaching a full load of classes. Veysey (1970) also noted the president's constant need to simultaneously attend to both an internal and an external constituency, stating that the American college president prior to 1900 played a dual role "as spokesman for an educational experiment and manager of a concrete enterprise" (310).

The rather sudden and certainly unplanned emergence of the modern American university at the close of the 19th and beginning of the 20th centuries, as nationalism linked with progressivism in the still-new nation, is another instance of the American college responding to the changing needs and aspirations of its constituent communities. Unlike previous shifts in the ideological firmament, however, this one provoked a radical revision of the mission of American higher education. This time the preservation, and more important, the generation, of knowledge for the benefit of a self-consciously American civilization became its overriding purpose. This shift also provoked a corresponding radical reorganization of the managerial framework of the classic American college, and most particularly in the role and function of the college president. Although, in 1902, Nicholas Murray Butler at Columbia would still be performing the dual tasks of president and dean, the era in which the college president would serve as both spokesperson for a particular educational experiment and manager of a concrete academic enterprise was already coming to a close (see Veysey 1970, 305–307).

With regard to fund raising, the post–Civil War era also marked a corresponding shift away from "church-affiliated and individual and personal solicitation to direct institutional appeals of an organized and professional nature" (Worth and Asp 1994, 13). The nation, too, was about to undergo a corresponding shift away from charity as it had been traditionally understood for thousands of years, toward philanthropy, with its emphasis on gifts as investments valued in noncharitable terms. In the modern era, a gift increasingly would be valued according to its impact on society, its investment value to corporations, and its tax advantages to the wealthy. In this sense, a gift became less a one-way beneficence and more an exchange—that is, the trading of tangible wealth or goods for an intangible influence or presence. Even so, no one could have foreseen how this shift would facilitate the widespread acceptance of fund raising throughout American institutions of higher education and move fund raising into the predominant role it plays in all aspects of modern-day university life (see Worth and Asp 1994, 13–14).

Fund Raising in the Modern American University

The era of the modern American university—and the era of the modern American university presidency—arrived in essentially two stages. The first occurred in the 1860s and 1870s with the presidential appointments of, for example, Andrew D. White to Cornell, Charles W. Eliot to Harvard, and James B. Angell to Michigan—all of them brandishing the new Ph.D. degree from German research universities and committed to reinventing the American college in their image. Their aggressiveness, their concern for budgets and public relations, and, most important, their interest in expanding their base of institutional support marked a new style and standard of academic executive. It also signaled which of the traditional dual presidential functions the modern university president would emphasize.

The second phase of administrative transformation began in the 1890s when various new services conducted by the president's office began to spin off into separate satellite administrative centers. Eventually, they settled into the solar system of bureaucratic infrastructure that exists in most American universities today (see Veysey 1970, 267–268, 305–307). It was during this second phase that the modern central development office emerged—but it was by no means a straight-line evolution. In developing the business side of the university, the American university was responding once again to changes in its relevant constituency. The Industrial Revolution had created enormous new wealth, establishing for the first time a class of American nouveaux riches with considerable disposable income. The great exemplar of this class was Andrew Carnegie. In his famous essay, "Wealth," published in 1889 in the *North American Review*, Carnegie argued that those with the ability to acquire extraordinary means had a God-given duty not simply to pass along their fortunes to their families, but to administer them as public trusts for the well-being of the nation.

This creed ushered in an era of what historian Cutlip (1965) called "big-scale philanthropy." Gifts by the new wealth transformed old institutions like Harvard and Yale. They also founded whole new institutions like Duke, Vanderbilt, Cornell, Chicago, and Johns Hopkins, creating the new American university model and catapulting higher education into new realms of socio-cultural power and influence. It was a heady time, and because, as Veysey (1970) observed, "money had to be wooed," the newly empowered university presidents became increasingly enamored—and accomplished—suitors of wealth.

In the same period essentially all the modern professions were formalized and credentialed by the academy, including medicine, law, and business management (see Bledstein 1988, 288–290). The expanding wealth and influence of the professional and business sectors of modern American society naturally attracted the attention of modern university presidents ever in search of resources to support sometimes-grandiose schemes for institutional expansion. In turn, the increasing presence of these new professionals on university boards of trustees and in newly formed alumni organizations constantly reminded the modern university of its obligations to the real-world constituencies outside the academy (see Veysey 1970, 308, 346–351). The implicit give-and-take of this new dynamic crystallized during the early decades of the 20th century, particularly with regard to the method and the manner in which universities sought new financial support.

A pivotal figure in the evolution of these new mechanisms of support was Bishop William Lawrence, a graduate of the Harvard Class of 1871. Although he was by trade and tradition of the old school of clergy-dominated Harvard overseers, by vision and inclination Lawrence was at the forefront of what John D. Rockefeller called the "business of benevolence," especially as it pertained to universities. To his eternal credit (or blame), Bishop Lawrence was the first to conceive the idea of petitioning alumni to support their alma mater en masse and in an organized and sustained manner. In response to President Eliot's vision of a Harvard that would be national in scope and research-oriented in mission, Lawrence, upon his election as president of the Harvard Alumni Association in 1904, called on fellow alumni to contribute some $2.5 million to increase the salaries of professors in the liberal arts. The 1904 Harvard campaign—or "appeal," as the Bishop preferred to call it—became a watershed in the history of university resource development, marking the beginning of the large-scale alumni drives that came to dominate educational fund raising over the course of the 20th century.

As the architect of this campaign, Bishop Lawrence stressed the importance of soliciting large lead gifts up front, of implementing organized and systematic peer-to-peer donor solicitations, and of conducting the appeal over a protracted but fixed period of time. If other aspects of this prototypic campaign seem dated—he decreed that there was to be "no crowding or jamming for subscriptions" and thought it best "not to complete the full amount" of the goal rather than risk losing "the good will and confidence of the alumni" (see Cutlip 1965, 35, 50–53)—it is because subsequent fund-raising founding fathers asserted even greater influence.

Contributing equally to the debut of modern fund raising were Charles Sumner Ward and Lyman L. Pierce, contemporaries of Bishop Lawrence produced by the same genteel Yankee society and moralistic Christian upbringing. Like Lawrence, both began their careers in religious vocations, in their case as executives in the YMCA movement, which at the time was enjoying a tremendous surge in growth and popularity as a tangible manifestation of the "muscular Christianity." As general secretary of the YMCA in Grand Rapids, MI, in 1890, Ward grew frustrated with the organization's scattered and inefficient manner of fund raising. "Out of this irritation," wrote Cutlip (1965), "was born Ward's methodical plan for getting the fund raising chore done all at once, and done quickly" (41). In short order, Ward's success at raising money in Grand Rapids caught the attention of YMCA executives, and soon he was being loaned out to other chapters to fix their ailing fund-raising mechanisms as well. In 1899, his fund-raising prowess landed him a position on the national headquarters staff in Chicago, where aiding various YMCA fund-raising efforts became his full-time job.

In 1905, Lyman Pierce, secretary of the Washington, DC, YMCA, invited Ward to help complete a stalled campaign for building expansion. Their collaboration yielded a fund-raising methodology that would revolutionize charitable giving and give birth to modern professional fund raising (see Cutlip 1965, 40–50). This campaign set the pattern for what became known as the "whirlwind campaign." Unlike Bishop Lawrence's alumni campaign, which lasted more than two years, the whirlwind campaign took place over an extremely short time span—typically a month or less—amidst a flurry of activity and publicity.

Planning a whirlwind campaign involved several distinct stages. After months of careful organizing, the campaign itself would be launched with a grand kickoff dinner. By promising not to solicit guests at the event, campaign managers enticed community leaders and officials—one of whom had been persuaded beforehand to chair the appeal—to attend and endorse the campaign's goals. The kickoff dinner typically culminated with the announcement of a large, previously secured lead gift—usually somewhere between one-tenth and one-third of the goal—that would be forthcoming only if the remaining amount was raised in the timeframe allotted. In addition to community leaders and officials, Ward and Pierce invited a carefully screened list of prospects to the kickoff dinner. To follow up on the impetus of dinner, they organized volunteer solicitors into competitive teams, complete with captains and quotas, to call on these prospects, and they carefully monitored their activities daily.

Cutlip (1965) quoted a newspaper account of the 1905 Washington YMCA campaign that noted, "It was easily to be seen yesterday by a visit to the [campaign] headquarters that no energy was lacking. The work of officials and clerks reminded the visitor of the stirring times at national headquarters during the recent [presidential] campaign" (43). Events and activities were orchestrated to build in intensity as the campaign progressed toward the deadline. In a calculated race against time, suspense as to whether the campaign would meet the goal was relieved by the dramatic announcement of a last-minute gift that put the campaign over the top. The tension was such that "tears of joy and cries of exultation" (43–44) would greet the news of success. The Fremont, OH, *Daily News* reported that, upon the announcement of the success of a Pierce-led campaign for a hospital building, "Men and women stood upon the chairs and cheered until the . . . building shook from wall to wall. Such a demonstration was never before witnessed in the old town" (91).

The whirlwind campaign became the backbone of the "Ward Method" or "Pierce Method" of fund raising as promulgated by the consulting firms they and their protégés established later. Its key was the skillful employment of the tactics and techniques of public relations, a field that itself was in its infancy. Ward and Pierce understood its importance to their endeavor from the outset, hiring a full-time publicity agent to support the Washington YMCA campaign. As Ward explained, "The job of these publicity men was to make sure that the newspapers were supplied with the day-to-day material necessary to keep a campaign on the front page. Headlines, front-page editorials, and cartoons aroused the city's team spirit" (cited in Cutlip 1965, 45).

Ward and Pierce also pioneered the use of paid advertisements for campaigns, with sponsors picking up the costs. Typical of these ads was a full-page spread in the Washington *Times* on Sunday, April 23, that used a mock news-story format with the headline, "The Y.M.C.A.'s Fight Against Time to Raise $50,000." To set the stage and create the mass tension necessary to a successful advertising campaign, Ward invented the campaign clock or thermometer to display at a glance the time elapsed and amounts raised. This device became a hallmark of his later campaigns and, indeed, of all whirlwind-style campaigns even today (see Cutlip 1965, 45–46).

With the dramatic success of the 1913 YMCA Campaign in New York City, which raised $4 million in two weeks with no other than John D. Rockefeller offering the initial lead gift, Ward became nationally famous as "the whirlwind collector." In 1914, after witnessing the success of the Ward Method in the New York, Chancellor Samuel Black McCormack, then in the throes of transforming the old Western University of Pennsylvania into the new University of Pittsburgh, engaged Ward to lead a campaign to raise $3 million in 10 days for a new campus. Although the legend probably exceeds its actual achievement, the campaign for the University of Pittsburgh nevertheless marks the first whirlwind campaign on behalf of a university. The University of Pittsburgh campaign of 1914 also marks the only occasion where the four early giants of professional fund raising collaborated on a project: Ward; Pierce, who advised Ward from his position as general secretary of the Central Pittsburgh YMCA; Carlton Ketchum, a University of Pittsburgh student assigned to the campaign; and Arnaud C. Marts, Pierce's assistant—collaborated on a project (see Cutlip 1965, 85–86, 88).

The successful use by Ward and Pierce of public relations and advertising was not lost on other fund raisers—even Bishop Lawrence. In a 1914 campaign to replace a building destroyed by fire at Wellesley College, where he was a trustee, Lawrence received a lead pledge from John D. Rockefeller. Having just participated in Ward's successful whirlwind campaign in New York, Rockefeller made his gift conditional on Lawrence completing the entire Wellesley campaign within a year. Only through considerable "crowding and jamming for subscriptions" was Lawrence able to meet Rockefeller's deadline.

Lawrence did not fully embrace the techniques of public relations, however, until he took up the definitive campaign of his career—the Episcopal Church Pension Fund Campaign of 1916–1917. The campaign was significant not only for the sheer size of its goal—an unprecedented $5 million—but also for its scope. It sought to solicit the entire nation for support of a single cause—the establishment of a pension fund for widows and families of Episcopal clergy. As he later wrote, "Up to this time . . . there had been no campaign like it. Young Men's Christian Associations and other organizations had, of course, carried many drives of smaller amounts. There were no professional campaign firms, and but little skilled publicity. There were no precedents for the organization of our work, which covered the Church throughout the country and in the mission fields. . . .We had to blaze paths in many directions" (cited in Cutlip 1965, 94–96).

After a few weeks of "wandering through a bog," as he put it, Lawrence decided to adopt the whirlwind-campaign approach, building his campaign on a platform of public opinion conditioned by persuasive publicity. Frustrated in his initial attempts, however, he eventually engaged the services of Ivey Lee, a professional public relations counselor in New York whose chief client was John D. Rockefeller. Lee advised Lawrence to run a simple publicity campaign based more on facts than emotion. Lawrence rejected the advice, ultimately concluding that charitable giving was almost entirely driven by emotion.

Nevertheless, the conversations with Lee awakened the Bishop's own considerable gifts for promotion. In a famous moment of inspiration, he sent a telegram to newly inaugurated President Woodrow Wilson urging him to show leadership on behalf of charitable causes, the release of which received considerable coverage in Boston and throughout New England. With similar cunning, he shrewdly scheduled the announcement of his Church Pension Fund Campaign on a Monday, generally a slow-news day. This stratagem enabled him to place on the front page of most daily newspapers the sermons delivered by local Episcopal bishops the previous Sunday that, orchestrated by Lawrence, urged support for a fund to alleviate the dire state of clerical salaries and pensions. Realizing, too, that the Episcopal Church pension system was a comparatively small cause in the eyes of the public, Lawrence guaranteed maximum coverage by linking his appeal to a problem touching everyone: the support of elderly citizens.

By wedding such public relations techniques to the careful organizational structure he had developed in previous campaigns, Lawrence created a juggernaut of public sentiment. The campaign reached its announced goal of $5 million a full month before its March 1 target, raised $6 million by the deadline, and ultimately rolled to $8.75 million before it finally ground to a halt in September. This success established Lawrence as the nation's premier charitable fund raiser prior to World War I (see Cutlip 1965, 96–97). Moreover, the Church Pension Fund Campaign served as a model for two national campaigns for Harvard that followed, including the 1919–1920 endowment drive and the 1923–1924 Opportunity for National Service Harvard campaign. Targeted to raise $10 million from non-alumni, the latter campaign was the last appeal personally directed by Lawrence on behalf of his alma mater.

In other colleges, early campaigns like those of the University of Pittsburgh patterned after the whirlwind campaign were short-lived and locally focused. But as more colleges transformed into universities and others invented whole cloth, their constituent communities expanded as well, both geographically and demographically. Accordingly, by the mid-1920s it had become clear that the timeframe and local focus of the whirlwind campaign was insufficient to generate the momentum necessary to sustain a campaign of regional or national scope. Although campaigns for smaller colleges and even some universities continued to use this model, more and more university campaigns patterned themselves after those led by Bishop Lawrence and his protégés, chiefly John Price

Jones, whose consulting firm was to dominate university fund raising until after World War II.

A journalist by trade, Jones was working for a New York advertising agency when he was assigned to help with publicity for the Liberty Loan campaign of 1917–1919, the second of five World War I war-bond campaigns that together raised almost $14 million. In this and two subsequent Liberty Loan campaigns, Jones worked under Guy Emerson, who, as campaign publicity director, had learned his trade in turn from Bishop Lawrence in the Church Pension Fund Campaign. During the Liberty Loan campaigns, Jones pioneered the use of celebrities to promote bond sales, enlisting Douglas Fairbanks, Mary Pickford, Charles Chaplin, and Lillian Russell. Jones also convinced utility companies to print appeals on bills, milk companies to put slogans on bottle caps, and banks to insert patriotic petitions with their monthly statements and innovated the use of special events to generate interest and enthusiasm for a cause. He was so successful that when Robert F. Duncan, secretary of the Harvard endowment fund campaign of 1919–1920, called fellow alumnus Emerson for guidance, he immediately directed him to Jones, Harvard Class of 1902. Duncan hired Jones as general manager of the campaign, which reached its $10 million goal in just two years, an unprecedented amount and timeframe for a university (see Cutlip 1965, 170–173).

But Jones did much more than deliver a large sum of money quickly and efficiently. As Cutlip noted, the 1919–1920 campaign "not only made fund-raising history but changed the course of American higher education" (1965, 173). With this campaign, Harvard announced to its sister colleges and to the nation that the old methods of financing higher education were passé—that, indeed, the old American college was passé. Previously, as Guy Emerson would later observe, colleges had launched campaigns with only a sketchy idea of their purpose: "They knew in a general way that they were after money and the net result of their appeal usually was 'Please give us some money because we want it.'"

In dramatic contrast, the Harvard Endowment Campaign of 1919–1920 used intensive, intelligent publicity to document the service that "the university, by the training of young people and the research work of its professors, had furnished the nation" (Cutlip 1965, 173). Instead of entering a beggar's plea for charity, Harvard presented its alumni with a bill for services rendered and asked for payment in the form of an investment to support even more and better service to future alumni and so the nation. Thus, rather than simply documenting campaign activity and whipping up mass enthusiasm, Jones used publicity to position the campaign to leverage its deep-seated moral appeal. From this point on, the solicitor's road would be paved by the campaign publicity director.

Just three years after the 1919–1920 Harvard alumni campaign, Lawrence again showed his facility for acquiring new tricks by using Jones's methods in a brilliant last display of his marketing genius to get a national constituency of non-alumni to support Harvard. The campaign to establish the Graduate School of Business was a tour de force performance that represented the first standalone capital campaign in America on behalf of a university college or sub-unit. Fueled not only by the combined total of the $20 million they raised but also by the hope and pride they inspired, the complementary campaigns of 1919–1920 and 1923–1924 catapulted Harvard into national prominence.

The lesson was not lost on the presidents of other national universities, who promptly followed Harvard's lead in cashing in on the post-war affluence of a nation just emerging as an international political and economic power. University campaign quickly followed university campaign, with Jones reporting in 1923 that at least 64 universities had conducted fund-raising drives since the end of World War I. Between 1920 and 1950, 51 of the most active fund-raising colleges and universities had received a total of more than $1.7 billion in gifts and bequests, mostly via campaigns led by professional fund-raising firms such as John Price Jones, Ketchum, Marts and Lundy (see Cutlip 1965, 243, 265–268).

By using the tools of public relations and mass marketing to communicate with the constituent community and to make a case for support, these campaigns paved the way for the modern American university. At this point, in fact, the idea of the modern American university and the practice of modern professional fund raising become inextricably linked. Alumni-based capital campaigns develop into the funding mechanism of choice by university presidents who saw them as a way not only of raising substantial sums of money but also of bonding their vision of the university to a new generation of graduates whose success (as they would be frequently reminded) they at least partly owed to their university. Combined with careful and detailed organization, this message captured the post–World War I wave of affluence and the rising national aspirations of its constituent communities as no other and propelled the university into an era of unprecedented power and affluence.

That being said, the ascent of the university to this new level of prestige was not achieved without some loss of institutional innocence and perhaps integrity as well. The old American college was a place where faculty and students pretty much exemplified Horace Mann's dictum regarding the ideal teaching situation: a log with a teacher on one end and a student on the other. It was an intimate setting for learning, with many of the emotional trappings of a family, and the students who graduated from it by and large continued to maintain a familial relationship with their alma mater and among themselves throughout their lives. In this context, charity began at home: The few financial obligations to their college that alumni observed were usually those of a well-to-do family member extending a helping hand to a penurious parent or guardian.

The new American university changed the basic chemistry of this relationship. Increasingly, the paradigm for higher education was business. Universities became analogous to corporations; likewise, university presidents became CEOs and "captains of erudition," as the academic scourge Thorstein Veblen wryly dubbed them, in spiritual kinship with the captains of industry with whom they filled their boardrooms. As universities grew larger, richer, and more bureaucratic, the familial culture became more a façade and, with the student revolution of the 1960s, finally irrelevant. No longer members of an extended family, the alumni of the modern university instead became essential corporate assets, whose collective political and economic weight and individual influence and wealth could be wielded, channeled, or tapped by the institution that granted them the educational and professional credentials increasingly necessary for success in modern American society. And for good or ill, no component of the new American university bore more responsibility for this fundamental transformation than did modern professional fund raising, the parameters and methods of which were just beginning to be defined formally by early practitioner-scholars such as Seymour in *Design for Giving: The Story of the National War Fund, Inc. 1943–1947* (1947) and especially in his classic *Designs for Fund-raising: Principles, Patterns, Techniques* (1966/1992).

The Role of the Fund Raiser in the University

With modern professional fund raising becoming instrumental to the modern American university, professional fund raisers became more and more a fixture of university bureaucracies. Their entrance into the university, however, took place piecemeal, gradually, and almost by stealth. In fact, the role of the modern development officer as it exists today is actually an assemblage of three fund-raising functionaries, each of which made its way into the academy through very different portals.

The first was the "campaign manager," of which Bishop Lawrence was the great prototype. Other institutions would occasionally have a trustee like Lawrence with the vision and leadership skills necessary to manage a campaign. But in most institutions these responsibilities fell to the president, who typically would employ a professional fundraising consultancy to direct the campaign. Inasmuch as most university presidents envisioned a massive campaign as a one-time or at most highly infrequent occurrence, they saw no need to incorporate a campaign manager into their permanent staffs. Thus, the campaign manager makes a first appearance in the academy as merely an itinerant operative employed by a president on a temporary basis to conduct a fund-raising campaign.

Inasmuch as presidents did think that the public relations and publicity aspects of campaign had long-term and ongoing utility, the second fund-raising functionary to enter the modern university—and the first to gain a permanent place therein—was the "public relations officer." This position began appearing on the staffs of university presidents as early as 1913. With the appearance of the public relations officer, universities merely reflected the nascent condition of modern fund raising in society as a whole where fund raising per se was typically viewed as a specialized branch of public relations or publicity and whose operatives were drawn predominately from the ranks of journalism and advertising. For this reason, prior to 1960 the chief public relations officer in a university often served double duty as the chief development officer, in part because these tasks were seen as integral and in part because role of campaign manager was still viewed as both extraneous and temporary.

Ironically, the role most commonly ascribed today to the modern university fund raiser—that of the "paid solicitor," who as one observer put it, possessed "gluelike persistence" (cited in Cutlip 1965, 64)—was actually the last to infiltrate the academy. The role of the paid solicitor combines two types of early fund raisers. The first was that of the paid clergy-cum-agent-solicitor, a role that evolved in the wake of the great success of Whitfield in raising funds for colleges and other charities during the Great Awakening in the 1730s and 1740s. Working on commission, such agent-solicitors continued to ply their trade on behalf of American colleges until the early decades of the 20th century. The fact that pioneers of professional fund raising such as Ward and Pierce and a number of their protégés—along with talented amateurs like Bishop Lawrence—began their careers as fund raisers in service to a Christian charity links them at least circumstantially with this tradition.

The role of paid solicitor, however, probably derives even more from the role of "paid collector," which was devised by local charities and welfare societies in the first decade of the 20th century. Writing in 1906, Walter S. Ufford, general secretary of the Baltimore Federated Charities, noted in a report that "The Charity Organization Society of Baltimore . . . has found it necessary to use a collector throughout the year. This collector works upon a salary, not upon commission. The salary basis is less open to criticism, as it does not meet with the objection that a certain proportion of the amount received is to be subtracted from every contribution" (cited in Cutlip 1965). This brief mention of the Baltimore Charitable Society's nameless collector is the earliest known record of an agent performing in a role that we would recognize as central to that of the modern development officer working for a charitable organization or institution.

In another part of the same report, Mina C. Ginger, financial secretary of the Newark Bureau of Associated Charities, described a related dimension of the collector's role: "The collection of funds for the society should represent educational work, and *each contribution secured should indicate an understanding of the work and approval of it by the contributor*" (cited in Cutlip 1965, 60, italics mine). In other words, each gift to a charitable organization or institution was understood to be more than simply a contribution to its operations. Implicit with the gift was an affirmation by the donor—a member of the organization's constituent community—of the effectiveness and continued relevance of its mission and purpose to that community. Thus, the organization or institution, initially by means of its annualized solicitation and later by means of federated campaign drives such as the Community Chest or United Way into which these separate solicitations collectively evolved, received not only the funding necessary to conduct business but also confirmation of the social contract between the institution and its constituent base to ensure its social relevance. In short, such gifts provided a charitable organization with both the means and license to operate. And from the onset, the paid collector as educator was understood as the agent implicitly empowered to obtain both.

In universities, because individual campaigns initially occurred infrequently, the various professional consulting firms that ran their campaigns and then moved on usually provided paid collectors. Liaison between the institution and a consulting firm would be performed by the university president's office, usually via the public relations officer if there was one. During drives, the public relations officer worked closely with the itinerant campaign manager. Afterwards, the campaign manager would help the president maintain key relationships begun during the campaign and solicit any subsequent gifts and bequests. As the pace and goals of campaigns began to increase in the decades following World War II, universities assumed more and more of their own campaign management and operation. In so doing, they began hiring their own itinerant paid collectors, perhaps keeping on one or two to help with follow-up initiatives.

The practice of hiring dedicated professional collectors or solicitors on a permanent basis was rather slow in coming, however. Northwestern University became perhaps the first to have a unit dedicated to ongoing institutional fund raising when it established a Department of Development in the 1920s. But the idea of establishing discreet and permanent development offices within the university did not begin to have widespread appeal until after World War II. Only two respondents to a survey conducted by the American College Public Relations Association (ACPRA) in 1949 used the title "director of development"; three years later, only 13 respondents to the same survey used the title (see Worth and Asp 1994, 9).

But during the post–World War II economic expansion and then the globalization of the economy during the Cold War era, the need of the university to maintain its social contract with its constituent community created an almost insatiable demand for ever-higher levels of funding. It became increasingly clear, therefore, that fund raising needed to assume a larger role than had heretofore been envisioned. Implicit in this new role was the need to obtain both operational support for the mission of the university and strategic complicity in expanding it. To describe its functions and functionaries toward these new ends, Northwestern University coined the term "development," which was gradually adopted by other institutions to describe the comprehensive role of fund raising within the modern academy.

By the late 1950s and 1960s, "development offices" began to appear in increasing numbers throughout American higher education, staffed full-time by professional collectors or development officers. And once institutionalized, these development offices evolved rapidly. In decentralized universities like Harvard, university colleges and schools were especially quick to establish their own development offices, often staffed with more dedicated professional fund-raising personnel than the president's office (see Mason, this volume).

In more centralized institutions, permanent development officers typically made their first appearance under the aegis of the public relations office before coalescing their own units in the growing bureaucracy. Among public universities, particularly in the West, centralized fund-raising units had existed almost from the beginning, whereas others, especially those in the East and South, effectively evolved development offices only in the later three decades of the century (see Worth and Asp 1994, 10–11). Sensing a lack of direction and leadership, ACPRA and the American Alumni Council co-sponsored a study in 1958 designed to find better ways to structure the various offices that linked universities to external constituents. The findings of this study were reported at a famous meeting at The Greenbrier resort in White Sulphur Springs, WV. The report called for strong coordination of the three functions of public information, alumni relations, and development, and implied that it would be most beneficial to unify them under a single leader who would be a member of the university's senior administrative team.

Despite the wide influence of the "Greenbrier Report," as the study became known, the shift to a centralized model and the elevation of "advancement executives" to top administration status occurred slowly. But the need to have better links to external constituents was strong, and over time most universities did create unified, centralized university relations or advancement offices, usually under the leadership of the chief public relations officer. Yet even after the widespread formation of central development or advancement offices, development officers per se were still widely perceived as products of a different culture, "gypsy professionals" who spent two to four years at one campus before picking up shop and moving on. Only gradually, as institutional relationships with alumni, legislatures, and the public at large became more complex and involved, did institutions begin to see the value of having such professionals permanently on staff to mediate the university's growing public role and to acquire the funding to support it.

After the Greenbrier Report, the trickle of development officers became a stream as the newly formed or recombined offices of "University Relations" or "Advancement" began appearing, but development officers still played minor roles. The stream became a river only as presidential fund-raising activities began to coalesce into campaigns, and campaigns became large and frequent enough to render the gypsy campaign mode cumbersome and inefficient. By the end of 1960s, permanent cadres of officers dedicated to fund raising had become a fixture of the hard-charging modern university.

Although the focus of these officers initially seemed rather narrow, their role expanded rapidly in the 1970s and beyond as the value of "development"—with all its attendant meanings and functions—became more and more apparent to universities strategically as well as operationally. As a consequence, by the mid-1980s the leadership of university relations or advancement offices for the most part had shifted from the chief public relations officer to the chief development officer, as development or advancement moved finally into the university's top management circles.

Emergence of the Unit Development Officer

During the 1960s, the first unit development or advancement officers also began to materialize. One of them, Bayley Mason, took his first job in 1960 as the public relations officer for Harvard Medical School, which was just beginning a standalone capital campaign. By 1965, he had become associate dean for resources and reported directly to the dean of the medical school. He had only a loose reporting line to the assistant for resources, the member of the president's staff who operated as the university's chief development officer.

Mason wrote that other units at Harvard, particularly the "big tub" professional schools like law and business, also had their own development officers. They paid even less obeisance than did he to the central office, which was widely perceived as exclusively serving the development needs of the undergraduate college of arts and sciences. Mason's story illustrates how the unit development position evolved in so-called decentralized universities such as Harvard, where strong constituent units were attached to a relatively weak central office.

In more centralized institutions, especially those where the political power of the president and the central administration predominate, unit-based development often began by assigning central-office development staff members to carry out fund-raising projects for a specific college or unit. My own experience is a case in point. In 1976 I was the public relations officer in the dean's office of the College of Liberal Arts at the University of Tennessee, Knoxville. As my duties also included grant writing, in 1978 I was assigned to write a National Endowment for the Humanities challenge grant proposal on behalf of the humanities program of the college, which subsequently was funded at the $1 million level. In accordance with the terms of the grant, the college and the university were required to match with $3 million in new private giving.

"Seeing as you're on a roll," as he put it, my dean then rather cavalierly assigned me the responsibility of raising the matching gift money—thus launching my career in unit development. With some financial support from the dean's office, the Knoxville campus development office hired a development officer to work with me, and together we raised the necessary private support. The concentrated four-year mini-campaign we conducted, which finished in 1984, marked the first such effort on behalf of a single college in the university's history.

This story illustrates the rather casual, almost accidental way in which unit development operations sometimes came about. It also illustrates what Hall called the "hybrid" university approach to unit fund raising, wherein both the central development office and the unit contribute to the support of a unit-based development office, and the officer reports both to the dean and the central office. In more centrally controlled universities, the distribution of development officers—and of the responsibility for unit fund raising—is less formal or widespread, residing mainly within the purview of the central development office and vice president.

At any rate, within a decade of the completion of my first campaign, virtually every major university—public or private—employed a unit development or advancement officer for at least their most prominent colleges or schools. Indeed, as Hall also noted, unit development officers have been and remain the fastest-growing segment of the development profession. Despite its demand and evident success, the evolution of the unit development officer position has often been viewed with a jaundiced if not hostile eye.

Politically, the formation of separate advancement offices within a university college or school possesses something of a grassroots, anti-establishment quality. By their very existence, unit offices challenge the centralized advancement system formulated by the Greenbrier Report. Consequently, some vice presidents think they challenge their right to direct the university's fund-raising strategy and operations. As Hall notes in Chapter 2 (this volume):

> Many of today's senior development officers, presidents, and prominent consultants began their careers before development was at the top-management table. They are aware of the struggle to centralize development offices into a cohesive, influential force within the university. They recognize that centralization increased development's power to offer the university access to the philanthropic resources of its community and to offer the community access to the professional resources of the university. Resounding discussions about current and future decentralization are the lessons of how institutional advancement programs were less effective when they were decentralized before the Greenbrier Report.

Yet, in light of the historical context of university advancement before the past half-century, the movement to establish unit development operations is clearly a contemporary manifestation of a long-established tradition of private-gift solicitation. Mega-campaigns aside, fund raising for U.S. higher education was born of a tradition of *collegiate* fund raising in the ancient colleges of Great Britain. Moreover, colleges remained the focus of fund raising for higher education essentially until the 20th century. Only with the onset of the German research university model in the late 19th century—more than 250 years *after* President Eaton solicited his first gift for Harvard—did the focus and locus of fund raising begin to migrate from the college to the university level.

Within university colleges, the fund-raising function has fluctuated with the role of the college dean. The role of the modern dean became defined only during what Veysey called "the second phase" of administrative growth in the modern American university— a phase that began in the 1890s and has not ended yet. At older, more decentralized universities like Harvard, deans became powerful spokespeople for increasingly professionalized and affluent alumni constituencies. Conversely, at new institutions such as Johns Hopkins and the University of Chicago that consciously exemplified the modern American university, deans were initially little more than extensions of the preeminent power of the president. Nevertheless, during the first half of the 20th century these divergent power bases managed to converge to make the deanship of a modern university college or school a locus of leverage and influence, arguably second only to that of the presidency itself. As the modern university continued to devolve into the contemporary "city state of the multiversity," as Kerr (1982) notably described it, it has become a "complex entity with greatly fractionalized power" wherein deans of every stripe have become the fulcrums of force.

Today, the modern deanship resembles in many ways the presidency of the classic American college—especially in the dean's manifestly dual role as spokesperson for and manager of an academic enterprise. Given the college's increasing visibility and autonomy—and its insatiable appetite for funding—deans also have to take the matter of resource development into their own hands. Indeed, the decentralized or distributed model for unit development that emerged in the 1950s and 1960s and came to predominate the university in the 1980s and 1990s stemmed from the seemingly spontaneous and unrelated decisions by individual deans to acquire their own development officers, either by hiring them outright or by browbeating the central office into assigning them. In so doing, they collectively and intuitively were—are—reclaiming a decanal function dating back to the founding of university colleges in the 11th and 12th centuries.

As manifested within the university college, the unit development officer position mirrors the dual role of the modern dean. With regard to the dean's role as manager of an academic enterprise, the unit development officer bears the responsibility of cultivating and soliciting gifts, grants, and bequests. With regard to the dean's role as spokesperson for the college, the unit development officer shapes the terms of such giving and thereby ensures the continued relevance of the college and its mission. By means of the gift, the unit development officer in turn transmits the values and priorities of the donors and constituent communities to the academy, thereby incorporating them into the institutional mission, faculty, and even curriculum. This exchange makes the college or unit stronger and more competitive, all while creating a constituency supportive of its service, teaching, and research. As the officer delegated to manage this function, the contemporary unit development officer thus brings to bear both the professional skills of the modern fund-raising practitioner and the historic agency of fund raising within the academy.

In conducting this exchange—which many educators argue is the most vital challenge facing the modern university worldwide today—the unit development officer must address a set of duties and responsibilities distinct if not unique from those of other development officers. Given the urgency of this challenge, the need now is to articulate these distinctive duties and responsibilities, identify best practices, and, in so doing, reclaim our history and our manifest purpose. It is this need and intent that motivates and justifies this Handbook.

References

Abrams, Deborah Blackmore & Travers, Linus. "Making the Ask." CURRENTS, September 2000.

Bledstein, Burton J. *Culture of Professionalism: The Middle-Class and the Development of Higher Education in America*. Harvard University Press, 1988.

Bremner, Robert H. *American Philanthropy*. University of Chicago Press, 1960.

Brittingham, Barbara E. & Pezzullo, Thomas R. *The Campus Green: Fund Raising in Higher Education*. ASHE-ERIC Higher Education Report, 1990.

Cutlip, Scott M. *Fund Raising in the United States: Its Role in America's Philanthropy*. Rutgers University Press, 1965.

Hall, Margarete Rooney. *The Dean's Role in Fund Raising*. The Johns Hopkins University Press, 1993.

Hofstadter, Richard & Wilson, Smith, Eds. *American Higher Education: A Documentary History*. University of Chicago Press, 1961.

Jones, John. *Balliol College: A History: 1263–1939*. Oxford University Press, 1988.

Kerr, Clark. *The Uses of the University*. Harvard University Press, 1982.

Kuhn, Thomas S. *The Structure of Scientific Revolutions*, second ed., University of Chicago Press, 1970.

Rudolph, Frederick J. *American College and University: A History*. Vintage Books, 1962.

Seymour, Harold J. *Design for Giving: The Story of the National War Fund, Inc., 1943–47*. Harpers, 1947.

Seymour, Harold J. *Designs for Fund-raising: Principles, Patterns, Techniques*. Fund Raising Institute, 1988. (Original work published 1966)

Veysey, Laurence R. *The Emergence of the American University*. University of Chicago Press, 1970.

Worth, Michael J. and Asp II, James W. *The Development Officer in Higher Education: Toward an Understanding of the Role*. ASHE-ERIC Higher Education Report No. 4, 1994.

I

BACKGROUND

CHAPTER I

The Distinctive Role of the Unit Development Officer

F. A. Hilenski

Director of Development and Communication,
Ivan Allen College, Georgia Institute of Technology

Modern-day unit development officers (UDOs) play roles similar to those played by development officers in the past (who were often presidents or deans—see the Introduction, this volume). Like their historic counterparts, they must often perform as educators and negotiators as well as fund raisers, and the skills needed to perform these roles are similar. Because of these similarities, the present-day role of UDOs is sometimes misunderstood. On one hand, they are often viewed simply as variants or extensions of a large central development or advancement operation. On the other hand, they are often thought of as being responsible only for development or advancement in small shops, that is, small-sized institutions. In reality, the job of today's UDO is unique in several ways, which I describe in this chapter.

A Special Relationship with the Dean

In *The Dean's Role in Fund Raising*, Hall (1993) suggested that the relationship that exists between UDOs and their deans or unit heads in unlike that between central development officers and their deans or unit heads and, in fact, may be different from all others except for that between development officers and the vice president and president. Hall considers this special relationship the aspect of the UDO's job that others—ironically, vice presidents of development in particular—are least likely to understand or appreciate. Indeed, in her book (which is based on the only extant empirical study of academic unit officers), she reported that UDOs rate their reporting relationship to their deans or unit heads as the single most important factor contributing to their success or failure, whereas vice presidents of development, generally regarded such a reporting line to be of little.

I have described the UDO's role less formally as "the care and feeding of deans"; to maximize the dean's impact, the UDO must manage at least a portion of the dean's time, energy, and well-being. And, too, the perceived closeness of the relationship between the dean and the UDO may lend additional authority to the UDO—a phenomenon Halton calls "borrowed clout" (see Chapter 4, this volume). Although borrowed clout certainly has its uses—particularly in sorting out conflicting priorities—Halton warns that if it is not wielded judiciously, it can bring great harm not only to the UDO but also to the dean and college. Moreover, even a strong relationship between the dean and the UDO does not automatically result in borrowed clout.

One aspect of the relationship UDOs definitely should avoid is that of becoming a "general factotum"—becoming the dean's aide-de-camp, as it were. Overburdened deans are often tempted to assign their UDOs duties extraneous to development, especially if UDOs are bright and capable, readily grasp the subtleties of policy and situation, and write and speak effectively. To escape this pitfall, the best defense is a good offense. UDOs must be ever vigilant about unilateral extensions of their prescribed duties, because once UDOs become general factotums, extricating themselves from the role will be difficult to effect without damaging their relationship with the dean or their effectiveness as development officers.

While maintaining a special relationship with the dean or unit head, UDOs must also maintain complex internal relationships. As Croft makes clear (see Chapter 6, this volume), to keep up with educational objectives or to exploit a hot topic or researcher, UDOs have to constantly reassess their relationships with faculty and unit heads. They also must learn the subtle art of saying no to faculty whose activities do not align with college or unit priorities, or whose needs do not justify the efforts of a major gift officer.

At the same time, UDOs often function as catalysts to create a synergy of mutual interest sufficient to attract additional support, a strategy not unlike that of the integrated income generation model employed in British universities (see Chapter 9, this volume). UDOs must maintain these interests in harmony with myriad other relationships involving institutional development officers and key staff members in alumni, public relations, and special events, not to mention individual and corporate donors, potential donors, and ordinary non-donor alumni and friends.

In summary, to be most effective, UDOs must establish and maintain a special relationship with their deans (or the equivalent) at every level—personal, professional, and ideological. These levels, in fact, are linked: remove, erode, or corrupt any one, and the others become dysfunctional. Correspondingly, UDOs also must establish and maintain an appropriate professional relationship with relevant sub-unit heads and staff directors and perform their tasks with a professionalism that earns the respect of the faculty and staff with whom they interact. For no other category of development officer are such organizational relationships as vital a factor for success.

Organizational Complexity

Organizational complexity represents another major difference between the work of the UDO and other development officers, small-shop officers in particular. Although two- and four-year colleges certainly have become more complex of late, they still cannot compare in complexity with modern American research universities, which undoubtedly are among the most labyrinthine institutions in the world. Hall (1993) argued, in fact, that it was the growing organizational complexity of the university that engendered the need for UDOs in the first place, and that the role of the UDO implicitly reflects this complexity. As the modern university evolved into the contemporary "multiversity," she contends that the role of the UDO evolved to provide the more complex and decentral- ized management approach that burgeoning institutions required. As evidence, her research discloses not one but three basic types of UDOs currently operating in American universities, each defined by their organizational contexts.

On one end of the spectrum are the *centralized* UDOs who are paid by the central development office and assigned or distributed to a unit or set of units. On the opposite end, *decentralized* UDOs are hired and paid for by deans or unit heads, and thus operate with varying degrees of independence from the central development office. In between these extremes are the *hybrid* UDOs, who are supported by both the central development office and the academic unit or units jointly and have dual reporting lines to both the central office and the unit.

Although UDOs are normally charged with advancing only one or two units within a university, they cannot function effectively at this level unless they are fully informed about the case and the operations of the central office and any unit- or institutionally related foundations. UDOs also need to be familiar with the case and operations of the many other units, programs, services, and centers that intersect with or impinge on their development operations, plus a multitude of faculty research projects as well. And if their role is truly advancement rather than simply development, UDOs also need to integrate their operations with public relations, alumni relations, and even governmental relations at the institutional level.

A Disciplinary Focus

As important as relationships and management are, the primary difference between UDOs and both university central officers and small-shop officers lies in the programs they advance. Small-shop officers and university central officers primarily advance an institution—a unique, holistic, and independent entity with a campus, buildings, students, faculty, curricula, alumni, history, and traditions. UDOs, on the other hand, advance a specific discipline or set of related disciplines or, alternatively, a profession or set of related professions. They may also advance the mission of units that support or enhance these disciplines or professions, such as a library or museum. Although these disciplines and professions often constitute a discrete intellectual entity and may even be housed in a distinct facility such as a theater or a laboratory, they constitute only a part of the total university experience—not standalone institutions.

Because UDOs advance just a part of a whole, major differences exist between the provision of development services for a small, independent liberal arts college and that for a liberal arts college within a large university. The case for the independent college typically focuses on its undergraduate program and special sense of community—the symbolism of specific buildings, the beauty of the campus, quaint communal rituals and traditions, and the technological state of the library or athletic facilities, not to mention the quality of the course of study. Individual academic units or sub-units, if they figure in the small-shop case at all, are usually promoted only in terms of their contribution to the institution's general education rather than their singular programmatic prominence or excellence. Consequently, the case for support of independent colleges typically tries to focus potential donors on improving or enriching the total living and learning experience of undergraduate-age students.

In large universities, development based on promoting the total living and learning experience is ordinarily the province of the central development office. The unit development office of the liberal arts college in a large university thus typically highlights the demonstrable quality of specific disciplines, units, or facilities with regard to its standing within the field or its graduate or postgraduate value to the student. As such, the case for support normally focuses potential donors on the quality of its faculty and research or of its graduate education or training provided in a specialized area of study, as well as the impact that this research or training has had, is having, or will have on society or a community, the economy, an industry or profession, or a corporation or group of corporations. Consequently, such a case for support of university units typically emphasizes improving or enriching the specialized learning experiences of students, recruiting or retaining the faculty necessary to direct their training and research, or erecting or upgrading the facilities to do both.

Negotiating the Social Contract

As I discussed in the Introduction, fund raising in American institutions of higher education has always been the currency of the social contract between the institution and its constituent community. If that contract is intact and each party understands its terms and feels satisfied that the other parties are honoring its obligations, then all things being equal (e.g., the economy, the state of the nation), fund raising will go well. If, however, the potential donor does not perceive the social contact as being intact, the donor may not recognize the obligation or agree that other parties are honoring theirs. In either case, fund raising probably will not go well, even if the economy and the times are propitious.

On a holistic scale, a strategic and policy scale, the establishment and maintenance of this social contract is the province of presidents, deans, boards of trustees, advisory boards, and the like. But on an individual, "street-level" scale (Lipsky 1983), this contract is very much the province of advancement officers, that is, public relations, alumni, and development officers, and especially unit development officers. Why UDOs especially? First, they are the officers who, as educators, have to instruct arguably the most essential segment of the constituent community—donors—about the state of the social contract with regard to the most essential elements of the university, its curriculum and research. Second, UDOs are the officers who, as negotiators, structure the individual gifts that update and maintain the social contract for donors, albeit individuals, corporations, or foundations.

An episode from my experience as a UDO at the Georgia Institute of Technology (Georgia Tech) provides a good illustration of these roles in action. While I was the UDO for the College of Architecture, one of our regional officers called me about an alumnus of my college with whom he was having great difficulty communicating. During his initial contact call, the alumnus had posed a series of in-depth questions regarding the profession of architecture that the regional officer was unable to address to his satisfaction. He then abruptly ended the meeting, stating in essence that the officer obviously had not come to update him about the college. "You're here just because you want my money," he charged.

Clearly, this alumnus—who had never been called on in person previously by anyone from Georgia Tech and who now was being visited for the first time by a fund raiser—believed that the social contract with his alma mater had been broken; less clear was whether he felt that it could still be repaired. On the one hand, taking the regional officer's call and agreeing to the appointment appeared to confirm that he believed at least some vestige of the contract was still in effect. On the other hand, the long period of neglect obviously had made him cynical about the institutional sense of obligation to the terms of that contract. Having failed to acknowledge or honor him appropriately in his current status as a practicing professional, he might justifiably have felt that the institution had forfeited any obligations it might claim of him as an alumnus and potential donor.

Suspecting that there was at least a chance at reestablishing the contract, the regional officer asked me to join him for dinner with the alumnus. At that occasion, I, too, was confronted, not surprisingly, with the same barrage of questions the regional officer had faced. Fortunately, as a unit officer who dealt with architects daily, I knew the major issues in his profession and, more important, understood the jargon used in his profession. Thus, as I addressed his questions, almost at once his demeanor began to change. By being able to speak his language, as it were, I was able to educate him as to how the college had evolved since his day, how it was addressing the professional issues he had raised, and how he could begin to participate in the current life of the college. In addition, by acknowledging and honoring his present status as a professional, I was able to renegotiate the terms of his social contract with the college and institution, effectively reinstating it so that he was now at least willing to discuss an obligation to his alma mater.

My success with this alumnus stemmed from the perceived authority vested in my position or office as a representative of the institution. Although the validity of this authority appears obvious and unquestioned, considerable controversy persists as to where this authority should be grounded. Hall contended that, to be most effective, a development officer cannot be merely an agent-solicitor for a college. Rather, "As a bridge between the college and its external constituents, a development officer can represent the college well *only as an integral member* of its management" (1993, 45–46, italics mine). In support of her position, she cited data showing that most UDOs think it very important to have a title that places them in the hierarchy of a college rather than in the central development office—for example, to be the "associate *dean* for development" rather than the "*director* of development." Vice presidents for development, however, may not deem such unit-based academic titles for UDOs to be important.

This seemingly petty disagreement over titles actually reflects a much more substantial division that goes to the very heart of UDO functionality. If the UDO title links the development officer to the collegiate hierarchy, then the authority the officer brings to the table as an educator and negotiator is that of a member of the management of the college, deriving thus from the intrinsic mission of the college. If, however, the title links the development officer to the central advancement office hierarchy, the officer's authority is not that of a member of the management of the college but rather exactly that of an agent-solicitor, deriving instead from the mission of the institution, that is, an entity extrinsic to the college or unit.

Even if never manifested explicitly, a title that effectively disenfranchises the UDO from membership in the college hierarchy implicitly erects an ideological barrier between the unit and the position. This barrier may or may not contribute to the creation of barriers between the officer and the dean or, by extension, between faculty and other staff members, but it certainly does add to the organizational complexity of the position, placing the UDO—already a somewhat suspect entity within the academy—in a permanent ideological Twilight Zone, *in* but never *of* the college, destined forever to being a marginally benign presence at best or a "corrupting influence" at worst. More important, disenfranchising UDOs from membership in the hierarchy of the units they serve alienates them from their historic functionality within the university college, thereby diminishing the authority of their roles as educators and negotiators.

Conclusion

What differentiates academic UDOs from other types of development officers is not the type or manner of their fund raising. Rather, they differ from other officers in terms of the organizational contexts and constraints in which they must operate. Thus, unlike central development officers in a large university, UDOs must develop and maintain a special relationship with their deans or unit heads, and to a lesser extend with other academic administrators and faculty as well. Unlike small-shop development officers in independent colleges, UDOs must manage fund-raising tasks in a highly complex organizational context. And unlike either central officers or small-shop officers, UDOs must articulate and present a case for support for the units or facilities under their charge based on the relevance of these units and facilities to the disciplines, affinities, or professions of their constituent communities.

In addition to these fund-raising functions, UDOs also serve as educators and negotiators for their units, teaching external constituencies about the mission and programs of the unit and formalizing with each and every donor the personal terms of the social contract by which he or she will agree to provide support for the unit. As such, UDOs in large universities complement the role of central development officers, providing a special unit-based perspective, expertise, and advocacy to supplement, enhance, and enrich the overall case for support of the institution.

References

Hall, Margarete Rooney. *The Dean's Role in Fund Raising.* The Johns Hopkins Press, 1993.

Lipsky, Michael. *Street-Level Bureaucracy: Dilemmas of the Individual in Public Services.* The Russell Sage Foundation, 1983.

CHAPTER 2

Evolution of the Unit Development Officer

Margarete Rooney Hall

Associate Professor, Department of Public Relations,
College of Journalism and Communications, University of Florida

Only 40 years ago, the debate at almost all colleges and universities was about centralization. Alumni, public relations, and fund raising were separate from each other and often distant from the president and other top administrators. By today's standards, the language of that discussion sounds somewhat quaint:

> It is impossible any longer for the president to perform well and promptly *all* the duties he has historically performed and is today expected to perform. By far the largest number of his day-to-day duties and distractions are in the broad area of public relations, internal communications, fund raising, and other demands not directly connected with the formal educational program. . . . It is both important and urgent to determine and evaluate various means by which the physical and mental burdens of the presidency may be lightened. (American College Public Relations Association [ACPRA] 1958, 2)

> The fact that current tenants of the posts [of fund raiser, public relations officer, and the alumni executive] are good friends of equal status who operate efficiently without formal structure is no guarantee that the system will work well if the friendships break up or men move on to other jobs. In fact, even a sincere desire to co-operate does not insure [sic] continuous communication and effective co-ordination. (ACPRA 1958, 52)

> The fund raiser should, in most cases, have status equal with that of the public relations officer and the alumni executive. . . . The fact that the fund raiser has but one principal objective does not make him a mechanic who should be subordinate to the big-picture planners of the public relations and alumni offices; nor does the fact that he sometimes produces spectacular and tangible results make him superior. (ACPRA 1958, 53)

Now, the debate focuses on the decentralization of development programs at universities. This decentralization discussion forces us to debate issues related to process, such as how to ensure two-way communication between the central office and the unit offices and how to manage multiple contacts with potential donors. It is also helpful to consider the historical and conceptual contexts that create the framework within which these process debates take place. Toward this end, in this chapter I provide an overview of how the position of unit development officer (UDO) evolved philosophically and pragmatically.

Historical and Conceptual Context

Many large universities today have some degree of decentralization in the management of their development programs. This has not always been the case. In fact, the history of managing development contains several stories of centralization and decentralization.

In the beginning, all management was centralized: Presidents did everything. They raised the funds and built the relationships that sustained the colleges. They found the students, established curricula, and taught, and they solicited philanthropic and public support for the colleges. This situation was not perfect. John Witherspoon, shortly after taking over the presidency of the College of New Jersey (now Princeton) in 1770, noted that "the short lives of the former Presidents have been by many attributed to their excessive labours" (cited in Curti and Nash 1965, 36). Their tasks then were similar to those of presidents today: They traveled, delivered speeches, and invited potential donors to campus. They also built personal and professional friendships with potential donors based on shared interests in the content or the process of higher education—friendships that often resulted in philanthropic support.

As the management function became more complex, universities hired staff members in alumni outreach, public information, and development—just as they had earlier hired professionals in teaching, student supervision, and business. The development professionals worked out of the president's office, seeking small gifts from many people. Occasionally they identified a potential major donor whom the president then cultivated, with varying amounts of assistance and counsel. Public relations and alumni relations officers, although somewhat more established in the academic hierarchy, were often more removed from the president and the top management team than were the development staff. The three outreach officers had little interaction with each other and even less with the top administrators.

Many of today's senior development officers, presidents, and prominent consultants began their careers before development was at the top-management table. They are aware of the struggle to centralize development offices into a cohesive, influential force within the university. They recognize that centralization increased development's power to offer the university access to the philanthropic resources of its community and to offer the community access to the professional resources of the university. Resounding in discussions about current and future decentralization are the lessons of how institutional development programs were less effective when they were decentralized before the Greenbrier Report (see Introduction, this volume, for a description of the report).

The Decentralization-Centralization Conundrum

The current debate is not about bringing boundary-spanning perspective and expertise to the management table, as in the past. The decentralization debate is about bringing those qualities to the major units. In a sense, the reason for today's decentralizing of development is quite similar to the Greenbrier Report case for centralizing it.

In the former decentralized system, fund raisers functioned more like agent-solicitors for presidents. They possessed strong technical skills but were not well connected to the institution's top management, which they represented to stakeholders. The argument for the new decentralization is that central office fund raisers are like agent-solicitors for deans. They possess excellent skills but are not well connected to the management of the unit they represent to the stakeholders. Because the shared interest between potential donors and the university is vested in those units, the development officer should be part of the management of the unit. Moreover, like the presidents before them, deans and directors need the expertise of development professionals to guide them and help them manage time spent on development activities.

A decade ago, I did a study of the three patterns for managing development activities at research universities: centralized, decentralized, and hybrid. Through interviews with presidents, vice presidents, deans, and development officers at universities with development programs that were managed differently, I identified management issues related to centralization and decentralization. Based on a follow-up survey of more than 300 development officers and vice presidents, I determined that presidents and vice presidents were reluctant to shift away from centralized development. Their reluctance was often philosophical, connected to their knowledge of—and in several instances participation in—earlier battles to centralize development and bring it to the management table. They worried that decentralization represented a step back toward a system that was less effective.

The study (Hall 1993) demonstrated that neither centralization nor decentralization provides a "best-practices" model for structuring university development programs.

When the institution needs greater involvement of deans and wants to increase support for their units, decentralization helps. When the institution needs additional support for programs that cross over the unit boundaries, centralization helps. The planning for Harvard's $2 billion campaign exemplifies the difference. Having always urged units to raise private support through UDOs, the university decided on a more centralized campaign that would focus on societal needs, such as improving schools or curing AIDS (Pulley 1999) Although it did not prescribe best practices, my study did clarify key operational issues that are at the heart of the centralization-decentralization discussion.

Key Operational Issues

The choice to decentralize the management of development programs must be compatible with the institution's overall management system. After presidents had generally transferred decision-making responsibility for academic and financial issues to the deans, greater decentralization of development also seemed appropriate. One president said that it would be wrong to superimpose a centralized bureaucracy for fund raising on deans once you have given them as much freedom as possible to run their units and have transferred most decision making to the dean's level. In contrast, if a president has maintained tighter control over academic and budgetary decision making, it would be inconsistent to delegate management of development activities to the dean.

Deans seldom bring fund-raising expertise to their positions. For the most part, deans arrive with strong teaching, research, and service credentials but without a clear understanding of their role in seeking philanthropic support. They have a responsibility to raise funds but only a vague, often incorrect, idea of how to do it. In a centralized system, deans often lack necessary professional staff to counsel them and the authority to begin working with potential donors.

Deans and vice presidents for development are both responsible for finding private support, but they may not have adequate authority to do so. Although fund raising is now one of the deans' responsibilities—and they are eager to have the authority to fulfill it—fund raising is the primary responsibility of vice presidents for development. Centralized systems grant vice presidents the high level of authority that matches their level of responsibility. In a centralized system, the deans feel powerless; in a decentralized system, the vice presidents do. No wonder tension develops.

Donors hold the institution accountable for providing an appropriate return on their philanthropic investments. Gifts are a social exchange. The donor and the institution share a concern or interest. The institution brings professional resources to bear on the shared concern, and the donor brings financial resources. Each side receives a valid return on its investment, although donors do not experience the return as directly, because they are not on campus every day. To compensate, the institution provides donors with as accurate as possible an accounting of the return. Because they are not stationed in the unit offices, development officers in centralized systems have difficulty supplying strong accountability. Decentralized systems are better prepared to provide adequate accountability for major gifts.

Gifts support academic priorities and have the potential to change them. In my study, deans raised concerns about the potential for gifts to be uneven exchanges with the donors and to encroach on the institutions's autonomy to set its own priorities. When the donor contributed more philanthropic resources than the institution had professional resources to provide, the balance tipped. Deans told of times when donors, in good faith, wanted the institution to initiate a program for which no professional resources existed. There was no shared interest in the field. By accepting a gift large enough to actually establish the program, the dean would have essentially ceded to the donor the right to set the institution's priorities.

The potential for relinquishing autonomy was a concern in both centralized and decentralized systems. The deans who possessed the greatest responsibility and authority for making decisions about programs and budgets were particularly unwilling to let central development officers manage relationships with potential major donors. They feared the central development officers would accept gifts incompatible with the unit's priorities. Where decision making was more centralized, presidents would have parallel concerns and be reluctant to permit decentralized development systems in which deans might accept gifts that skewed the institution's priorities.

In decentralized systems, presidents and vice presidents wonder whether they have all the information they need about the units' development activities. In centralized systems, deans and directors are convinced they do not have it. Universities are rather loosely linked organizations. They have many units, each operating in its own sphere of political, social, and academic influence. One unit can shrink or expand in size and influence, without dramatically affecting the well-being of the others. And yet all of them are better off for being part of the whole than they would be standing alone.

Because a unit operates in its own sphere, it is difficult for one unit to stay attuned to the other's needs and concerns. Everyone values coordination, and even control, of overlapping areas like fund raising, but recognition of value does not easily translate into an acceptable program. In my study, I found that deans and UDOs believed that they coordinated and communicated well between the colleges and to the central officers. The vice presidents seldom agreed; they believed they communicated well to the deans and effectively coordinated activities. The deans and UDOs rarely agreed. In centralized systems, the deans felt as if they were out of the information loop and hamstrung by centralized efforts at coordination.

Philanthropic support alters the balance of power. Deans have told me that the possession of private support gives them more power with other deans in their institutions. One president said that private support altered the power balance between the deans and the president because the units were less dependent on the central budget for every penny. Philanthropic support is also a measure of a unit's off-campus power. A unit will not attract support if it fails to meet the needs of the community, if it does not listen to its stakeholders, or if it cannot commit to mutually beneficial undertakings. The relationship between a unit and its donors expands the unit's power in the spheres where the donors are influential.

Recent Developments

In the past decade, several authors have helped explain how decentralization affects universities and their units. Estey and Wilkerson (1994) found that centralization works best in institutions that have focused missions, no graduate or professional schools, and strong internal communication systems and that decentralization works best in large universities that have many components, clear rules, strong administrative support from the central advancement office, and enough resources to cover the additional costs associated with decentralizing. The authors pointed out that this system, however, may be more bureaucratic and less nurturing for junior professionals. Sabo (1994) added that decentralization also assumes that deans are used to cooperating with each other, that the central advancement office is prepared to provide abundant service to the deans and UDOs, and that development officers at all levels communicate frequently on substantive issues.

Ryan (1994) asserted that centralization provides better prospect management and avoids the excessive competition that leads to withholding information. It seemed to her that centralized systems result in fewer missed opportunities and lower costs, and that rich units are less likely to grow richer while poor ones get poorer. Grunig (1995) studied aggregate cost and contribution figures and concluded that decentralization does not affect the cost-per-dollar-raised.

Kelly (2000) found that centralized systems focus on "the overall needs and strengths of the university" (349) but that development officers in centralized systems may lack understanding of the core activities of the units they represent. Similarly, Kelly saw a disadvantage to decentralization if UDOs lack a strong understanding of the institution's goals and mission. For those reasons, he prefers a hybrid system. Ryan agreed that some level of decentralization is practical for large institutions because, as more donors are cultivated, units assume more initiative and deans get a professional staff to guide development actions.

I have shown that UDOs and chief advancement officers (CAOs) have agreed on important issues (Hall 1993). Both said that the central office should maintain alumni and donor records, acknowledge all gifts (although the unit might also acknowledge them), and provide research. They agreed that, to succeed, UDOs must belong to the management team of their units, have easy regular access to the dean, and interact well with the faculty and with the unit's volunteer board. Ryan reached similar conclusions.

My study also showed significant disagreement in other areas. UDOs and CAOs disagreed about whether, to succeed, a UDO needs to be paid by the dean, have an office in the unit, possess good rapport with the CAO, or possess an academic title. They disagreed about which office should have primary responsibility for setting development priorities, providing gift stewardship, preparing the case statement, and managing the unit's annual fund and major gifts programs. The most dramatic disagreements focused on the effectiveness of coordination and control measures, communication between the central office and the units, and communication between CAOs and faculty.

Other authors have indicated recently that tensions persist. Writing about the special needs of libraries at research universities, Paustenbaugh and Trojahn (2000) and Martin (2000) discussed the value of having UDOs help directors deal with internal and external development-related issues, especially because libraries are seen as having "no alumni" and "no students" and therefore no claim on any potential donors in the management systems. Sabo (1994) mentioned inherent tensions caused by prospect assignment systems that rely on "our" criteria instead of donor criteria and about the "snatching" of prospects by the central office after they are identified by UDOs.

Duronio and Loessin (1990) provided case studies of successful fund-raising programs. In their discussion of a public doctoral program, they expressed strong concern about moving to decentralize before organizing a central infrastructure to support additional, remotely located professionals. In an insightful discussion about fund raising for graduate professional schools within universities, Ashton (1993) pointed to the major differences between professional education and undergraduate education and the resultant differences between the schools, their alumni, and other potential donors. Ashton also discussed the relation between schools and the other units within an institution.

In addition, two authors have provided insight into the conceptual framework for decisions and actions related to decentralization. According to Orlansky (2000), decentralizing government is highly desirable when there is a large population, a large geographic area, higher per capita wealth, and a high degree of income inequality. Similarly, Lauglo (1995) suggested that decentralization usually relates to the scale and complexity of organizations as well as to power, conflict management goals, and crises of legitimacy. Lauglo offered four political rationales for decentralization:

▶ Decentralization promotes the use of market forces to achieve maximum potential.

▶ Decentralization creates checks and balances against the concentration of power.

▶ Decentralization challenges organizational dominance by established elites.

▶ Decentralization reflects the right of workers to be the decision makers.

Both Orlansky and Lauglo made points that seem to have applicability for all education institutions.

Conclusion

The positions that the vice president for advancement and the UDO hold share philosophical roots. One is chief officer of a major unit, the other is chief officer of the parent institution to which the unit is loosely coupled. Each is expert in both the technical and management skills necessary to manage relationships between the organization and a set of its key stakeholders. Each also supplies experienced counsel to a CEO and plays a role in the overall management team. Each is a boundary spanner who gives others in management the data they need about their stakeholders and negotiates mutually beneficial agreements between the organization and the donors. Despite these similarities, however, tensions are inherent in these positions because of differing responsibilities, perspectives, and, often, levels of experience. Ways to minimize tensions and maximize the UDO's professional success are discussed elsewhere in this book.

References

American College Public Relations Association (ACPRA) and American Alumni Council. *The Advancement of Understanding and Support of Higher Education*, 1958.

Ashton, R. "Fund Raising for Professional Schools Within a University." *Educational Fund Raising: Principles and Practice*, Michael J. Worth, Ed. Oryx Press, 1993.

Curti, Roderick, and Nash, Merle. *Philanthropy in the Shaping of Higher Education*. Rutgers University Press, 1965.

Duronio, M. A., and Loessin, B. A. "Fund Raising Outcomes and Institutional Characteristics in

Ten Types of Higher Education Institutions," *Review of Higher Education*, 13, 1990.

Estey, Gretta P., and Wilkerson, Steve. "Harmonious Arrangements," CURRENTS, June 1994.

Grunig, S. D. "The Impact of Development Office Structure on Fund-Raising Efficiency for Research and Doctoral Institutions," *Journal of Higher Education* 66, no. 6, 1995.

Hall, Margarete Rooney. *The Dean's Role in Fund Raising*. The Johns Hopkins Press, 1993.

Kelly, Thomas F. "Organization of the Development Program." In *Handbook of Institutional Advancement*, Buchanan, Peter McE., Ed. Council for Advancement and Support of Education, 2000.

Lauglo, Jon. "Forms of Decentralization and their Implications for Education," *Comparative Education* 31, no. 1, 1995.

Martin, S. K. "Academic Library Fund-Raising: Organization, Process, and Politics," *Library Trends* 48, no. 3, 2000.

Orlansky, D. "Decentralization Politics and Policies." In *Critical Issues in Cross-National Public Administration: Privatization, Democratization, Decentralization*, Nagel, Stuart S., Ed. Quorum Books, 2000.

Paustenbaugh, J., and L. Trojahn. "Annual Fund Programs for Academic Libraries," *Library Trends* 48, no. 2, 2000.

Pulley, John L. "How Harvard Raised $2.3 Billion While Trying Not to Look Greedy," *Chronicle of Higher Education*, November 5, 1999.

Ryan, Ellen. "Too Many Hooks," CURRENTS, June 1994.

Sabo, Sandra R. "Hybrids in Bloom," CURRENTS, June 1994.

CHAPTER 3

Characteristics of the Successful Unit Development Officer

James W. Asp II

Executive Director of Development, Memorial Sloan-Kettering Cancer Center

I attended my first CASE conference in 1982, just a few months after entering the development field. At the time, I was working in Manhattan in a development office with professionals who possessed all the stereotypical characteristics (positive and negative) of New Yorkers. I looked forward to meeting colleagues from around the country, naively assuming that they would resemble my colleagues back home. I still remember my surprise when, after looking around the room at the first session I saw individuals of every description. I recall in particular seeing a man wearing a lime-green leisure suit and thinking, "I'm not in Manhattan anymore."

I got to know that man better during the next few days. He was smart, professional, and an effective fund raiser within his community. I learned a valuable lesson at the conference: Successful development officers have many different types of personalities, character traits, and styles. What works in New York's Manhattan may be different from what works in Manhattan, KS, or Manhattan Beach, CA.

Those outside the development field—and that includes university presidents, deans, and the other academic administrators who hire us—find this variety of styles confusing. How can radically different types of people all be successful at the same job? Or, to put the question another way, how can a development officer be very successful at one institution and not so successful at another? To resolve this confusion, we need to know what makes a good development officer, and, particularly, whether development skills are innate or learned. In other words, are good development officers born or made?

In fact, development skills are both innate and learned. However, those aspects of the job that are learned tend to be similar for all of us in development, whereas innate characteristics differ greatly among individuals. This is why a development officer can be effective in one situation but not in another. Personality traits that are assets at one institution might be detrimental at another. As unit development officers (UDOs), you particularly need to understand these factors, because you work simultaneously in a variety of environments within your own institutions. In this chapter, I describe several ways to think about the role(s) you play and about how you can meet the expectations your organization places on you.

Four Types of Development Officers

In *The Development Officer's Role in Higher Education*, Worth and I (1994) posited four types of development roles, each requiring a different set of skills, talents, and approaches. We referred to those who personified these roles as follows: the salesperson, the catalyst, the manager, and the leader. The first three types (salesperson, catalyst, and manager) derive from innate individual characteristics. Each of us adopts a basic approach to life, a kind of worldview that determines what we regard as important. These approaches influence the way we respond to professional challenges and opportunities. Our approach to work is also shaped by what feels comfortable to us.

The Salesperson, the Catalyst, and the Manager

Dedicated to securing the gift, the salesperson receives considerable satisfaction from the thrill of the chase. With his or her ego highly invested in the success of this enterprise, the salesperson tends to personalize the effort: "I need to raise $1 million this year," "I need to close this $50,000 gift before June 30." The salesperson spends his or her time with as many donor prospects as possible and gains job satisfaction by closing the deal. One fund-raising consultant has said, "The most effective fund raisers, I find, are motivators—men and women who inspire others to give at the very highest level . . . Great fund raisers have the glorious capacity to touch the heart and set the stands roaring" (Panas 1998).

Engaging others in the cultivation and solicitation process, the catalyst is effective at recruiting and motivating volunteers to work on behalf of the institution. They are more likely to remain in the background (although they are usually very engaged in planning strategy for the gift and may be involved in the actual solicitation). Thus, the catalyst tends to use "we" language and give credit to others. Often, the catalyst spends time with institutional leaders, such as members of the board of trustees, the Dean's council, and other volunteer groups. His or her satisfaction over a job well done comes when teamwork results in a gift. According to Pendleton, "The role of the development director tends to be that of a background person . . . The director is an enabler—one who, realizing the paramount importance of the volunteers, enables them to perform their fund-raising assignments with ease and dispatch. The director does not solicit, but prepares the way for the solicitor" (1981).

The manager focuses internally on the effective and efficient management of resources—both human and financial. The manager spends more time with staff members both within the dean's office and in the central advancement office. To the manager, job satisfaction comes from having a well-run shop, which means one that has programs that run in a professional and organized manner, clearly articulated plans that reflect institutional goals, and closely monitored and effectively utilized budgets. According to Greenfield (1999), "There is more to fund raising than asking for money. The development office must be managed so that all operations run smoothly throughout the year. . . . Success as a manager of fund development means success as a manager of the fund development office."

There is no right or wrong approach to development (although a particular approach may be right or wrong for a particular institution, a particular prospect, or a particular time). But it is useful to recognize the distinct approaches typified by the salesperson, the catalyst, and the manager as we analyze our own fundamental strengths and weaknesses and determine which functions best fit our natural abilities. However, keep three things in mind when conducting your analysis:

▶ Very few individuals are exclusively one type of development officer. Most people's skills and interests reflect some blend of characteristics. Do not apply labels to support a limited and biased view of the individual, but rather use them as a tool for understanding a person's talents and areas of natural ability.

▶ To define someone as a particular type is not to render judgment on an individual's effectiveness as a development officer. For instance, a development officer who has a natural tendency to be a manager may not be good at training staff or balancing the budget. Another development officer who possesses the characteristics of a salesperson may be ineffective at actually securing gifts.

▶ Labeling someone a catalyst or manager or salesperson is not a value judgment; no approach is good or bad per se. However, knowing when to take which approach does require experience, judgment, and discernment. This is where the fourth type of development officer—the leader—enters the scene.

The Leader

The attributes of the salesperson, the manager, and the catalyst come naturally. But a good leader is someone who has learned—through experience, training, observation, and continuing education—how to use all three approaches in the appropriate way at the appropriate time. A mature and experienced development officer will know when to pay attention to management issues and when to spend time on the road nurturing relationships and soliciting gifts. He or she will have the ability to switch with facility between these roles, even on short notice. For instance, when a development officer and a volunteer solicit a prospect together, the experienced development professional will know how to read the signals and act accordingly. If the volunteer moves effectively toward making the ask, the development officer will play the catalyst by acting as a good staffer (which may mean remaining silent). If, however, the volunteer stumbles and does not move toward the solicitation, the development officer may need to step into salesperson mode and directly make the ask. To be a leader, in this sense, means applying experience and judgment to a situation and then acting accordingly—even if this means acting outside of your comfort zone.

A Vector Model of Development Officers' Roles

How do these issues play out in the day-to-day life of the UDO? First and foremost, a clear correlation exists between the three areas identified in Chapter 1 as unique to the UDO position—articulating a unit- or mission-based case, managing complexity, and maintaining key relationships—and the roles of salesperson, manager, and catalyst. The UDO must be a salesperson to formulate and communicate an effective case for support. He or she must be a manager, concerned with the effective and efficient administration of financial and human resources within the dean's office and among the central advancement, marketing, public relations, and alumni relations offices. Last, a UDO must be a catalyst who engages, recruits, and motivates others within and outside the unit or institution.

Worth and I (1994) used a vector model to illustrate how these different approaches relate to an individual's responsibilities—and how they may describe a career path. As development officers, all of us inhabit two worlds. Internally, we work with faculty, staff, and fellow colleagues within our institution; externally, we work with prospective donors (the alumni base, local or national foundations and corporations, and the local community). Figure 1 depicts these two worlds as vectors on which are charted our various job responsibilities. Responsibilities at the lower end of the vector are narrower in scope. Typically, UDOs enter the field at the lower level and gain broader responsibilities as their careers mature (illustrated by rising to higher levels on the vector).

Characteristics of the Successful Unit Development Officer

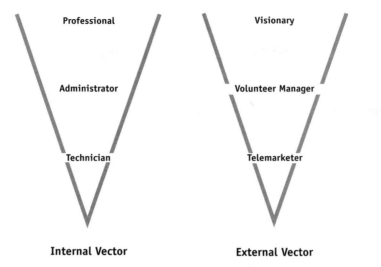

Figure 1. The vector paradigm.

Internal Vector

The internal vector demonstrates responsibilities within the institution. At its narrowest point, the responsibilities are more detail-oriented and tasks are similar day in and day out. Staff members who function in this area are technicians, and their duties are limited in scope. For example, a technician would be the person who enters information into the database or someone who prepares routine gift acknowledgments to donors. I do not suggest that these responsibilities are unimportant—in fact, they are key to the functioning of the office—but the individuals at this level typically have little influence on institutional policy making and seldom have direct contact with external constituents.

Tasks with a greater degree of responsibility are plotted higher on the vector, and the staff members responsible for these tasks may be called administrators. Although this is a common term, here it specifically refers to individuals who do have influence on policy and who are charged with implementing policy. These are internal matters, however, and administrators do not necessarily have much contact with external constituents.

Situated at the broadest part of the internal vector, the professional is an individual who must have a broad understanding of the institution. The professional influences or sets policy and thus possesses the broadest and most varied day-to-day responsibilities. He or she is also expected to comprehend industry standards and be able to benchmark the institution against its counterparts. The professional is acquainted with development practitioners at other institutions and is aware of trends in the field. Accurately viewed as "the pro" by deans, faculty, and other officials, the administrator is a valued advisor in this area of expertise.

External Vector

A similar broadening of responsibilities from bottom to top is evident in the external vector. But whereas all of the tasks on the internal vector are associated with making the office run, tasks on the external vector concern relationships with prospects and, ultimately, bringing in gifts. In general, the higher up the vector they are, the more time staffers spend on relationships with prospects and the larger the ask. As on the internal vector, the day-to-day tasks on the narrow end of the external vector change little; job responsibilities at the broader top of the vector have far greater variety.

Situated at the narrowest end of the external vector, the telemarketer is expected to make contact with hundreds of individuals every year and to close gifts with a significant percentage of them. Although, in a sense, the telemarketer is expected to develop relationships with prospects, this connection must happen in a matter of minutes and lasts only a short time. There is no period of cultivation, and the staff member is not expected to obtain a real understanding of the interests and motivations of the donor. The gifts received, of course, are typically small (which is not to say they are unimportant).

At mid-level on the external vector, volunteer managers have management responsibilities—just as on the internal vector—but their attention is focused on the external constituency: volunteers. A volunteer manager, for example, might be the person responsible for staffing and securing gifts from the dean's council or some other group of volunteers. The volunteer manager has responsibility for fewer donors than does the telemarketer, but expectations are higher. The volunteer manager must engage in cultivation and be in contact with the donors several times over the course of the year. He or she must have a much better grasp of what motivates the donors, their values, and their understanding of the institution and its needs. A volunteer manager requires more training and experience than a Telemarketer must possess.

At the highest level of the external vector, the visionary has a broad grasp of what constitutes excellent cultivation and a keen sense of the right time to solicit. The visionary will necessarily work with a much smaller group of key prospects—those who can make transformative gifts to the institution. He or she will work hard—and possess the skills needed—to understand the donor's interests, motivations, opinions, and values. Because this takes considerable time, the visionary needs to meet frequently with prospects to present the institution's hopes, dreams, and aspirations—to paint the big picture of the institution's vision—and often works closely with faculty and academic leaders.

Overlapping Vectors

These two vectors delineate the division between internal and external responsibilities. Most of us, however, work both internally and externally. Figure 2 show examples of how these vectors overlap. Generally, in larger development operations, overlap occurs farther up the vector. In central advancement offices of large research universities, for example, more individuals specialize in working with only internal or external constituents. Relatively few development staff members have responsibility for both, and those who do tend to be the most senior members of the organization (see Figure 2, Example A).

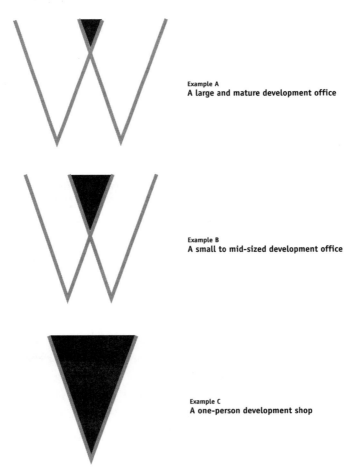

Example A
A large and mature development office

Example B
A small to mid-sized development office

Example C
A one-person development shop

Reprinted from Worth and Asp (1994) with permission.

Figure 2. Overlapping vectors.

Most unit development offices, however, have fewer specialized staff and therefore a greater degree of overlap between the two vectors. Staff members of small-to-medium-unit offices typically are responsible for a wider variety of tasks. Many larger development units within a research university (for professional schools, business schools, and engineering schools, among others) are essentially mid-sized offices, as is illustrated in Figure 2, Example B. Although they generally have fewer and less specialized staff than does the central office, they may have a substantial complement of staff working in a variety of areas of expertise.

At the extreme is the one-person shop (see Figure 2, Example C), in which one individual has complete responsibility for both internal and external tasks—and the overlap is total. Some unit development offices—even some within very large research universities—are one-person shops. Obviously, the pressures on the unit's sole development officer will be very different from those on his or her counterpart in a large unit or in the central advancement office.

Development Types and the Vector Model

To identify their day-to-day tasks, the four types of development officers—the salesperson, the catalyst, the manager, and the leader—may be charted on these overlapping vectors. The salesperson (Figure 3, Example A) predictably focuses on the external vector. Within the central advancement office or large unit office, they will not concern themselves much with internal matters, or with volunteer management. Rather, the salesperson will either concentrate on those areas of the vector that represent the telemarketer (e.g., junior staff members responsible for smaller gifts) or higher on the vector in the area of the visionary (e.g., more experienced staff who deal with major donors). Within smaller unit development offices, however, the salesperson works the entire range of internal and external vectors.

Because the catalyst as a central advancement officer (Figure 3, Example B) typically concentrates on volunteer management —the mid-range on the external vector—and internal administrative concerns related to volunteers, there is some overlap onto the internal vector. Conversely, the catalyst as a UDO, regardless of unit size, spends considerably more time and effort in the internal vector than does his or her central counterparts, initiating and maintaining networks and relationships, chief among them with the dean or unit head.

By contrast, a manager's efforts in a central office focus almost exclusively on the internal vector (Figure 3, Example C). Depending on his or her level within the organization, the manager may spend time on tasks that run the full gamut of the vector—from

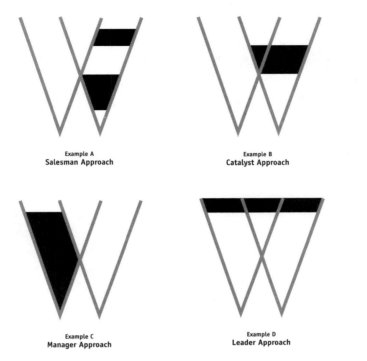

Example A
Salesman Approach

Example B
Catalyst Approach

Example C
Manager Approach

Example D
Leader Approach

Reprinted from Worth and Asp (1994) with permission.

Figure 3. Integrating the literature with the vector paradigm.

narrowly defined tasks at the bottom to broad and significant responsibilities at the top. The manager in the unit advancement context, either large or small, must manage considerably more complexity and thus spend significant time and effort on tasks that both span the full range of the internal vector and overlap onto the external vector as well, especially at the top.

In the context of the central advancement office, those who have enough experience and knowledge to act as leaders will find themselves promoted to positions of the broadest responsibility (Figure 3, Example D). These responsibilities will completely overlap both vectors, a tribute to the leader's ability to integrate all aspects of the advancement profession in a skillful way. Likewise, UDOs in large and small shops occupy positions for which responsibilities clearly span both vectors, thus making the ability to integrate skillfully all aspects of the profession an everyday necessity. Consequently, they must understand how and when to employ each of these approaches, and they must also master the skills necessary to advance the unit in both vectors. It can be argued, therefore, that a successful UDO is a professional who, almost as a prerequisite, has achieved leadership status.

Evaluation and Assessment

The vector model is a useful paradigm for a UDO who is evaluating his or her aptitude and responsibilities as well as a useful way to chart a career course. Figure 4 illustrates how an institution might position different job titles on a vector model. The vector model can also help the head of the unit responsible for hiring the UDO (dean, director, or other administrator) determine the kind of development officer the unit needs. And the dean and the UDO who share responsibility for matching institutional needs and individual strengths can use the vector model to conduct this analysis and guide this discussion.

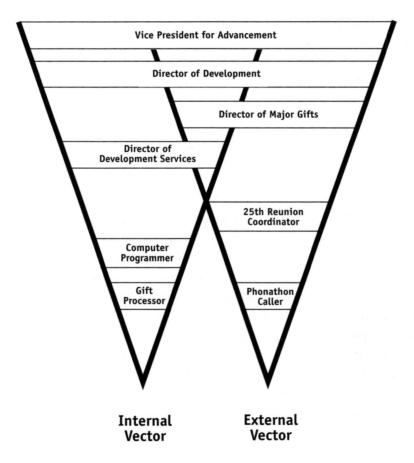

Figure 4. The vector paradigm and specific job descriptions.

The UDO's Self-Assessment

UDOs should consider the following factors when determining how to succeed in their current position or when assessing new career opportunities:

▶ Assess your basic personality candidly and objectively. Know your strengths and weaknesses to determine how you would rate yourself as a salesperson, catalyst, or manager. For example, when you call on an important but difficult prospect to test a draft case statement, do you feel exhilarated (a trait of a salesperson), or do you have to psyche yourself for the call? When you are asked to formulate a thoughtful and complex budget to support your program, do you accept the task willingly (a trait of a manager), or do you procrastinate because you would rather be in touch with a prospect? When a dean or department chair requires a great deal of hand-holding, rehearsal, and preparation for making a call, do you accept this willingly as a good use or your time (a trait of a catalyst), or are you irritated because it feels like a waste of time? If you are irritated because you would rather do the solicitation yourself, perhaps you are a salesperson at heart; if you are irritated because you would rather spend the time developing your unit's strategic plan, perhaps you are a manager.

▶ Develop the professional skills that will make you a leader. Once you know your weaknesses, figure out how to compensate for them. This may involve gaining more experience or education. For example, if you are not a strong manager, volunteer to serve on the budget committee to learn more about internal financial management. Or if direct solicitation makes you nervous and uncertain, get some practice by actively soliciting smaller gifts under the tutelage of a mentor.

▶ Assess your own institution—both the central development office and your unit—to determine its needs. Then be honest about your own fit. For instance, if a unit operates solidly established programs in annual, major, and planned giving but has no fire in the belly for expanding these programs, then a proactive salesperson approach is probably called for. A unit in which enthusiastic but ill-trained staff haphazardly conducts hit-and-miss solicitations may be better served by a manager who can introduce a systematic and effective program. For a unit with a history of effective volunteer leadership that has stagnated in recent years, a good catalyst may be the one to reinvigorate the program and recapture the good will of the faculty. Assess where your unit works well and where it needs improvement, then take the following step.

- Determine how to compensate for these shortcomings—either by improving your own skills or (if the budget allows) by hiring others who have strengths in your areas of weakness. For example, if you are impatient dealing with volunteers, find someone else on staff who has those skills.

The Dean's Assessment

The dean is also responsible for assessing and meeting the unit's development needs. As was previously noted, classifying a development officer as a salesperson, catalyst, or manager is not a value judgment: There is no right or wrong way to approach the development field. But there *is* a right way at the right time for the right group of prospects. And it is the dean's responsibility to hire the development officer who is right for a particular unit at a particular time. When making these determinations, deans should keep four factors in mind: constituency, culture, partnership, and personal fit.

Constituency

What donor constituency is most likely to provide significant resources for your unit? Are your best prospects among alumni who might give major or planned gifts? Or does building corporate relationships between faculty researchers and local industry represent your greatest opportunity? Or perhaps you should concentrate on developing grants from national foundations. Determine the constituency with the most potential, and find a development officer with skills and experience that match.

Culture

Be aware of the culture of your unit, and be honest with the UDO about these issues. Do your faculty regularly collaborate? Is teamwork encouraged, or are unit members competitive and individualistic? Is there general agreement about the direction and focus of the unit, or does the environment demand sophisticated political skills? Look for a development officer who will operate well within the culture and can work with a wide array of faculty members.

Partnership

Just as development officers should be aware of their strengths and weaknesses, so should deans be realistic about what development work they are willing and able to perform. Development officers should complement the dean's style. If you enjoy donor contact and thrive on sharing your vision, you may be better off with a good manager who can put in place thoughtful plans that best utilize your time with prospects. But if you frankly do not enjoy the hunt, you should find an experienced salesperson who is skilled and eager to close gifts.

Personal Fit

The entire development profession is ultimately about relationship building, and one of the most important relationships is between the dean and the UDO. If you are truly engaged in development work, you will be spending a great deal of time with your UDO, possibly traveling and attending social functions together. It is important to trust and respect each other—and this trust and respect will be enhanced if you enjoy each other's company. Look for a person you can feel comfortable with as a professional colleague, a sounding board, and (when necessary) a constructive critic.

References

Greenfield, James M. *Fund Raising: Evaluating and Managing the Fund Development Process.* Wiley, 1999.

Panas, Jerold. *Born to Raise: What Makes a Great Fundraiser; What Makes a Fundraiser Great.* Precept Press, 1998.

Pendleton, Neil. *Fundraising: A Guide for Non-Profit Organizations.* Prentice-Hall, 1981.

Worth, Michael J., and Asp II, James W. *The Development Officer in Higher Education: Toward an Understanding of the Role.* ASHE-ERIC Higher Education Report No. 4, 1994.

II

ESTABLISHING AND MAINTAINING KEY INSTITUTIONAL RELATIONSHIPS

CHAPTER 4

The Unit Development Officer's Key Relationships Within the Campus

John C. Halton III

Assistant Dean for College Relations,
College of Engineering, University of Texas at Austin

In the early 1990s I and Dr. H. H. Woodson, then dean of the College of Engineering at University of Texas at Austin (UT-Austin), who is now retired, attended a meeting of other deans and representatives of the university's central development office to learn about a new analysis of the giving potential of our 350,000-member alumni body. About mid-way through the meeting, Woodson started to make a comment and then paused for some reason without finishing it. Spontaneously, I completed his sentence for him. Not taking offense at my intrusion, he burst out in his robust and rolling laughter and repeated my words. Later, one of my colleagues who observed the interchange remarked about how closely we must work together, that one could finish the sentence of the other.

The ability to "finish the sentence" of your dean as well as those of as many of your colleagues as possible is one of the acquired abilities essential to establishing and maintaining key relationships if you are a development officer in any college or sub-unit setting. Success in development depends on anticipating the impact of an action you intend to take or are expected to take. Anticipating what will happen next and being prepared for it—even if your boss is not—is what you are paid for. Such anticipation also is what prompts you to practice your solicitation presentation before you make it, even to choreograph the seating arrangements at key meetings.

Moreover, what-is-ahead thinking applies not only to actions today and tomorrow but also to actions next year or in the next five years. Strategically, the question then becomes, "What impact in the more distant future will the program we are designing now have on the organization, and what adjustments or plans do we need to make to achieve the best future outcome?"

In fact, this theme of anticipating what is going to happen next will be the thread that holds this chapter together. It is the key to successful relationships with your dean, your department heads and faculty, and the people who support your work, as well as colleagues whose support is key to your success even if they have no reporting relationship with you. Allied to looking ahead are two related concepts: the awfully official sounding "doctrine of completed staff work" and the less intimidating idea that "quality is free."

Practicing Anticipation

The Doctrine of Completed Staff Work

A former colleague, Claudia Woody, introduced the doctrine of completed staff work to me, but it is really just common sense. Simply, it involves giving the person for whom you are working a finished product. It means that a staff member has studied a problem and presented in such a form that all your dean or unit head needs to do is to indicate his or her approval or disapproval. In this definition, "completed action" should be emphasized because the more difficult the problem, the greater the tendency to present it to your supervisor in piecemeal fashion. Although this impulse is natural, it is one you should strongly resist. As the staff member assigned a particular task, it is your job to research the details and present an acceptable position for action, considering alternatives and the implications of such action on various constituencies.

In reaching your decision, you may need to consult with other individuals, peers, your staff, other agencies, and even the dean if necessary to obtain the information you need to determine the appropriate course of action. Indeed, making sure that your dean is on board with your decision may save time and effort later, both yours and the dean's. This does not imply that you are asking your dean to solve the problem, but rather that you are seeking advice based on the dean's larger information base. The final product, however, whether it involves the pronouncement of a new policy or the modification an established one, should, when finally presented to the dean for approval, be worked out in finished form. Your job is to advise your dean, who needs answers not questions. If necessary, study, write, restudy, and rewrite your recommendation until you have evolved a single proposed action—the best alternative.

Writing a memorandum to your dean does not constitute completed staff work. Writing a memorandum for him or her to send to someone else does. Ideally, your views should be placed before the dean in finished form so that he or she can simply sign. In fact, in most instances completed staff work results in a single document prepared for the signature of your dean with only a brief accompanying comment or, in many cases, no additional comment. However, do not hesitate to point out areas or aspects of your decision that might be sensitive or confidential in nature. Let your dean know where the tender points are so that he or she can prepare ahead of time to deal with any negative reactions or alter your work to deflect or avoid them.

The doctrine of completed staff work does not preclude a rough draft; in fact, providing a draft document gives your dean an opportunity to add his or her own personal touch. A rough draft, however, is not the same as a half-baked idea. Nor should it be used as an excuse for shifting to your dean the burden of formulating action. Rather, the draft must be complete in every respect except that it lacks the requisite number of copies and need not be in final form. In keeping with finishing-the-sentence principle, learn your dean's writing style and presentation sequence.

Time deadlines are essential in completing staff work. Always obtain a clear indication from your dean about the urgency of an issue. If a task must be done today, then information collection may be limited. If you have time, use it to do a better job. If you are going to present a draft of the document, give your dean enough time to edit and still complete the task by the final deadline. If the document is to be sent on by the dean, draft a transmittal letter to accompany it and provide the addresses of individuals who are to receive copies. To save time for your dean, have any attachments included with the draft as well as any original correspondence on the topic. If the draft refers to other documents, include a copy of the pertinent sections so that your dean will not have to scramble to get the needed information as he or she reviews your work. Anticipate the work your dean is going to have to do to complete this task, and prepare as much of it as you can. Your job is to support your dean's efforts.

The doctrine of completed staff work will generate more work for you, but it accomplishes three important things:

1. Your dean will not have to consider half-baked ideas, voluminous memoranda, and inadequate oral presentations.
2. The dean will receive the best advice from the most expert source.
3. The unit development officer (UDO) who has a good idea is motivated to think it through and lay it out thoroughly, so as to more readily find a market for it.

When you think you have completed your staff work, put it to one final test: If you were the dean, would you be willing to sign the material you have prepared and stake your professional reputation on its being right? If the answer is no or maybe, take it back and work it over, because your staff work is not yet complete.

Quality Is Free

In the early part of the 20th century, the first dean of engineering at UT-Austin, T. U. Taylor, would place a check mark on lab assignments signifying that he had read them. At some point in the early 1900s, he began to curl down the right-hand side—the long side—of the check mark. The mark began to resemble the logo on the helmets of the St. Louis Rams football team, but with not quite as radical an inward turning curl. Students who saw this mark on their papers and lab assignments began calling it the ram's horn, after the headdress of a male sheep. They learned that to receive it meant that the dean had judged that paper or assignment as outstanding. In other words, the student had satisfied or delighted the customer—the dean. In the early 1990s, when "quality" was the latest management buzzword, we began telling our audiences that our ram's horn was the earliest symbol of quality in continuous use in the United States.

Perhaps you can see how this idea of quality as satisfying the customer fits well with the principles of finishing the sentence and completed staff work. Anticipate what your boss needs, do a thorough job of whatever is required, and offer it in the way that he or she can make the best sense or use of it. The ability to think ahead of your dean should apply to your work with donors as well. A final thought on quality: If you do not have time to do it right the first time, when will you have the time to do it right later? If you think of it this way, quality is free.

Key Relationships

The Dean

In addition to completed staff work and quality, the overriding concept of what-is-ahead thinking applies to what is perhaps a UDO's most fundamental job: establishing and maintaining key relationships within and outside the campus. Among these relationships, none is more key than your relationship with your dean. What are the secrets to cultivating that special relationship with your dean? These four ideas all involve anticipating what is going to happen next.

Learn what your dean values. The last changeover of deans in my college took place over a weekend. The retiring dean left the office for the last time at about four o'clock on a Friday afternoon, and the new dean officially assumed his duties the next Monday. Over the weekend, the new dean rolled up his sleeves and applied furniture polish to all of the walls (stained woodwork is the wall treatment in the dean's office) and did some other repairs. The message: "I'm willing to apply 'elbow grease' to take care of this place and, to do it, no job is beneath me." As a rule, deans are masters at sending signals and clues about what they value. Successful UDOs learn to read these signs and adjust accordingly.

Do what it takes to get the job done. Not long after receiving the elbow-grease message, I had the opportunity to let the dean know of my willingness to "polish the furniture" as well. Some maintenance had been performed in our office area, which includes well-apportioned meeting room space. A conference was to be held there Monday morning that involved our largest donor. As we were working on Saturday to prepare for the meeting, the dean and I noticed that the maintenance crew had not cleaned up its mess and had scratched the large conference room table. Thus, for a good part of that Saturday morning, the dean of a top-ten engineering school and I ran the vacuum cleaner and took turns polishing that table. When Monday arrived, not only was our presentation in good shape, but the room in which we were to meet looked first class, too. There is a true shortage of people who can find ways to get the job done. Those who demonstrate "plenary capability" are, when push comes to shove, progressively accorded "plenary responsibility."

Tell the truth. Simply put, this means saying what you think is right even if it differs from what the dean thinks. The way an idea, or a difference of opinion, is presented *always*—not sometimes—influences its acceptance. Learning how to tell your dean that you disagree is truly important. Inevitably, if you are a person of integrity, you will have the opportunity to do so. Spend time deep in thought about how to speak the truth as you see it. Observe intently your dean's interaction with others, and learn from it. Practice telling your dean that you disagree. Practice in front of a mirror—out loud. Record your practice sessions. Play them back. Always tell the truth, and always work to present your different opinion in the way that it will best be received.

Look good. Successful development rests on gaining and holding credibility with your stakeholders, constituents, and alumni. To gain their trust you first have to *do* good. Then you have to be sure that you also *look* good. In the end, the best thing you can do to make your institution look good is to make your dean look good. That means permitting no unpleasant surprises for your dean. All events in which the dean participates should be well planned with the dean's role thoughtfully orchestrated. The law of randomness means that every once in a while events that are not planned well somehow turn out well. But more often they will not. Plan well to reduce uncertainty—and foul-ups. Obviously, great commitment is demanded of those who seek to excel. To be the best, it takes hard work, persistence, and determination—and what-is-ahead thinking.

Department Heads, Chairs, and Others

As much as I try to read the mind of the dean and chart the political winds of the dean's office, I endeavor to stay out of departmental politics. My job is to serve the dean, the individual, as well as the dean, the institutional head. But with regard to departments, I think it best to serve the departmental head and not the individual.

A concept derived from the Old Testament of the Jewish and Christian book of Holy Scripture informs me here. The Hebrew word *sadaq* or *tzeh-dek*, translated into English as "righteous" or "righteousness," appears more than 500 times in that compendium. Although today we understand the term to speak primarily of a righteous person as "being good," the ancient Hebrews understood the idea as "fulfilling the demands of a relationship," a different concept. A companion idea is that of "the covenant" or contract, governing the specific terms of the relationship. He who kept the covenant was righteous. He who was righteous was therefore good.

The idea of having a contract with a departmental head or chair clarifies what you can and cannot do for a sub-unit director. It also lets that person know your expectations for a development relationship. When you are "righteous," that is, when you fulfill the terms of the relationship, a relationship of trust is established. Building and maintaining relationships of trust is the key to operating successfully in an environment where you have multiple and overlapping and sometimes conflicting direct-line supervisory bosses such as deans or central development vice presidents—not to mention "virtual supervisors" such as "star" faculty and research center directors as well as departmental heads or chairs. Try to keep the terms of the contract simple and consistent, employing the same terms and conditions for all the people with whom you are relating.

Remember, too, another concept: borrowed clout. As UDOs, we have no standing in the academic hierarchy, that is, no one in the academic faculty ranks reports to us. But that does not mean we are without authority in this realm. Precisely because of the special relationship UDOs are perceived to have with their deans, they are also perceived to operate in the academic arena with the dean's assumed authority—the borrowed clout. Thus, the contract you have with a school chair or department head is built not only on trust in your professional abilities, it is also built on the authority you bring to the relationship as an agent of the dean.

When you are righteous with your chairs, they also will perceive a need to be righteous with you, because you are an extension of the dean's power and leadership. Although such borrowed clout can add weight to your relationship with them, you must at the same time be mindful, in representing the deanship, not to misuse or abuse this authority. Once lost, it is virtually impossible to regain. Borrowed clout is best thought of, in fact, as a passive rather than active power. I think of it not as a license to do something—I would never say "the dean would like it if you would do this or that"—but as a value added to my position as UDO beyond my personal skills and abilities as a development professional. The art of managing borrowed clout is a fine one, but once mastered it can bring more vitality and creativity to your key relationships with chairs, directors, and other academic managers in your institution.

Faculty

If your job is to serve the dean as both an individual and institutional head, and to serve department chairs as organizational heads but not as individuals, what is your job with regard to faculty? How do you stay righteous with them?

To start with, you need to recognize that all faculty are not alike. At the top of the food chain, as it were, are the faculty superstars. In my College of Engineering, we have almost 40 endowed chairs and 140 professorships and faculty fellowships. About half of the chairs have market values of more than $2 million. As a result, we have many faculty members who are superstars—and almost all of them are great fund raisers. Although most need little help from me, I nevertheless like to keep them happy, in part because whatever gift money they bring in makes my development operation look even better with very little effort on my part. In addition, I believe I also have a "contractual" responsibility to them—to support their fundraising as it fulfills the strategic goals of the college.

For the most part, this responsibility entails handling for them the details of the institutional development process. In general, I find that faculty superstars have little awareness of or patience with the minutiae of the gift-approval and tracking process. I add value to my fund-raising stars by helping them negotiate that maze. I almost always can do it quickly because I know where the shortcuts and dead ends are. My assistance means a modest time investment for me, but it yields high value for them. Different stars require different value-added elements, and no two can be "handled" in the same fashion. But with all of them, anticipate how you could help them—and then be sure to follow through. Always remember that your university has made a tremendous investment in the success of its superstar faculty, especially those holding endowed positions. Therefore, almost anything you can do to improve the return on that investment is well worth your time and attention.

Keeping righteous with faculty other than the superstars is more problematic. If UDOs are responsible to a dean on both the institutional and individual levels, and to department chairs and faculty superstars only on the institutional level, then they are responsible to other faculty members only on a project-priority level. In these cases, I apportion my services strictly in terms of institutional priority and time versus return. Toward this end, I avoid at all costs becoming the arbiter of the relative worth or merit among faculty or projects. Thus, in order to keep things simple, I ask my dean and chairs to identify and prioritize the faculty or projects I need to attend to. Or, if faculty members come to ask my help or support, I always ask them if they have discussed their request with their department chair, because I will certainly be seeking the approval of the chair and perhaps even the dean before doing anything on their behalf.

Even with such approval, a UDO still needs to assess carefully the time versus return on a given faculty project. In this situation, you need to pinpoint exactly the type of professional activities or services the project requires, because your chairs or dean might not be able to do so for you. If you are in a hybrid or dual-reporting position, you might need the help of your development-side supervisor to complete or confirm this analysis; if you are in a truly decentralized position, then seeking the advice of UDO colleagues might prove helpful. In any case, once you have assessed to the best of your ability the time and effort the project will require over and against its projected return, you then need to review this assessment with the relevant chair and possibly your dean. This will give him or her a clear idea of what the project will entail with regard to your services. He or she can then assign its proper priority and approve the appropriate level of your professional involvement.

Determining the exact terms of the contract with a particular faculty member or project is delicate and intricate process at times more akin to a dance than a negotiation. As in all relationships with individual faculty, no two dances are the same. In any new dance, when the partners are unknown to each other and each is still moving to his or her own music, missteps are bound to occur. Often, not only the nature of your role but also the nature of the project will evolve and change by the time you find your rhythm. At this point, the contract might then be sealed either informally as a verbal agreement or formally with an exchange of memos—but you must always keep an eye turned toward what's ahead in the relationship.

Your Staff

What about the staff members who report to you? How do these concepts apply to them? As you might guess, the execution of the principles described earlier often requires a considerable amount of extra effort. This high expectation trickles down to people who have to do the work. A few years ago, rumors surfaced of a Fax Friday, which was spoken of with dread and sighs. When I asked what the term meant, I was told that those who worked for me counted on a very busy day of faxing documents as, on that last working day of the week, I tried to complete all the week's projects yet undone. In other words, it was a busy week that day. Was I finishing the sentence for the staff who reported to me? Obviously not, but I did finish my week!

In all fairness, should your support staff have to pay the price week after week for your inability to plan ahead? I think not, although I personally always feel challenged in this area. How can you avoid unfairly taxing your staff? A big part of finishing a sentence for a boss is knowing what he or she is going to say. But knowing that requires thinking ahead and planning ahead. At the beginning of the week, sit down and figure out both what you need to accomplish that week and how these tasks relate to what is ahead. What must happen this week to move you toward the goal you set for the month or the year? This is the basic question you must constantly ask yourself, and you should constantly share the answers with your support staff.

I have discovered that a spontaneous management style, which many development officers prefer, puts me on the road to a destination other than where I intended to go. I am easily diverted from my goals and must work constantly to stay on-task. Many UDOs, in fact, favor the development of a written strategic plan for the year and often involve their staff in the planning process. Short of that, planning your activities can make clear both to you and your staff what needs to be done week in and week out to meet your goals for the year.

Regarding your personal activities, you know at least three things. First, you know you must get out of the office to make calls. Second, you know that you will be seeing someone for the purpose of moving him or her toward a gift. Third, you know that you will want to take your dean along to close a gift. Using just these three basic parameters, create a calendar for the year that contains your travel dates, who you will be seeing on each trip, and the dates your dean will be traveling with you. Slot in two or three times the number of people you actually will see. Start with your best prospects early in the year and move to the individuals who will need more work as the year progresses.

How will this help relations with your staff? In my case, creating a plan and sharing it with them has encouraged my staff to believe that Fax Fridays are a thing of the past. Not only does it allow them to prepare me better for my visits, but it also lets them feel like they are participating in fulfilling the overall goals of the development office. All of us like to own things, including what we do with our time. Likewise, those who support you need to own as much of their work as possible. Thus, besides having them participate in planning my activities, I assign them specific tasks for which they are responsible, such as gift acknowledgment and special-event coordination and planning. Owning these specific duties will help your staff take ownership of the bigger goals and help them do for you what I want you to do for your dean—finish your sentences. In addition, I am extremely fortunate in having a staff that has taught me quite a bit about completed staff work and checking and rechecking to be sure the job is done right the first time—that quality is free.

Signs of Trouble in Relationships

Not being perfect, none of us enjoy perfectly harmonious relationships with others. I will not even attempt to elaborate the myriad ways any relationship can sour. But here are three clear signals that, for whatever reason, something is indeed amiss in one or more of your key relationships:

- ▶ Acknowledged failure to communicate effectively with your dean and other key individuals

- ▶ Constant variance between what you think should be done and what your dean wants you to do

- ▶ Persistent and perhaps escalating problems in getting along with the dean's closest associates, either staff or faculty

Assuming competence in fundamental professional tradecraft, the UDO who apprehends any of these signs needs to realize that serious trouble lies ahead. Do not be lulled into thinking that excelling in your fund-raising duties alone will compensate for trouble in your key relationships. Any competent officer can do the tradecraft, but only the UDO can provide the individual support the dean needs—and only the dean can provide, in turn, the authority the UDO needs. Thus, no matter what else you may do, get righteous—and stay righteous—with the dean.

Recommendations for Best Practice

- Set a goal to finish the sentence of your dean.
- Commit yourself to the doctrine of completed staff work.
- Quality is free, but it takes daily, diligent dedication to do something right the first time.
- Be a righteous person: Make commitments you can keep, and keep the commitments that you make.
- Find where you can add value to the work of other people, and serve them as you accomplish your own goals.
- Be mindful of the borrowed clout your position entails, and be wary of the potential for its abuse.
- Apply what-is-ahead thinking each day to improve the processes and performance of your organization in its pursuit of long-term goals and objectives.

CHAPTER 5

The Unit Development Officer's Key Relationships with the Central Advancement Office

Bayley Mason

Director (ret.), Corporate and Foundation Relations, Harvard University

I recently reviewed a memorandum that the chairman of Harvard University's committee on governance had asked me to write in my capacity as associate dean for resources at the Harvard Medical School. I and colleagues throughout the university had been asked to appraise a faculty report on Harvard's time-tested, decentralized fundraising system. I commented that although the centuries-old system engaged the "motivation, energies, and expertise of those most directly concerned" within a single faculty or school, it encouraged duplication of staff and services, a tendency to horde prospects without regard for their optimum interests, and counterproductive inter-school competition. My critique concluded that fund raising should follow Harvard's basic decentralized management ethos, but that more cooperation, training programs, central services, and structured central major gift clearance "would improve overall fund-raising effectiveness." That date of the memorandum: December 18, 1970.

Over the ensuing 30 years, I left Harvard for vice presidential stints at Oberlin and Boston universities, returned to Cambridge to head development at the then-new Kennedy School of Government, and ultimately retired from the central Harvard University Development Office. Very little had changed when I returned in 1981. And although progress had been made by the millennium, underlying tensions regarding fund raising persisted between unit advancement offices and central administration. To a lesser degree, tensions linger between the central and unit public relations and alumni offices. In fact, that strain continues not only at Harvard but also at hundreds of universities across the country—wherever there is a satellite development, external affairs, or advancement office.

In this chapter I address some inherent sources of internal conflict and suggest ways out of the thicket. I also examine how related units such as public relations and alumni affairs can better collaborate with each other and with the process of development. The underlying goal of most unit development officers (UDOs) whom I have met and whose writings I have studied is not how to win the battle for autonomy. Rather, they want to learn how best to blend the front-line, entrepreneurial spirit of the units with the greater resources, broader vision, and mission commitment of the parent central administration. Those officers do want to learn how to work better together. At the same time, central advancement management recognizes that the creation of climates, policies, and procedures to foster that spirit of cooperation will assure the central support and coordination that leads to institutional advancement success. Toward that end, some campuses appear to be moving toward greater centralization, especially in their fund raising, whereas others are becoming more decentralized. Whatever the mode, most campuses are searching for equilibrium to minimize inherent tensions.

Sources of Tension Between Unit and Central Offices

By definition, universities are bodies of learning united in pursuit of common goals. In reality, universities resemble confederations, although not all confederations look or act the same. Section I of this book reminds us that fund raising at the level of undergraduate colleges and professional schools or institutes—even organizational subsets such as libraries, athletics programs, theaters, museums, arboretums—take their cue from the institution's culture and history. Wherever I served, most policy decisions at either the school or the central levels were highly culture-dependent.

My view from Harvard's medical school, for example, varied from my view from its school of government—the sheer size, budget, and clout of the medical school dwarfed that of the Kennedy school for many years. Similarly, when I was in central offices my professional relationships with the various units at Boston University and Harvard were tempered by the nature of the unit. The Boston University law and medical schools were far more autonomous, for example, than its schools of communications or education. Harvard, which calls its units "tubs," has long recognized a distinction between the big tubs (Harvard College and the law, business, medical, and, lately, government schools) and the smaller tubs (education, divinity, public health, design, and satellites such as the art museum, arboretum, and others). The unit differences affect not only the bargaining chips that deans may use with their respective presidents, provosts, and vice presidents, but also the units' dependency on central administration for development services and, most important, for assistance in finding prospects.

We must recognize not only that units are not equal in their power or dependency, but also that the ties that bind central development to units may be tight or loose, with varying degrees of tautness in between. At one end of the spectrum sits an institution such as Harvard with a powerful tradition of confederacy, and at the other end lie institutions like Boston University with a tradition of strong central control. The degree of on-campus autonomy granted to professional schools and academic support units—and their respective deans and directors—coupled with their size, prestige, alumni base, budget control, and history, shape the culture in which development, public relations, alumni offices, and institutional foundations function.

Just as each university has its own idiosyncratic history and culture, so each has its own idiosyncratic bureaucracy. Although Harvard's development operation has historically seemed like an ad hoc confederacy of professional schools, institutes, and other quasi-independent units with an undergraduate college at its core, the university was never as anarchical as it appeared to the outside. When I joined the public relations staff of Harvard's $58 million medical school campaign in 1960, I was told that the president and other members of the Harvard Corporation had postponed the campaign since 1956 in deference to a campaign for Harvard College (an $82.5 million effort). However, when the college campaign was successfully concluded in December 1959, then-President Nathan Pusey steered volunteer leadership to the medical school, unflaggingly contributed his own time in cultivation and solicitation, assigned some support staff, and provided prospect research. Harvard's fund-raising history before and since provides ample examples of presidents setting institutional fund-raising priorities, especially in allocating their own time and persuasions.

Nevertheless, by 1965 when I became the medical school's chief development officer, competition for private funds was rising at Harvard. The dean had appointed me, and the two central governing boards had ratified the nomination only perfunctorily; the dean also evaluated my performance and paid my salary. Thus, I had no doubt to whom I reported and who would set our office's fund-raising priorities. But even though the medical school was in Boston and the president in Cambridge, I still knew my way to Massachusetts Hall, home of the president and my other at least nominal boss, the assistant to the president for resources. I always readily answered phone calls from Massachusetts Hall, and I met regularly with the assistant for resources to discuss policy and especially overlapping prospects.

I do not recall that he ever actually ordered me to steer clear of particiular prospects—he never had to. Mutual trust guided our relationship. Trust, in fact, always seemed to be the essential ingredient in the institution's unit-central balancing. Because I conscientiously worked to honor that trust in all transactions with the assistant to the president for resources, he and his small staff gave me wise counsel, identified new prospects and volunteers, provided introductions, and squeezed out time with the president when I needed it.

When I returned to the Kennedy school in 1981, the relationship between the units and the parent university had become more tense. Throughout the 1980s, fewer people seemed willing to share prospects, and useful information was transmitted into central files only with reluctance. Certainly the level of trust had diminished since my previous stint. Harvard's UDO had always included the faculty of arts and sciences, the annual fund and capital gifts group, plus planned giving and research, and it was then focused on a large drive for the undergraduate college. Understandably, the graduate and professional schools tended to view the UDO as the college's handmaiden. Cooperation and coordination between the units and the central office were minimal and fraught with tension. Various units also competed for funds among themselves. Competition between universities and with other charities is to be expected, but when internal competition becomes too intense it dampens productivity throughout the institution.

In most universities, only the undergraduate college and the professional schools of business, law, and medicine have built-in constituencies (alumni), which often serve as the epicenter of fund raising. Those groups cultivate wealthy non-alumni, foundations, and corporations to round out their funding needs. Schools such as education, divinity, public policy/administration, public health, and architecture that have fewer wealthy alumni gravitate toward the corporate and foundation sector as well as to wealthy concerned individuals. Pursuit of wealthy individuals is fine—as long as they graduated from other universities. That is known as "new money." But when, for example, a school of education tries to enlist law or liberal arts alumni in its cause, academic internecine warfare can erupt.

That form of academic cannibalism can pose a special problem at large universities that may have dual or even multiple degree holders. The alumnus with an A.B. and J.D. from Stanford, for example, inevitably triggers a potentially unhealthy competitive situation. The prospect can become irritated and head for the nearest symphony or be steered to a cause of lesser interest and thus make a smaller gift. Without thoughtful central prospect review, a university may ignore the fact that some prospects may be interested in a part of the university that they had not attended. That is when UDOs must deal honestly, trustingly, and yet aggressively with the central office—and vice versa. In that give-and-take, all sides must remember that the goal must be to obtain the maximum gift for the institution that best meets the interests of the donor.

The past decade has seen the growth of still another potential source of tension between central and unit operations—the regional officer. The rise of national and now international mega-campaigns with mega-goals, coupled with dramatic improvements in information and communication technology, has prompted more universities to add new officers to manage institutional development in locations beyond the immediate vicinity of the university. Typically, those officers either reside permanently in the region they service and occasionally make visits to the host campus, or they live permanently near the host campus and visit their regions on a regular and protracted basis. Although the role of regional officers is usually limited to development, sometimes they also have responsibility for alumni relations and even public relations and marketing functions, such as recruitment.

In development, regional officers often are assigned to be lead solicitor or moves manager for all alumni in their region, regardless of their majors or unit affiliations. Ideally, the regional officer and the relevant unit officer work as a team to cultivate and solicit prospects in the region. But that ideal frequently is honored more in the breach than in the observance, especially when rules for crediting gifts in those circumstances are unclear, biased, or nonexistent. A more likely cause of tension, however, is when a small unit—or even a big unit with a small but critical need—cannot attract the attention of the relevant regional officer. The regional officer may focus on the needs of the larger units because most of the alumni in the region are from those units, or the office may focus on the solicitation of a relatively small cohort of potential major donors. In those situations, unit officers may have to actively court and cultivate the attention of regional officers to get them to focus on their unit's potential donors or unit needs. In a worst-case scenario, they may need to involve their dean or unit head to leverage the necessary attention.

Resolving Tensions in Development Between Development Operations

In the 1990s, the search for institutional equilibrium to minimize inherent tensions led many major research universities with centralized advancement operations to distribute those tasks and responsibilities to their constituent units. At the same time, for much the same reason, several universities with historically decentralized advancement organizations moved toward greater constituent unit parity and control. The latter trend surfaced at Harvard during the 1990s, when the institution undertook its first university-wide campaign. Although essentially the sum of multiple unit campaigns, the university campaign included a sizable niche for central initiatives. In addition, influential alumni from large schools, such as business, were encouraged to take volunteer campaign roles with smaller schools, such as education. More significantly, that course brought all the deans together in planning the campaign and pulled development officers, communications officers, and alumni officers into more focused and frequent contact. Consequently, the central UDO was empowered to arbitrate all inter-university competition for top prospects.

The simple management tool of controlling presidential access can also aid central prospect control. At Harvard, as at many universities, the vice president for alumni and development, and the central principal gift officer guarded access to the president and the campaign chairs on development matters. When I was at Boston University in the 1970s, John Silber, the powerfully charismatic president (now chancellor), sealed most major gifts. Reasonably firm supervision over access to his office kept unit development officers reined in. Such door keeping, which was necessary to protect the president's time and maintain priorities, especially affected the management of those top prospects who expected his cultivation and benediction for their favorite projects. In addition, that device, along with joint committee meetings between unit officers and central officers, tended to moderate the ability of school development officers to do solo marketing.

Other management tools exist for stiffening central control. During its most recent campaign, Harvard's university committee on resources, a volunteer development committee that for years had been a Harvard College-based group, added many alumni from the professional and graduate schools. In a similar move, the central UDO itself, although not diminishing its work for Harvard College, added services for the smaller units, supported core and interdisciplinary fund-raising efforts, and brought all schools into closer communication. Even kickoff events and the celebration for concluding the campaign were promoted as university-wide, not unit-focused, affairs. The units lost none of their individual identities but rather prospered in the more cooperative climate. Indeed, Harvard's in-house historian, John Bethell (1998), noted in his history of the university in the 20th century that greater cooperation and collaborative planning were having a positive impact, particularly on fund raising.

Whereas Harvard worked to tighten central administrative control of advancement, other universities in the 1990s moved to loosen centralized operations and cede more autonomy and control to units. At those institutions, many deans and unit heads, especially those who had achieved high visibility, began to command the loyalty of top prospects, and, consequently, to assume responsibility for soliciting them for gifts. Once started down that slope, many institutions found the route very slippery indeed. In more cases than not, the strategizing in the cultivation of top donors quickly shifted from central to the relevant unit offices, as did solicitation efforts. Universities in that situation typically adopted at least a de facto matrix organization, with certain specialized development functions remaining centralized, such as constituent research, planned giving, and corporate and foundation relations, whereas most major gift functions migrated to the units.

As a consequence of that gravity shift, the role of the central major gift officer has changed as well. In some universities, to mine and steward the many new prospects and donors turned after a decentralized or distributed advancement model was implemented, central officers have been assigned or reassigned to work for various units or even to other geographical regions. Other universities have maintained a semblance of a central major gift office, either by capping the size of a gift that the unit could handle or by centrally managing a limited portfolio of major donor prospects whose interests clearly are institution-wide, intercollegiate, or simply unknown. The end result is that unit autonomy and control of advancement gained at the expense of the central office.

In such a climate, the least controversial strategy for a UDO is to seek out individual prospects with no other affiliation within the university. If you are the UDO of a professional school with a sizable body of wealthy alumni, such as business or law, you can focus on your own alumni and bargain over only those with overlapping undergraduate degrees. Moreover, professional schools in particular are also problem-solving organizations, which can appeal to non-alumni philanthropists, foundations, and corporations. With the exception of large national foundations that require presidential approvals or exclusive, time-defined institutional priorities, most of those sources will support multiple parts of your university (depending on their interests) and require minimal central arbitration.

Historically, prospect research has been both a means of encouraging central- and unit-office cooperation and a potential source of prospect security-control concerns. In theory, the central advancement office should be able to supply units with much of their requisite prospect research. In reality, although central development offices certainly do provide the bulk of constituency information, many unit offices still want to be relatively self-sufficient in order both to ensure timely research tailored to unit-specific prospects and to enhance security. However, some of the mistrust that permeates universities can easily find its way into the research realm. One of my deans, for example, preferred to use our own research staff in case the central office learned of our interest in a prospect before we had staked out a claim. But as central development offices continue to increase research capacity and improve information flow, the cost of maintaining a strong research capacity at the unit level overrides any residual mistrust.

Resolving Tensions in Public Relations and Alumni Affairs

The organizational models for institutional advancement vary on the macro level, just as they do for the development component. Many institutions package the three external affairs departments—alumni, development, and public relations/communications—under one umbrella. Some universities add community and governmental relations along with admissions. In other instances, each functional body has a single identity. In another variation, a news office reports to a vice president for community affairs and leaves publications and events to be dealt with primarily at the unit level. With public universities, there is the added phenomenon of the institutional foundation.

Whatever the organizational model, and whether it grew by accretion or design, there must be policies, procedures, and agreements for bringing public relations, alumni, and development into concert. *Educational Fund Raising: Principles and Practice* (1993) addresses that topic, notably in Chapters 26 and 27, within a discussion of the interfaces between public relations and alumni and development. Academic administrators generally understand that effective fund raising depends on powerful communications and an informed alumni constituency. The issue worth reemphasizing is not whether cooperation is the goal, but how to balance the values of decentralization and central authority.

In my personal experiences and based on discussions with colleagues and from what I have read, tensions between unit and central offices on development matters do not carry over into public relations and alumni. Most academic units and large support units, such as museums or libraries, attend to their own alumni or members and conduct their own public relations. Those activities are usually performed with requisite attention to overriding image expectations and other policies of the university. Rather, conflicts are more likely to erupt because of a disequilibrium between public relations and alumni affairs offices and a development office—whether central- or unit-based—whose mission seems to have institutional priority over their own.

Communications professionals (including those who are integral development-office staff members) sometimes believe that they are expected to put too much of a marketing spin on publications, news releases, and events. Similarly, the familiar conflict between alumni and development officers revolves around the relative value of "fund raising" versus "friend raising." And the "they-only-come-to-me-for-money" syndrome troubles many alumni. For example, during the 1960 Harvard Medical School campaign, one alumnus wrote that the "money changers had entered the temple." That letter prompted the dean to publish a strident denial in the alumni magazine. The anxiety level is much lower today, but that type of friction lingers. Development officers must remember that advancement is a partnership in which all elements merit respect, and that fund raising is usually more effective when equilibrium remains among and within the advancement and academic units of an institution.

Alumni associations can build loyalty that ultimately translates into dollars. In today's heady mega-gift environment, alumni associations can involve and reward alumni who give lesser gifts, recruit students, promote legislative programs, and assist in career placement. Similarly, encouraging the public relations office to develop stories that generate interest in a faculty member or in timely research programs contributes to the background information crucial to the early stages of relationship building.

UDOs can profit by establishing regular meetings with relevant alumni and public relations officers that keep them apprised of operations of their college or unit and serve as a forum for dialogue when conflicts arise. That communication is especially important when a department or school operates its own constituent alumni group or publishes its own newsletter; the schedules and operations of such unit initiatives must be aligned with the mission, policies, and procedures of the institutional office. But when those matters cannot be resolved, or when new or proposed activities require policy changes, wise unit officers do not attempt to resolve those conflicts by themselves. The best course for UDOs is to leverage their power by invoking the clout of their dean or assistant vice president.

Conclusion

From my comfortable perch in retirement, I can reflect on the unnecessary tension that exists in the academy between central administrations and various divisions. I do not support Henry Kissinger's postulate that the political conflicts in universities can be vicious because the stakes are so small. Rather, those tensions arise because parties on all sides fail to realize that their self-interest lies not in endless conflict but in seamless cooperation. As my colleague, Scott Nichols, dean for development at Harvard Law School, points out, centralizing advancement is largely a matter of trading efficiency for effectiveness. Having a central advancement office perform research, assign prospects, and oversee spending is efficient. But UDOs, who are a lot closer to their faculties and their market, can be more effective. Which do you want? Both, of course, but attaining both requires building a consensus about process and an almost intuitive sense of institutional balance—qualities difficult to attain in an advancement operation always at war with itself.

Building a consensus about how an institution should handle advancement and obtaining the institutional equilibrium between the whole and the parts to enable advancement to move the institution forward are not either/or propositions. Rather, they result from an ongoing process of give-and-take, a never-ending dialogue, and a functionality that weighs the well-being of the unit or institution against the well-being of the donor. One can go through life cynically putting down age-old maxims rooted in philosophy, politics, or religion. Some are mere platitudes; most turn out to be true. Our business is ambiguous at best, sloppy at its worst—and humble in all cases. Institutional advancement might not be able to produce the sound of one hand clapping. But it can give voice to the aspirations of a donor, assemble those voices into a choir, and conduct that choir in a concert that can make an institution soar. All it takes are advancement officers who put the unit and/or institution above themselves, think strategically, and see the forest *and* the trees.

Recommendations for Best Practice

- Understand the mission of your institution. And appreciate the truth behind the weakest-link theory.
- Universities are by definition collegial. The central administration should not assume a Mussolini-like role. Do not treat professional schools like colonies. They may not revolt, but the existence of sullen members in your corporate body will disrupt the whole institution.
- Strive for common ground and set up regular systems of communication—down as well as up. It may be true that more good ideas have died in committees than have been born there, but committees (working groups or task forces) are generally effective in a university environment. They afford units a sense of parity with the central administration and permit information to flow. Their weakness is that they take time, so impose action timetables on an agenda.
- Prospect review sessions are vital. They may involve only the central office and a single unit, or they may involve as many interested parties as appropriate. The trade-off is between free and open exchange of information and efficiency. The more prospects are discussed, the greater the likelihood of an optimum prospect assignment.
- Listen to your prospects. They are not "owned" by anyone. The wealthier they are, the more likely they are to have specific objectives for their philanthropy. Assume nothing—certainly not that they will support only that part of the university from which they graduated. Listen to them carefully, but do not be afraid of persuading them to support an institutional priority that strikes them as foreign. Back off when you become more of an irritant than an asset.
- Unit development offices must serve their school's mission, support their deans and faculty, develop new prospects, and protect the prospects they have. They perform

these functions in a spirit of cooperation and with respect for the university and the units but with a healthy stubbornness. You should be able to advance your unit while you remain a responsible academic citizen. Schools and other units that acquire a reputation for collegiality are, in the final accounting, more likely to receive their fair share of central support and cooperation from other schools. That notion may require the faith of a gambler, but, in my experience, collegiality yields higher returns than bunker management.

- American colleges and universities are remarkably durable. They have successfully raised funds for about 365 years in a variety of organizational modes. As professional schools have achieved greater eminence and impact, the temptation has been to opt for a highly centralized or decentralized fund-raising model. The middle way holds the greatest promise for gaining the fruits of cooperation while advancing the unity of the whole institution.

References

Bethell, John. *Harvard Observed*. Harvard University Press, 1998.

Worth, Michael J., Ed. *Educational Fund Raising: Principles and Practices*. ACE/Oryx Press, 1993.

CHAPTER 6

The Unit Development Officer's Key Relationships with Disciplines and Institutions

Molly Ford Croft

Director of Development, Department of Biomedical Engineering,
Georgia Institute of Technology and Emory University

Over the past 10 years, I have held the position of unit development officer (UDO) for two interdisciplinary programs. I was director of development for the college of computing at Georgia Institute of Technology (Georgia Tech), one of the first programs of its kind in the country. Its faculty comprised individuals drawn from a variety of academic disciplines. My current job is in the department of biomedical engineering, an unusual academic program administered jointly by two major research universities—Georgia Tech and Emory University. Because of the dual participation, my position has an added layer of managerial complexity and university politics that makes a difficult job even more formidable.

Establishing and maintaining key institutional relationships are pivotal to a UDO's success—it is that simple. But although forming relationships has been and always will be a constant requirement for UDOs, the institutions where they work are metamorphosing as never before. As the trend toward interdisciplinary and intercollegiate approaches to fund raising continues among universities, UDOs are increasingly called upon to create connections and coordinate publicity for unusual if not unique combinations of disciplines, programs, and even institutions. In programs that reach across traditional boundaries, managing relationships among faculty, organizations, and institutions is vital to the UDO's success. In this chapter I discuss how to establish and maintain good relationships at three specific levels: interdisciplinary programs, schools and colleges within the university, consortia and other multi-institutional partnerships.

Interdisciplinary Programs

When I first began fund raising, I assumed that my most important relationships would be with my donors. I was wrong. I quickly found out that if I had weak connections with certain non-donors, I would have no donors to worry about. Whether in an interdisciplinary program or not, unit development depends on solid ties with the *people who work in the unit*. Because every relationship is special and must be individually nurtured, each one requires a UDO's investment of time and emotional energy and none of them can be given short shrift.

In interdisciplinary programs, the task is more difficult because more constituencies—and often more people within each constituency—interact than in typical programs. Moreover, because of the unconventionality of the program's context, those relationships may spring from unusually complex personal and intellectual connections within the unit. Similarly, just as UDOs must have a strong relationship with the dean and department chairs of a standard college, school, or department, UDOs in interdisciplinary programs must work with academic leaders across several different disciplines. Given the sheer number and complexity of relationships, the primary challenge for the UDO of an interdisciplinary program is to develop a deliberate protocol to build and nourish multiple individual relationships and to map them organizationally.

Relationships with Faculty

In interdisciplinary units, more than in conventional units, it is critical to create and preserve relationships with influential faculty members. After all, they know their former students (that is, potential donors) better than anyone else. And because no normal institutional "ties that bind" exist, graduates of interdisciplinary units have bonds of loyalty to their alma mater only through their former professors. Faculty members are typically also the best connection to other potential funding, such as corporations and foundations. Indeed, the personal reputation of individual faculty members often constitutes the only real assets the UDO of a new or unconventionally defined unit can sell.

To connect with my faculty members, I needed to become a day-to-day presence in their lives. Toward this end, I discovered that the faculty members did not completely accept me until I asked if I could attend their monthly meetings. After attending a few meetings, I asked if I could deliver a short presentation on the importance of fund raising. Some members warned that I would bomb—but I did not. I made the topic fun. Instead of making a speech, I related specific success stories that had direct impact on them. After that meeting, I asked if I could deliver a brief update at the beginning of every meeting, which I did. The more they knew about what I was doing, the less of a mystery I was.

I also discovered that faculty members appreciate a sympathetic ear. In 1990, after Georgia Tech had completed its first major capital campaign, senior administrators had promised faculty members that the funds raised would have an immediate effect on their programs. And although the campaign achieved its monetary goal—and its success was ballyhooed near and far—the professors saw no difference. I should not have been surprised that three years later when I arrived on the scene some had lost faith in fund raising. Only by becoming a constant presence in their professional lives and showing continued interest in their work did I eventually overcome their skepticism.

I realized that not all relationships are equal and that I had a professional obligation to determine the relationships in which I could afford to invest time and emotional energy. I began to build rapport with the faculty more efficiently. Understanding that they had more needs than I could possibly satisfy, I initially worked with those faculty members who "bubbled up"—that is, those who sought my advice. My premise was that I was more likely to do well with professors who understood my role and saw how I could be of assistance. Accomplishing that, in turn, would help me gain the trust of other faculty members and lead to the cultivation of more relationships and, eventually, more successes.

My bubble-up theory worked well until my dean called me in and asked why I was devoting time to a project that was only a minor priority. The question shocked and embarrassed me: I had assumed that all faculty members were equally brilliant, their research projects and scholarship equally valid and important. Fortunately, my dean understood my confusion and generously instructed me about the unit's strategic priorities and how various research projects and professors aligned with those priorities. So I could determine when and where to concentrate my efforts, he helped me understand the timeliness of particular initiatives. As a consequence, by adding the vital trust-but-verify step to my bubble-up procedures, I regularly reviewed all current and anticipated projects with the appropriate dean or unit head.

Those periodic reviews also enabled me to formulate a third stage for my faculty relationship guidelines: mapping faculty-to-faculty relationships and tracing the connections between their research projects and scholarship and other projects within the unit and beyond. In a unit with minimal if not nonexistent organizational boundaries, diagramming functional bonds gave me a blueprint of the real organization driving the unit that was more vivid than any conventional organization chart. With the assistance of the unit head and other academic leaders, I learned to graph where one research project led to another and how the one laboratory's endeavors dovetailed with those of others. With those maps I could determine the various paths faculty members had to travel in the present and in the future. I improved my efficiency in building relationships by spotting junctures and predicting crucial partnerships. The more maps I drew, the more I noticed connections with funding sources. I could write more effective case statements, develop more successful proposals, and cultivate more suitable potential donors.

Relationships with Students

In addition to fostering strong faculty relationships, the UDO of an interdisciplinary program must develop dynamic relationships with principal *students*. Although students play an integral role, they are often overlooked. There is nothing donors appreciate more than thank-you letters from students. How do you get students to write letters? Make the task as easy as possible. Give them pre-stamped envelopes with matching cards. The same holds true for visitations. When donors come to campus, whom would they rather talk with: you or the students? The students win every time!

To get the students to work with you, feed them at every opportunity. (Remember *your* student days?) To thank them, order pizzas and Cokes. Trust me, they will like you and want to continue working with you. Occasionally, take a student who has been particularly helpful out to lunch. If one particular face just popped into your mind, that student probably deserves a lunch. Make reservations now.

Schools and Colleges Within the University

A UDO must have a solid relationship with the dean or school chair. UDOs employed by interdisciplinary programs need to work harmoniously with academic leaders for two reasons. First, the leaders can enable a UDO to operate efficiently within their unit. Second, when establishing priorities for a cross-disciplinary project or initiative, consult only those leaders who have the clout among their peers, their faculties, and the central administration to champion the initiative and provide support.

Throughout my career in interdisciplinary and cross-disciplinary programs, I have worked diligently to maintain healthy relationships with senior administrators. Why? Because those relationships are the foundation for my achievements with those programs. The key to those relationships is trust. Occasionally, I have said to my dean or school chair, "It's really important for you to attend this long and boring meeting. We will not see any immediate benefits, but it will pay off in the long run." Sometimes I assess a situation correctly and sometimes not. But I take solace in knowing that good deans and chairs, like all good leaders, accept input and advice from a variety of sources before they make decisions. So my advice alone—good or bad—is seldom the sole factor in a particular decision. Put another way, I do not have to get a hit every time at bat; I just need to maintain a respectable batting average.

Inevitably, a few leaders within interdisciplinary programs may not appreciate the processes of development. Indeed, I have often told myself that even if they were interested in fund raising, they would not be effective. But do not despair: Some deans and unit heads are willing to learn about the process. In such situations, instead of delivering lectures or assigning readings, I use a just-in-time pedagogical approach by wrapping advice about a specific decision or strategy into a general principle of development.

For instance, I frequently cite the five *Is* of fund raising—identification, information, interest, involvement, and investment—as the context for understanding the unit's position in a developing donor relationship. Ensuing conversations on what specific action to take can provide opportunities to introduce the concept of "moves management," or coordinating priorities. Also, circumstances change. One of my colleagues had a dean who had no interest in fund raising—until he married a fund raiser!

UDOs who represent a new or interdisciplinary programs, or seek support for an initiative that crosses school or collegiate boundaries, often find that potential donors are major contributors to other disciplines within the university. Consequently, it is important to develop good working relationships with fellow UDOs. Keep in mind, however, that you never want to create the impression that you are stealing donors away from UDOs in other departments. Rather, take pains to demonstrate how everyone can benefit if the donor sees UDOs coordinating their efforts. Such teamwork reassures donors and builds confidence in the program. The corollary is also true: At the first sign of competitiveness, everyone loses. The bottom line: Do not worry about who gets the credit. Get the donor to make the commitment, and let the credit take care of itself.

For example, a graduate (I will call him Bob) who had majored in electrical engineering had made millions as a computer scientist. Bob could be a candidate for either the electrical engineering or computer science department, or both. Obviously, Bob himself will make the final decision, but, obviously, if someone from electrical engineering gets to Bob first, he or she will promote electrical engineering. As the UDO of an interdisciplinary unit, however, I need to make sure Bob is exposed to a wide range of options. What if Bob is a basketball fan? Maybe he played in the band as an undergraduate. These are not conflicts—they are opportunities for collaboration. Put yourself in Bob's shoes.

Would you respond more positively to a coordinated effort or to several competitive proposals? Bob, like most donors, is smart. I could not trick him into believing I was working with another unit when, in reality, I was not.

Barrett Carson, vice president of development at Georgia Tech, teases that all fund raisers want to claim donors for their own purposes. According to Carson, donors should be a prospect for

- Computer science—if they have a computer in their office
- Athletics—if they watch *Monday Night Football*
- Electrical engineering—if they own a toaster oven
- Civil engineering—if they drive across bridges
- Biology or medicine—if they worry about dying
- Liberal arts—if they read

Those recommendations may seem far-fetched, but they make a point. In interdisciplinary programs, you can view the scene as either an opportunity or a source of frustration. I recommend looking at it as opportunity!

Consortia and Other Multi-Institutional Partnerships

When working for a consortium or other multi-institutional units, UDOs face one major additional challenge: conflicting (or at least differing) organizational cultures. Although all relationships within an institution are grounded in the fundamental values of the organization, UDOs usually deal with only the various behaviors those individual organizations manifest.

My current position within an academic program that is part of two institutions—Emory University and Georgia Tech—provides a good example. Emory is one of the nation's premier private liberal arts universities; Georgia Tech one of the premier public technological universities. If I am to perform my role effectively I have to understand and reconcile two very different organizational priorities.

The most obvious difference is the contrasting management styles. True to the values of a university focused on the liberal arts and aligned with the Methodist Church, Emory practices a collegial management style, where deans and unit heads are generally regarded as colleagues and peers. Georgia Tech, an engineering school conceived by the state legislature as an "engine of commerce" during the heyday of post-Civil War orator Henry Grady's New South progressivism, conducts business according to a more corporate management style than do most universities. At Georgia Tech, deans and unit chairs may or may not view one another as colleagues, but they are always executive decision makers.

Different management styles are also evident in the institutions' development programs. According to the nomenclature used in this book, Emory operates a decentralized development office: UDOs answer primarily to their deans and have "dotted-line" responsibility to central offices, hold decanal titles, and work in a loose confederation with other central and unit officers. UDOs at Emory deal primarily with the development aspects of the position, because most units have their own separate communications and alumni officers. Georgia Tech, by contrast, has adopted a hybrid style of development. Because the central office pays and distributes UDOs among the units, UDOs have direct dual-reporting channels to their deans and to the central development office. They hold the same rank and title as do central officers—"director" instead of "assistant" or "associate dean of development"—and collaborate closely with other officers. Although their titles indicate that they are development officers, in reality the UDOs at Georgia Tech by default carry out many of the communication and alumni-relations duties and functions of development officers. Both Emory and Georgia Tech are supported by just one institutional endowment, and specific functions—such as prospect research and planned giving—are centralized. However, in some decentralized universities, such as the University of North Carolina at Chapel Hill and the University of Virginia, even those functions take place at the unit level.

UDOs who have to operate on a day-to-day basis in two distinctly different organizational cultures have to learn quickly how to reconcile these differences. At the simplest level, they have to manage a new set of meeting schedules and reporting lines. In addition, they have to become acquainted with the personnel of another organization, as well as with the nuances of how those personnel operate. Most important, they have to develop a new set of relationships and gain the trust of a new set of colleagues, faculty, and donors. It can be quite challenging, but it is exciting and never routine or boring.

To manage such complex tasks and relationships, I divide my schedule into "Emory days" and "Tech days," concentrating all activities involving Emory players and events into one day, and those involving Georgia Tech players and events into another. Whenever possible, I refrain from bouncing between a Tech meeting and an Emory event, although on some days that agenda is unavoidable. Remembering which hat you are wearing at any given moment is especially important for maintaining relationships with faculty and students. Essentially, faculties are faculties and students are students no matter where they reside. By working with the faculty who bubble up, treating all faculty projects as unit priorities (but verifying their status with your dean or unit head), and mapping relationships organizationally, you can succeed in virtually any institutional setting.

In general, the differences reside in the nuances: manners of address and discourse, common nomenclature and jargon, formal and informal organizational structures, and topics of current institutional interest. Your tactics will yield success if you recognize that, for example, faculty members at one institution prefer to be addressed by their first names rather than by titles, and that "the Whitehouse" refers to a campus facility, not the residence of the U.S. president.

Another issue is trust. If units in the same institution do not trust each other, imagine the challenge of building trust between units at different institutions. Intercollegiate trust builds when, as in the case of Emory and Georgia Tech, there is a long history of collaborative projects and little overlap (and thus competition) in mission and curricula. In such situations, I have concentrated on projects similar to previous fruitful joint projects by focusing on corporate, independent, and family foundations. Because those sources are typically nonproprietary, Emory and Georgia Tech have combined their strengths to compete successfully for funds they would never have received separately.

I have avoided the sensitive topic of sharing donors. In my experience, some sharing has come about naturally, as the two staffs and I cultivate relationships with alumni and their families who play important roles in various foundations. The day is near when we will jointly identify a group of donors and cultivate them collectively on behalf of the intercollegiate unit we both serve.

Recommendations for Best Practice

- To manage the number and complexity of relationships across disciplines and institutions, install a protocol to cultivate relationships in an efficient and timely manner. Key elements of such a protocol include working with faculty and staff most amenable to development initiatives, distributing your time and effort to projects according to strategic priorities, and mapping relationships organizationally to anticipate needs and relate projects to the widest range of constituencies.
- Cultivate students, both for their future potential and for their immediate value in building relationships with donors, alumni, and the media.
- Establish and maintain good relationships with deans and unit heads when working across schools or colleges within a single university.

- A just-in-time educational approach when working with a dean who has little development knowledge or experience will give him or her a theoretical context for making an immediate decision.
- Avoid being territorial, and always be open in your dealings with the UDOs of other units. At all costs, avoid even the appearance of stealing donors.
- Be quick to share donors, projects, and credit. Be willing to sacrifice credit for the sake of institutional success.
- When working with two or more universities, pay attention to the different nuances of institutional culture.
- Concentrate initially on nonproprietary initiatives to demonstrate how both institutions benefit by working together.
- In all dealings, cultivate a personal reputation for scrupulous professional integrity.

CHAPTER 7

The Unit Development Officer's Key Relationships Outside the Campus

Amy Doonan Cronin

Chief of Staff and Special Assistant to the President, University of Virginia

One of the greatest challenges of working as a unit development officer (UDO) is navigating the terrain within one's institution. While working for the College of Arts and Sciences at the University of Virginia, I often cultivated relationships with UDOs for professional schools such as the Law School, the athletics department, the Jefferson Scholars merit scholarship program, and the alumni association. In fact, keeping tabs on the status of other UDOs' relationships with our constituents was an essential part of the job. A colleague jokingly characterized our constant monitoring of contact reports as "philanthropic voyeurism." But joking aside, such monitoring is particularly important because most of the people with whom UDOs come into contact have multiple relationships within and outside the institution. And, particularly with regard to relationships with individuals and entities outside the institution, UDOs must capitalize on the credibility and trust already established within the university.

This chapter focuses on relationship building with people outside the campus, from benefactors to professional associations. For this purpose, the UDO's credibility within the institution—and hence the ability to work freely with external constituents—will be considered a given because the chapter focuses on cultivating relationships with four key constituent groups: patrons and clients, peer institutions, trade and professional organizations, and international agencies.

Patrons and Clients

Unit development offices must first determine who falls into the patron/client category. For the purposes of this discussion, the most useful answer is donors or potential donors, a category that encompasses many subcategories. From the UDO's point of view, the patron/client category consists essentially of any individual or group—corporation, foundation, and others—that can offer the unit financial support.

For virtually all units, as for the university as a whole, alumni are the most promising donors. Although most alumni are the people who obtained degrees, do not overlook non-degree holders—those who attended but did not finish their degrees. The first eight-figure donor to the University of Virginia College of Arts and Sciences was a man who left the university to fight in World War II and never obtained a degree.

UDOs must also be mindful of corporate prospects and donors, as well as foundation donors. The best entrée to both corporations and foundations is through alumni who serve as their officers or directors. Often, however, faculty's research interests (and their knowledge of potential funding sources) determine whether the unit attracts support from corporate or foundation sectors. To successfully match faculty research projects or other funding needs (such as curriculum development or student programs) with corporations and foundations that have an interest in these areas, donor research is critical.

Nurturing a relationship between a unit and potential corporate or foundation donors is difficult, and the marriage cannot be forced. The unit must align its needs to the funding priorities of the donor and strictly adhere to the guidelines for proposal development. Many a development officer has received the skinny letter of rejection stating that "your request does not match our funding priorities." A simple rule of thumb: Assume that the organization publishes its proposal/funding guidelines for a reason. Do not waste your time and the program officer's time by ignoring the guidelines.

In addition to fund raising, relationships with corporations (and alumni employed by them) can be useful in other ways. These organizations may wish to work with your career development office to recruit students for jobs or internships. They may be interested in the unit's executive education or continuing education opportunities. They may also be potential sponsors for public programs—lectures or a concert series—or they may be vendors willing to sponsor programs or support the unit in other ways.

My working definition of patron/client also encompasses customers of the school or unit. For example, UDOs should be attentive to people who purchase tickets to plays, concerts, and other events; lists of season ticket holders often contain names of excellent donor prospects. UDOs can also increase the unit's cadre of patrons by becoming visible in the local community, perhaps by serving on the boards of local nonprofit organizations or joining civic groups such as a rotary club.

Peer Institutions

In the higher education marketplace, most colleges and universities regard other institutions as potential competitors for students, research support, and reputation, among other areas. Yet there are real incentives for institutions to overcome these biases and form relationships along lines of mutual interest. In Chapter 6 (this volume), Croft describes her experience as a fund raiser for an academic unit situated in two universities. However, a UDO does not have to occupy such a challenging and still rather unusual position to recognize the considerable benefits of establishing connections with colleagues in peer institutions.

Besides the obvious benefits of networking, such connections can be particularly helpful for developing joint proposals to foundations or individuals with ties to both institutions. To benchmark their organizations for strategic planning purposes, most universities and many of their units have identified peer institutions. Many universities already have longstanding relationships with other universities or colleges within the locality. Establishing professional relationships with colleagues in these institutions facilitates the development of joint funding opportunities and dissipates the distrust that might arise. In fact, such relationships might even be the locus for new joint funding ventures no single university could initiate on its own. Although it is still the exception rather than the norm among U.S. universities, networking and collaboration for the purpose of enhancing competitiveness for revenues is a long and established modus operandi of, for example, European universities. Another important reason to establish relationships with peer institutions is to share best practices ideas. A former colleague used to joke that CASE really stood for "Copy And Steal Everything." And unlike other professions, the development field lends itself to the sharing of ideas.

In virtually every discipline or profession, opportunities exist for UDOs to affiliate with colleagues. In the liberal arts, UDOs meet annually in dedicated sessions of the Council of Colleges of Arts and Sciences; in engineering, they meet at the Engineering Development Forum; in architecture, at the Workshop for Development Officers in Collegiate Schools of Design. In addition, UDOs meet in conjunction with national professional association meetings, which also bring together important groups of alumni. Many other venues obtain as well. Such activities offer opportunities to brainstorm creative solutions to common (and uncommon) problems, hear how others handle routine activities such as direct mail and alumni reunions, and establish a network of peers to call on for advice and counsel—and jobs.

Trade and Professional Associations

Just as the participation of the faculty and administration in national and regional organizations benefits the university, the development staff's external affiliations benefit the unit. Opportunities for memberships abound. The key is not simply to join an organization, but to actively participate in it by joining boards, making presentations at conferences, and writing for organization publications.

For higher education development professionals, CASE offers the best opportunities to stay current with best practices and issues in higher education. Many fund raisers in higher education also belong to the Association of Fundraising Professionals (AFP), formerly the National Society of Fund Raising Professionals. AFP has 24,000 members organized in chapters throughout the United States and Canada with a few newer chapters in Mexico. Because AFP includes fund raisers from all types and sectors of non-government organizations, it offers members the big picture of their profession. In addition, more fund raisers inside and outside of higher education are seeking AFP accreditation as a Certified Fund Raising Executive (CFRE). The Advanced Certified Fund Raising Executive (ACFRE) credential—the so-called Ph.D. of professional fund raising—is also available through AFP.

A growing number of UDOs, particularly those responsible for communications, also join the Public Relations Society of America (PRSA), an international organization for public relations professionals. Programs in PRSA's special-interest section for higher education offer a broad perspective on external relations plus opportunities to learn about effective strategies from the corporate and agency sectors. The International Association of Business Communicators (IABC) offers similar opportunities. Both PRSA and IABC combine strong national programs and a strong national presence with well-run regional and local chapters that provide professional development opportunities throughout the year. They also jointly sponsor an accreditation process that enables UDOs to acquire an Accredited in Public Relations (A.P.R.) designation, an internationally recognized credential. One caution: Although UDOs are encouraged to pursue opportunities for professional development in national organizations, it is easy to be drawn into those activities to the detriment of job responsibilities. As deans often advise students, extracurricular involvement should be taken in moderation.

International Agencies

As the unit's constituencies have spread around the globe, UDOs have become increasingly involved in development activities on an international scale. Because donors and prospects living or doing business abroad are likely to have an interest in international-izing the unit's programs, UDOs need to know about the university's and the unit's inter-national consortia and other global partnerships. UDOs also should be mindful of additional funding opportunities from international sources, including national gov-ernments, international service agencies (such as the Red Cross), and partnerships in international consortia (such as the newly formed Universitas 21). CASE-sponsored international development seminars and conferences can benefit both experienced and neophyte UDOs.

Communications officers at the unit level should know how to reach alumni and others who live and work abroad. International work by all UDOs affects development budgets, imposing travel costs to visit overseas prospects and increased mailing costs. The international arena provides excellent opportunities to make cost-effective use of e-mail to compensate for the diminished effectiveness of traditional methods, such as phonathons.

Conclusion

Unit development officers must recognize that relationships with external constituents can be complex and reach far beyond the donor relationship. A UDO must be conscious of—and attentive to—all the various individuals and organizations that can support the unit financially, help the UDO upgrade his or her professional skills and competencies, and extend the reach of the unit (and the university) well beyond campus boundaries.

Recommendations for Best Practice

- Build strong relationships throughout your institution. The greater the UDO's credibility within the campus, the greater the likelihood for cultivating successful relationships with a wide range of external constituents.
- Always be mindful of the potential impact—positive and negative—of external constituents on the unit and on the university.
- In addition to building trust as relationships deepen, focus on steward relationships to ensure the long-term strength of the bond with the unit.
- As good as a personal relationship between the UDO and an external individual or organization may be, the UDO should never forget that interests of the unit are cen-tral to the relationship.

Contacts

Association of American Law Schools (AALS), Section on Institutional Advancement, 1201 Connecticut Avenue, NW, Suite 800, Washington, DC 20036-2605, (202) 296-8851, www.aals.org/sections/ia.html

Association of Fundraising Professionals (AFP), 1101 King Street, Suite 700, Alexandria, VA 22314, (703) 684-0410, www.nsfre.org

Council for Advancement and Support of Education (CASE), 1307 New York Avenue, NW, Suite 1000, Washington, DC 20005-4701, (202) 328-2273, info@case.org, www.case.org

Council of Colleges of Arts and Sciences, P.O. Box 873108, Tempe, AZ 85287-3108, (480) 727-6064, info@ccas.net, www.ccas.net

International Association of Business Communicators (IABC), One Hallidie Plaza, Suite 600, San Francisco, CA 94102, (415) 544-4700, service_centre@iabc.com, www.iabc.com

National Agricultural Alumni and Development Association (NAADA), www.naada.org

Public Relations Society of America (PRSA), 33 Irving Place, New York, NY 10003-2376, (212) 995-2230, hq@prsa.org, www.prsa.org

CHAPTER 8

Hiring, Training, and Supervising the Unit Development Officer

Marta Garcia
Associate Vice President of Development, Georgia Institute of Technology

Authors of previous chapters have examined the history and evolution of the unit development officer (UDO) position, and explored the complexities of a development position based in an academic program rather than in a central development or advancement office, the traditional home of academic fund-raising professionals. Having served in both central and unit officer roles, I would definitely agree that, unlike the traditional central officer, the unit officer most assuredly carries a broader range of responsibilities that are an integral part of building and maintaining a successful development program. Therefore, no discussion of the recruitment, placement, training, supervision, and evaluation of UDOs would be complete without a thorough delineation of how the position differs from that of the central officer along with a complete cataloguing of the characteristics of those fund-raising professionals who have the privilege of serving as UDOs.

Requisites and Characteristics

The UDO is the acknowledged expert in his or her field. Because the role of the UDO is uniquely structured so as to be the primary link between the unit he or she represents and its internal as well as external constituencies, a much deeper knowledge and level of understanding of the unit's mission is required than one would expect of a development officer who represents the institution as a whole. Yet few UDOs represent programs in which they have training or expertise. At Georgia Institute of Technology (Georgia Tech), for example, only 2 of 15 unit officers were trained in the fields they represent. Most of our officers, in fact, majored in the liberal arts, although only one of us represents the liberal arts.

Imagine, therefore, the educational effort most of them have to expend to be able to represent competently to alumni fields such as quantitative and computational finance, polymers, theoretical physics, prosthetics and orthotics, CAD architecture, heat transfer, fluid mechanics, or avionics, just to name a few. (The reeducation of liberal arts graduates into technology has occasionally been referred to as "moving from Voltaire to Photovoltaics.")

A UDO educates several different communities. Although a UDO's primary responsibility is to secure private funding for the unit he or she represents, this unit does not exist in a vacuum. A prospect with interest in the Department of Modern Languages might not have numerous questions specific only to the discipline (e.g., number of faculty, degree programs, travel options, etc.) plus overarching questions about the institution as a whole (e.g., language requirements for engineers or business majors, campus living conditions, graduation rates, sports, computer resources, etc.) that all must be addressed competently. Hence, in addition to a strong level of understanding in a specific discipline, the UDO must master the same level of knowledge that central office generalists possess about the institution of which his or her unit is a component. Be that as it may, central offices rarely recognize the steep learning curve UDOs often face, much less provide any type of support for acquiring such knowledge.

Moreover, a good UDO must always be conscious of the possibility that, despite a prospect's field of study and career path, his or her interests may best be served by making a contribution to an entirely unexpected discipline or program. Thus, although the most obvious priority for UDOs is to obtain support for their unit, they must also understand that their first priority should be to obtain the greatest amount of support from a donor that will also provide the highest level of satisfaction, even if it means that that gift will not directly benefit their unit. It is important, therefore, to remind UDOs, almost continuously, that rather than compete with other unit colleagues for prospects, they should recognize situations where they must wear what we at Georgia Tech call the "Institute hat" and see things from a university perspective.

UDOs become knowledgeable about those fields or programs where such "crossover" giving is likely to occur—the civil engineer who now heads a construction company and wants to support the building construction program located in architecture, the business major who is now a developer and wants to give a chair in urban planning, or a mechanical engineering graduate who has made a fortune in biotechnology and wants to support the field of bioengineering. Often, crossover giving can be anticipated in areas where academic programs have already built cross-disciplinary bridges. Such crossover giving can be mapped over time, and the UDOs involved should be encouraged to become knowledgeable in their related program areas. Although difficult to perceive or anticipate at first, with time it will become apparent that "what goes around, does indeed come around!"

A UDO's responsibilities include a broad range of constituencies, external and internal. Most central or regional advancement staff members are primarily major gifts officers who spend the bulk of their time identifying and cultivating prospects likely to make major contributions to the institution. UDOs, in addition to working as major gift officers, must spend a considerable amount of time and effort establishing strong working relationships with members of the central development staff as well as with faculty and staff members within their units. In the latter case, and especially if the unit has not had an advancement program previously, the UDO often must first overcome a skeptical attitude on the part of academics, who frequently view fund raising as somewhat tainted in contrast to their own "purer" pursuits of teaching and research. Having overcome that barrier, they then face the task of training and coaching these same previously skeptical colleagues—now flocking to their office in search of support—in the fine art of cultivation and solicitation in order to keep them from jumping the gun.

As one of my colleagues puts it so well, much time and attention needs to be turned to preventing the fallacy of "Ready, *Fire*, Aim!" There are, as we all know, innumerable stories of deans or professors who, in the presence of a prospect with significant giving capacity, assume that anyone suspected of having millions of dollars at his or her disposal for philanthropic use would naturally be interested in supporting what is near and dear to the dean's or professor's heart. A premature ask or cavalier attitude toward the donor's interests could well ruin months of painstaking research and cultivation on the part of the UDO. The UDO, therefore, must identify those professors or students who are likely to make the most positive impressions and have the most in common with their prospects, and then train them in the skills and behavior that will enhance the coordinated effort to obtain a significant commitment.

In order to acquire resources for their units, UDOs must also find ways to build bridges to advancement officers working in broader, institutional arenas. The temptation is strong for regional, reunion, or planned giving officers simply to steer a prospect toward contributing to traditional university-wide initiatives that are easy for them to pitch and easy for the prospect to understand. Indeed, it is human nature to shy away from issues or topics that make us look uninformed. Thus, rather than enter into conversations about funding chairs in nanotechnology or graphic visualization, centrally based major gifts officers might focus instead on the need for athletic facilities, scholarships, or a student center. If they are to be effective, UDOs must be reminded to forge good collaborative relationships with their centrally based colleagues. Only when there is trust, respect, and appreciation *on both sides* are central or regional officers likely to go the extra mile to find or create a link between a prospect and a unit-based colleague who could potentially threaten their level of control over a prospect's decision.

A UDO can function in two or more separate departments without losing focus or identity. UDOs should be physically based in the department or school they represent, and most often they are. Their physical presence allows them to become part of the unit community and to gain those deeper levels of understanding that make them able to represent the discipline or profession with a sufficient degree of knowledge. Being part of a community also creates a certain degree of passion for one's home turf, and we all know how effective passion is as a tool for cultivation and solicitation!

But although the UDOs may live in an academic community, they are neither scholars nor researchers. And although they are development or advancement officers, they do not live with the other development officers of the university. Thus, without specific safeguards designed to avoid it, there is a clear danger that, in time, a UDO will feel isolated as opposed to an integral part of something large and important.

Simultaneously, pressures from the academic department might lessen a UDO's focus on the primary purpose, which is and should always be fund raising. Deans and department chairs are often tempted to take on extensive extraneous responsibilities that make it difficult for them to stay on target. Admittedly, unit alumni activities and communications programs are necessary foundations for healthy development programs, but development officers who spend more than 25 percent of their time organizing alumni gatherings, preparing newsletters, and arranging receptions for corporate recruiters do not have adequate time to cultivate major prospects or prepare proposals.

UDOs can use advancement activities as a step toward successful development. Many UDOs, in addition to their work with individual prospects, are responsible for working with the corporations that may also provide philanthropic support for their programs. Normally, these responsibilities do not involve representing the unit's or university's research activities: Those are negotiated through academic and legal channels. Rather, they focus more often on the initial research relationship that can and often does lead to broader philanthropic support. Indeed, as corporations become more diversified and international, and their relationships with the universities become more complex, managing the corporate relationship overarching these various research relationships might fall under the aegis of the UDO. Through careful stewardship and subtle education and cultivation, UDOs have raised a number of such companies to "graduate" from relatively narrow support for research to major or even principal gifts that benefit a broad spectrum of the university's programs.

A UDO generally operates with little or no close or continuous supervision. Most unit-based development programs are structured with reporting lines through both the academic department via a dean or department head and the development office via the senior officer responsible for unit-based programs. The danger is that that neither the academic nor development supervisor can be continuously informed of the UDO's whereabouts and actions. Unfocused or unscrupulous individuals can play one supervisor against another, accomplishing little and causing confusion and frustration in both the department and central office as well as to themselves. Conversely, the individual who successfully balances all of these often-conflicting interests to the benefit of the department and the institution is what I call the "total officer"—advancement's equivalent of the general practitioner. In addition to being experienced, entrepreneurial, focused, collaborative, and integral, the ideal UDO is also self-motivating and self-regulating.

Recruitment and Placement

Where then, is one to find the ideal UDO's unique blend of talents? After all, many of these characteristics are extremely difficult to measure, and most of them do not surface until an officer has already received single-handed responsibility for a program. Although not denying the obvious utility of search firms and national searches, the best place to look for talent is (as always) in one's own backyard. In institutions where the annual fund or the alumni-reunion fund is closely tied to or forms part of the development office, these programs provide a natural training ground for major gifts officers. This allows potential candidates to acquire knowledge of the university, attain successive levels of responsibility, and document talents and accomplishments that will become the foundation of a successful unit development professional.

Those who have graduated from the ranks of preparing annual appeals and organizing class reunion gifts understand the importance of a few key gifts in reaching a goal and raising a larger group's sights. In particular, an individual who has guided preparation for a major reunion toward the identification of a collective goal understands the process of negotiating, setting priorities, and focusing on a common objective. Someone who has made solicitations for "stretch" gifts, answered the questions that arise when donors are asked for more than they have considered in the past, or convinced a potential donor that structuring a gift through various investment instruments makes much larger gifts possible might well be ready to assume the challenges of a unit position.

Another part of your backyard is your own central office. It is not at all uncommon for major gifts officers who have worked in the central development organization to look to unit development as a way of enhancing their credentials while simultaneously taking advantage of the more focused and intimate nature of the community they join by virtue of a unit position. In this case, with all the requisite talent and experience already present, the key becomes finding the right fit between the officer and the unit, which I will discuss at length later.

When looking for talent, search both in your own backyard but also next door. Never overlook the wealth of talent that can be brought to a unit program by someone who has actually toiled in the field—albeit for an organization other than a university or nongovernmental officer. For a variety of reasons, professionals who have represented their companies or industries—most often but not exclusively in sales or marketing—might well look at development as a positive career change. Typically, such individuals bring industrial contacts, knowledge and passion for their field, and the perspective of age that enriches and diversifies a team otherwise remarkably similar in age, background, and professional level. One of Georgia Tech's most successful and respected UDOs is a former sales executive who, after 25 years in airplanes and boardrooms, joined the university as a school-based development officer. He has subsequently taught his new colleagues much about persistence and the art of closing a deal.

Ultimately, the question of fit cannot be ignored. Certainly, there is a huge difference in the cultures of academic departments. Who could miss the clearly identifiable differences between faculty and students of disciplines as disparate as physics, business, and art? These differences are not just superficial: Concentration in a particular discipline teaches the mind to think along unique patterns, and these thought patterns influence the culture of those professions. Even in closely related fields, I have noticed distinct nuances in the way people approach the same situation. When considering development, for example, a mechanical engineer might ask how the program would *fit* in relation to the rest of the university and other departments, whereas a chemical engineer might ask how it would *affect* the department or institution.

Reflecting these cultural differences, alumni and professionals related to these disciplines respond positively to individuals who are sensitive to and respectful of their modus operandi. I am reminded of a very verbal colleague who loved to hear prospects reflect on how their education affected their lives. As a generalist, he was immensely successful with alumni from political science, psychology, management, and the humanities. He was less comfortable and perhaps less successful with the scientists and engineers who wanted to "get down to business" much sooner than did their more communicative counterparts. This is obviously a generalization, but it illustrates the importance of finding the right fit for UDOs, who are likely to enjoy a stronger rapport with students, faculty, and alumni with whom they are simpatico.

Training, Supervision, and Evaluation

Key to the training and evaluation of UDOs is a clear and thorough job description. Normally, such a description is prepared before the position is posted. But in some schools, particularly those that are new to the decentralized or distributive model, development supervisors who may not have served in a unit see them as major gifts positions that just happen to be located on the other side of campus. Consequently, they do not understand the need for a distinct position description. Academic managers, however, may see the UDO as someone who should take responsibility for and thus can be asked to do anything related to the external world—newsletters, receptions, career placement, even admissions work.

The collision of these points of view can lead to numerous conflicts in expectations and a potentially disastrous working environment for the UDO when neither supervisor sees how this professional fulfills the program's mission. During job interviews, candidates for UDO positions can do themselves a major service by querying carefully about goals, reporting lines, and, most important, which one among their bosses is their immediate, day-to-day supervisor. If the candidate can get any of this in writing, so much the better.

The training process for UDOs should reflect the position's duality. UDOs need to master and thoroughly understand the structure, function, and responsibilities of the unit and central development programs. A basic knowledge of planned giving, clearance and reporting requirements, research capabilities, communications resources, and policies ensures both that the university is properly represented and that the development program is informed of activities and information that it must efficiently collect and coordinate. This training, focused on the development side of the job, is relatively standard throughout the profession. Continuing the training, it is important to provide not only guidelines but also field experience in the major gifts process, especially in the case of professionals who are graduating to the major gifts program from the annual fund, central development assignments, or even other professions.

Almost everyone who is acquainted with the profession knows the "five *Is*" of major gift solicitation: identification, information, interest, involvement, and investment. Although even fledgling major gifts officers usually know how to structure a solicitation, it is important to explain the need to involve the right individuals, to be direct, to make the case clearly and succinctly, and to place a number on the table. But it is no substitute for seeing the perfect execution of this script or for observing an experienced officer respond to the unexpected at a solicitation.

Moreover, even experienced professionals can benefit by having managers make calls with them from time to time. On those visits UDOs should receive every measure of respect and, if appropriate, be encouraged to take the lead. Where a UDO's training differs markedly from that of central office colleagues is in the degree of information that must be mastered regarding the academic department. Here, the degree of involvement by the dean or department chair sends a clear signal to faculty about the importance of development. The regard of individual faculty members for development is of prime importance, for it is these faculty members who must take the time to provide their new UDO with the rudimentary understanding of what goes on in the classrooms and laboratories. This is also where the development officer's fit with the unit begins to take shape and where the UDO begins to form crucial links with faculty and students. Even before the initial training period is over, the UDO becomes quickly immersed in an ongoing academic community filled with pressures that can easily distract inexperienced or unfocused individuals. At this point, the development-side manager needs to emphasize the UDO's need to get out and meet the constituencies that will ultimately provide support. Ideally, the supervisor and UDO should schedule regular joint visits. During these visits the supervisor can introduce the new UDO to important members of the community and take advantage of the new-kid-on-the-block novelty to meet individuals who have not been previously engaged.

In addition to joint visits, which reality and scheduling often limit, it is extremely important for new UDOs to meet regularly with their development-side supervisors—weekly at first, then biweekly, and ultimately monthly—on a permanent basis. A supervisor who interacts with a number of unit officers will need to keep track of the most important initiatives and prospects that are in play—to advise and supervise and help the UDOs avoid any untoward collisions with other units and the university, and, if appropriate, to step in. One of my colleagues had worked for months to arrange a visit with a principal prospect and his program—to bring him up to date on changes in the field and to meet with members of the faculty, students, and, most important, the department chair. The evening before the scheduled visit, weather conditions prevented him and the dean from getting back in time for the meeting. I was called (at home, at dawn!). Because from our regular monthly briefings I knew who the prospect was and what was at stake, the associate dean and I were able to successfully substitute for the stranded travelers.

In addition to regularly scheduled meetings with the development supervisor, UDOs need interaction and regular contact with other UDOs. Inevitably, they will have official contact with the central development staff and will participate in regular department meetings—usually solicitation clearance or tracking meetings. However, as usually the only development professional in an academic program, a UDO has limited opportunities to casually interact with other development professionals. While forging strong relationships with faculty and students in the college of arts and sciences, UDOs for that college miss opportunities to form analogous relationships with other development officers.

Regular meetings for all UDOs, organized either around similarity of experience levels or similarity of discipline, afford them opportunities to discuss issues of common interest and enjoy peer support and humor. Regular meetings also lead to shorter meetings between UDOs and their supervisors, because issues affecting all of them can be discussed within the group. In such meetings, it is important to follow an agenda and to keep the meetings on track, in case they turn into protracted gossip or gripe sessions. Each UDO should also have an opportunity to highlight individual issues and events of importance for the unit. At Georgia Tech, because these meetings, originally planned for one hour, rarely conclude on time, we have started budgeting two hours—usually meeting for breakfast. It is the only regularly scheduled meeting I know of that, if cancelled, becomes a real disappointment!

Keeping UDOs focused on fund raising amid the distractions and clutter is key to the success of both the unit and the officer. A monthly reporting structure (in addition to regular contact reports on activity) helps keep the UDO's sights on the immediate activities that are necessary to reach elusive long-term goals. A model report would include a chronological listing of the visits that have taken place, with columns to indicate whether the visit was individual, group, or corporate, plus space to record the nature of the visit—introduction, cultivation, solicitation, or stewardship. If the purpose is solicitation, then basic information on the amount and purpose of the ask are noted as well, as are gifts and commitments received. (A sample format is provided on page 112.)

There is endless debate over what kind of contact warrants inclusion in the report. My rule of thumb: It must be significant enough to move a prospect another step toward successful solicitation or closure. A simple phone call inviting Mr. Burdell to a football game does not qualify. But if the phone call and invitation lead to a description of a renovation project taking shape in the aerospace engineering department that moves him one step closer to a visit with the dean for solicitation, it is as significant as a personal visit and thus would qualify.

Unit Development Monthly Activities

Unit: _____

Director: _____

Month: _____

Date	Prospect's Name or Group Description	# of Contacts						Amount	Notes / Other
		U	I	C	G	Tx	S		
Total		0	0	0	0	0	0	$0	

U–Unit Activity   I–Initial Activity   C–Cultivation   G–Group   Tx–Thank you   S–Solicitation

Should UDOs be required to meet a monthly quota or minimum amount of visits? Having during the course of my career served as both a UDO and central development officer (CDO), I believe CDOs are usually able to execute more direct meetings with prospects than UDOs. Because of the nature of their jobs, CDOs can focus more directly on the process of development. In moving someone from the stage of identification to cultivation, solicitation, and closure, and ultimately stewardship, the major obstacles are travel complications, unexpected events either in their territory or on campus, or the coordination of visits by academic representatives of the university. Pulled in many directions by their academic bases, UDOs must participate in numerous on-campus activities that do not pressure CDOs.

The key to evaluating the efficacy of contacts and determining whether their numbers are sufficient is the age-old concept of quality versus quantity. Nonetheless, there should be an official goal. Much as prospects need a number on the table during solicitation, UDOs as well as CDOs need a number to raise their sights. At Georgia Tech we have settled on an expectation of 20 contacts per month, or 5 per week—not an unrealistic goal. (Note: Despite an extraordinarily successful campaign in which *every single unit* achieved its goal, there were relatively few months in which most UDOs achieved the goal of 20 visits.)

Ultimately, even with extensive reporting structures, joint visits, and training, a UDO supervisor can do little to motivate or support individuals who need constant prodding and supervision or who are inherently negative or pessimistic. UDOs are in many ways free agents and, as such, must generate virtually all of the motivation and energy they put into their work. Training and supervision are merely structures that allow them to function in concert with their colleagues in both the central office and in their department or school.

One more motivator worth mentioning is the role model. Because no teacher is stronger than example, a supervisor who sets a high bar and inspires others by virtue of his or her own professionalism influences the way experienced professionals relate to their less-experienced colleagues, creating a perpetual stream of mentors and protégés. To co-manage and support UDOs effectively and consistently, a UDO supervisor should maintain contact with all of the department heads or deans. Simultaneously, the unit supervisor must build bridges rather than walls between UDOs and their central colleagues and set achievable goals that have been established with the input and agreement of the UDO. Because of administrative responsibilities, the supervisor cannot make the same number of contacts or manage the same number of prospects, but UDOs should always be aware that their supervisors also participate in the major gifts process and face the same pressures and disappointments.

If good training and motivational relationships between UDOs and their supervisors are in place, the evaluation process becomes rather simple. A supervisor who is in continuous contact will not spring surprise evaluations on subordinates. In the case of joint supervision, it is both desirable and imperative that issues of concern to one supervisor be communicated to the other, and that they collaborate on the training and evaluation of the UDO. Evaluation should be ongoing, and items that need to be corrected should be presented in a positive, constructive manner, possibly involving the active participation of the other supervisor.

I am reminded of one UDO who had experience in the business arena and some exposure to the major gifts process. She enjoyed the process of cultivating prospects, but feared that if she asked them for a gift they would no longer enjoy her company. Both supervisors concurred that this needed correction and informed her of their concern. After a few joint solicitation meetings, with her supervisor acting first as the active solicitor and then as a passive observer, her self-imposed obstacles disappeared and she became a skilled and enthusiastic solicitor and closer.

Because most institutions require formal annual evaluations, it is my custom to prepare these with input from the deans or department heads, one or two key volunteers, and colleagues from central development. I usually distribute a brief questionnaire that can be submitted anonymously. The academic supervisor comments to the completed formal evaluation, which is then signed by both the development and academic supervisors. The final form is given to the UDO at a regular monthly meeting early enough in the year to allow the UDO some time to review it and discuss it with me or the academic supervisor. Then it is signed by the UDO and submitted through the appropriate channels. In the relatively rare case that evaluations clearly signal a drastic need for improvement, it is crucial for both the development and the academic supervisors to participate in the evaluation meeting.

Is the job complicated? Yes. Intricate? Yes. But the UDOs are actually the professional fund raisers who have the strongest link to the ultimate purpose of development. Their contact with and commitment to the academic program of an institution provides the greatest feedback and opportunity to see in action the fruits of their labors. They are privileged to see, in a way that few non-educators ever do, the effect of their efforts on the progress of education. For that, they are willing to work harder and put up with more complexity and challenge than most of their colleagues. In so doing, UDOs energize and enrich themselves and their development and academic colleagues, and they make working with them and for them indeed a pleasure and privilege.

Recommendations for Best Practice

- When hiring a UDO, pay close attention to the input of colleagues who will work at the same level as the candidate and interact with the position frequently. It is better to reopen the search than to settle for less. Pay attention to fit as well as to credentials and references.
- Once you have made a final, well-thought-out choice, give the UDO solid training and create a bond with the institution.
- Set clear, achievable goals in concert with the UDO and the dean or department head.
- Have faith—not everyone does things the same way you do, but everyone wants to succeed. Provide professionals with the tools to do their job, offer help if they need it, and they *will* succeed.
- Do not compete with your staff!
- Give your staff credit for their creativity, their energy, their loyalty, their hard work, and—most of all—for their success.

CHAPTER 9

The Durham Integrated Income Generation Model for Fund Raising

Scott Hayter
Director, Development and Alumni Relations, University of Durham, England

Peter Slee
Director, Marketing and Corporate Communications, University of Durham, England

Models of fund raising used in the United Kingdom are typically imported wholesale from North America. In these models, the director of development is the maestro, the conductor of a development orchestra in which every member has been classically trained (usually by CASE) and sticks closely to the printed score. At the University of Durham, however, we have formulated an indigenous model for income generation in which the director of development is more akin to a virtuoso soloist in an integrated income-generating improvisational jazz ensemble. It is an approach that has radical implications for directors of development and their teams—and it may have implications for the operations of unit development officers (UDOs) on both sides of the Atlantic.

In this chapter, we first examine the rationale for the Durham Integrated Income Generation (DIIG) model and then discuss synergy, which is a critical success factor for integrated income generation. We then present two case studies of actual projects to illustrate how the DIIG model works and conclude with a list of recommendations for best practice.

Rationale

Three historic developments in the UK funding mechanism for higher education underlie the rationale for the DIIG model. The first is in the amount and source of university funding. In common with all European countries, higher education in the United Kingdom is highly dependent on state funding. Across Europe, states provide an average of 75 percent of total university funding; in the United Kingdom this amount is 72 percent. At the same time, between 1990 and 2000, the percentage of young people in higher education in the United Kingdom has doubled. Lower funding, coupled with the increase in the number of students, means that the money universities receive per student has fallen by 40 percent over this period. Moreover, the UK government anticipates an additional 15 percent increase in students over the next 10 years with no additional increase in resources. According to recent estimates, in order to maintain current standards of teaching and research, universities will require an additional £900 million. Because the government has made it clear that this money will not be forthcoming from public revenues, universities must become better at raising money from nongovernment sources.

Second, although government funding for UK higher education has been capped, the nature of that funding has undergone an important shift. Twenty years ago, a UK university could typically count on receiving an annual grant equivalent to approximately 90 percent of its core funding. Today, with a deregulated income stream, universities are no longer assured of national funding for all core functions. Rather, they must compete in a fierce government marketplace for both students (and the funding that accompanies them) and research funding. In addition, to complement and complete their core funding, universities must bid for scores of challenge funds available from national, regional, and European governments.

As a result, Durham University today receives less than 40 percent of its income for core functions from state allotments. The rest—another £70 million annually—has to be earned in the government marketplace. Ultimately, this is a zero-sum game, because there is only a fixed amount of money in the pot, and increased success by one organization reduces the funds available to the rest. Within the general context of near-term annual reductions in state funding, the deregulation of those funds means there are big winners and even bigger losers.

This state of affairs has changed the nature of academic leadership. Deans of faculties and heads of departments are now managers of what are, in effect, small, or perhaps medium-sized, businesses. Similarly, the vice chancellor or principal is now the CEO of a massive, highly complex conglomerate that comprises these micro-businesses. To a large extent, the success of the conglomerate depends on the success of these micro-businesses, each of which operates in its own highly complex market. To succeed, these businesses must provide demonstrably top-class education and groundbreaking research. To do that, however, they must attract students to educate and money to fund research projects. Deregulation has led to more intense competition for these resources.

Academics can easily be drawn into spending more time chasing money, and, correspondingly, less time professing their discipline—which leads to the third element underpinning the DIIG model.

Synergy: A Critical Success Factor

The relatively recent pressure on academics to generate the resources they need to conduct their business has led to the development within UK universities of new business-support services, such as development offices. But in almost every UK university, these services face a dilemma. On the one hand, following funding "deregulation," university or "corporate" income generation is an illusion inasmuch as universities per se do not generate income. Rather, *academic departments* generate income from the delivery of specific services or initiatives. On the other hand, the theoretical income-generating needs of what might in a large university run to more than 100 such units are massive and undeliverable "in-parallel." In short, the DIIG model aims to address this dilemma.

Simply put, integrated income generation means the coordination of resource generation in support of strategic institutional or corporate advancement. The critical success factor of integrated income generation is synergy. This synergy needs to operate at three levels: strategic integration, structural synergy, and shared objectives.

Strategic Integration

Using a business analogy, strategic integration means, first, clear integration of institutional or "corporate" and departmental or "service" strategies and, second, a clear relationship between corporate strategic priorities and the operational plans for the services that will deliver them. Continuing with a business analogue, Durham has established three corporate strategic goals through 2007:

- To offer world-class learning and research
- To establish a closer fit between learning and research and the needs of 21st-century society
- To create a world-class infrastructure for our staff, students, and other clients who deliver and use our services

These goals shape the planning process in every academic department, which must then decide what they need to change and develop to deliver relevant world-class services. These needs in turn shape the agenda of the business support services.

In Durham, these income generation objectives are clear. Our departments need to do three things:

- Attract additional world-class academic leaders
- Develop an endowment to ensure that we continue to attract the very best students, rather than simply those who can afford to pay
- Increase investment in buildings and the information technology infrastructure

In short, integrated income generation bridges the strategic and operational levels, tailoring operational plans directly to strategic goals. It makes clear to everyone what are the specific priorities, what will be done to achieve them, and—by definition—what will not be a priority and what, therefore, cannot and will not be done.

Structural Synergy

The structure of the DIIG model addresses the perennial practical problems of an imbalance between supply and demand. Currently, 98 percent of our income comes from three main income streams:

- Human resource development activities (teaching and training)
- Intellectual property (research, consulting)
- Exploitation of physical resources (accommodations, meals, conferences)

Given the deregulation of UK higher education funding, every one of these income streams is competitive and requires highly specialized support. This support is generally of three types: market intelligence, promotion and selling, and networking and friend-raising.

In some cases, even within an income stream, universities may find that different academic disciplines require highly specialized, dedicated input. Nevertheless, many higher education institutions (HEIs) have found it difficult to release enough core resources to invest in broad-based specialist services, such as fund raising and advancement. It is this shortfall that has bedeviled philanthropic fund raising in the United Kingdom. To run a Rolls Royce fund-raising service, a university needs professional staff to address the following:

- Research and databases
- Alumni relations
- Annual fund
- Major gifts
- Fulfillment, donor recognition, and donor relations
- Events management, finance, public relations, and information technology

Handling these tasks could easily occupy a staff of 25, with an investment of approximately £1 million. But outside the ancient universities of Oxford and Cambridge, this level of investment has not been made.

Why not? Because, quite simply, Europe is not yet a mature philanthropic market. In 1998, universities in the United States generated twice as much income in philanthropic donations as did the whole UK charitable sector combined. Most established UK universities generate only 1 percent of their turnover from donations. Yet these universities will generate some 30 percent of their turnover from winning highly competitive research funding from the government. For management, the answer is clear: Investment in winning mainstream research funding is less risky and more likely to succeed than is a comparable investment in traditional development activity. Here, then, is the "cleft stick" or dilemma. HEI fund raising in the United Kingdom does not yet command the market to justify the investment it needs to create that market. The result is a hugely underfunded and generally weak profession in which overall level of expertise is low and success limited.

Shared Objectives

By developing a coordinated strategy for income generation that is related to clear strategic priorities and backed by an integrated support structure, one can begin to overcome this blockage. In an integrated structure, philanthropic fund raising can punch above its weight. Its role is not to be a major income stream in and of itself, but rather to leverage income from donations in order to attract matching funding generated by the actual major income streams—human resources, intellectual property, and physical resources.

At Durham, this income-generation strategy is applied at the project level. As such, each project is clearly defined and clearly related to the corporate strategy. Each project is also carefully planned, involving funding specialists from research, regional, European, and student recruitment teams. How does it work? Here are two examples.

Case Study #1: The Ogden Centre for Fundamental Physics

This project was part of the university's strategic vision to create a series of world-leading research teams. The Department of Physics at Durham had already established significant global networks in particle physics phenomenology and computational cosmology that aim to unlock the secrets of the universe. To develop a genuinely big-hitting center of excellence with a critical mass unmatched in Europe, the department required the sophisticated infrastructure to attract new staff and additional funding. Accordingly, the physics department developed a case for support that generated full departmental and institutional backing.

The development office worked with colleagues in Research and Economic Support Services (REDSS) and the physics department to devise an integrated funding strategy, thus creating structural synergy. Potential funding bodies included the Particle Physics and Astronomy Research Council (PPARC) and two other government challenge-based funding opportunities, the Joint Infrastructure Fund (JIF) and the Joint Research Equipment Initiative (JREI).

A communications plan produced by the university's corporate communications team that included proposals, presentations, events, and internal/external communications was instrumental in the success of the proposals submitted to PPARC, JIF, and JREI. The director of development led the team, ensuring that everyone was singing from the same hymn sheet (that is, sharing objectives). He took the vision to a prospective private donor, Peter Ogden, a computer entrepreneur and Durham physics graduate who had been well stewarded for several years since making a significant major gift. The university's demonstration of strategic and financial commitment—an indication that this was a major project with full backing of the institution—was crucial to him.

Results

Proposals were then submitted to the various potential funders. Timing was critical, in particular for the JIF bid, because it required a firm pledge from Ogden before it would make a commitment. Because the JIF commitment led to commitments from other funders, his gift, in effect, became the lever that opened the door to all of the other funding pots. In November 2000, the University of Durham announced the establishment of the Ogden Centre for Fundamental Physics. The project included the following:

- A four-story building
- Institute for Particle Physics Phenomenology (IPPP)
- The Institute for Computational Cosmology (ICC) and Ogden Chair in Fundamental Physics
- The Centre for Nano-Technology
- A Condensed matter laboratory

The sources and amount of integrated income generated for this project are illustrated in Table 1.

Table 1. Integrated Income Generated for the Ogden Centre for Fundamental Physics

Source	Gift	Value
Private donor (Ogden)	Leadership Gift—ICC	£2 million
JIF	Building	£2.9 million
PPARC	IPPP	£10 million
PPARC	ICC	£1.3 million
EC/Royal Society	ICC	£.3 million
JREI	Supercomputer	£.7 million
SUN Microsystems	Matching JREI	£.7 million
Private donation	Centre for Nano-Technology	£2.2 million
	TOTAL FUNDS RAISED	**£20.1 million**
University	Building and staff	£5 million
	TOTAL PROJECT COST	**£25.1 million**

Case Study #2: The Wolfson Research Institute

This project is part of the university's strategic vision to develop the capability to conduct world-class research in health and medicine to address the healthcare needs of one of the United Kingdom's most economically deprived regions. The project started by establishing at its newly founded Stockton campus a research institute consisting of an interdisciplinary research team drawn from existing high-quality departments. Once in place, this institute would provide the basic infrastructure to underpin a submission to the Higher Education Funding Council for England (HEFCE) for the establishment of a new medical school. The school's first phase would involve a pre-clinical medical program for 100 medical students. The combined program would sustain and enhance university research and teaching in health, medicine, and the environment while providing a critical service to the region.

In creating structural synergy, the challenge lay in the simultaneous presentation of the case for support of infrastructure (buildings, equipment, and new programs), staff, and students. The problem we encountered initially was that potential funders all wanted agreement from the others before making their own commitment. The approach we adopted was to go after a leadership gift that demonstrated enough support to lever out funds from other prospective funding bodies. Toward this end, cultivation began in 1999, with the Wolfson Foundation as the prime prospect. The foundation had a long and supportive history with the university, but it had never made a major gift.

Once again, the university development office worked with REDSS to identify other potential funders based on the high potential in terms both of research outcomes and the regional economic impact. The scope of the initiative indicated that regional funding opportunities and the European Regional Development Fund (ERDF) were the best prospects to match the leadership gift. Advice on gaining the support of local and regional partners was crucial to the project's success. REDSS staff played a key role in this regard, working closely with the senior leadership team at the Stockton campus.

The corporate communications team developed a communications plan based on shared objectives (media, press releases, proposals, and events). The student recruitment team formulated a plan for the HEFCE bid to secure 100 funded medical-student places. Proposals were then submitted to various potential funders. On December 30, 1999, the vice chancellor secured a lead gift from the Wolfson Foundation for the building. And on December 31— the deadline for ERDF funds—an additional significant gift was secured from the ERDF.

Results

In January 2000, the University of Durham was able to announce the establishment of the Wolfson Research Institute. The project included the following:

- A research building at the Stockton campus
- Hiring faculty in health, medicine, and the environment
- A pre-clinical medical school
- Research centers for waste management, land reclamation, and land and water pollution

The sources and amount of integrated income generated for this project are illustrated in Table 2.

Table 2. Integrated Income Generated for the Wolfson Research Institute

Source	Gift	Value
The Wolfson Foundation	Leadership gift	£4 million
ERDF	Matching gift	£3.5 million
Stockton Borough Council	Land	£.5 million
One North East	Land reclamation	£1.5 million
	TOTAL FUNDS RAISED	**£8.5 million**
University	Building contribution	£.9 million
	TOTAL PROJECT COSTS	**£9.4 million**

Recommendations for Best Practice

- The whole institution needs a clear vision and strategic objectives to which everyone subscribes. The development office must establish what needs to be achieved to deliver the strategy and then win institutional consensus. To this end, a jazz ensemble plays both to its own strengths and to the needs of the audience.

- Use a major gift as a leadership gift to leverage funds from other well-researched sources. The best music highlights virtuoso soloists who then draw out the best from the rest of the band.

- Share priorities to work as an advancement team. All the specialties involved—development, research grants, industrial liaison, corporate relations, public relations, communications, regional affairs, and student recruitment—must avoid parochialism. The critical mass formed by close collaboration provides the expertise and knowledge essential to optimizing the institution's fund-raising prospects.

- The best development teams focus on major gifts for big-picture ideas in areas that have reached critical mass in terms of top-quality staff, teaching, and research. Large gifts for priority investment areas take advantage of existing strengths and provide strategic support for the institution's long-term future. For the most part, prospective major donors will support a vision only if it is unique, will make a difference, and, in most cases, possesses world-class quality. A world-class jazz ensemble is a perfectly tuned team that knows its music, takes full advantage of the talent of each member, and keeps the beat regardless of the situation.

III

HANDLING THE COMPLEXITY OF UNIT DEVELOPMENT

CHAPTER 10

Starting a Unit Development Office

Pamela Cook
Philanthropy Consultant

Dwain N. Fullerton
Senior Associate Dean Emeritus, School of Engineering, Stanford University

THE FIRST THING PRUDENT PILOTS DO IS TO MAKE SURE
THE PLANE WILL FLY. THEY HAVE A CHECKLIST FOR EVERY
KEY ELEMENT THAT MUST BE WORKING PROPERLY.

There are libraries of full of how-to books on fund raising, but not many good check-lists exist for anyone planning to become a development officer in a unit such as a school, department, or college of a university. Fund raising for a unit can be one of the most personally rewarding and exciting jobs in the world. It is an occupation that per-mits you to have lunch with a Nobel laureate on Monday and dine with the head of a corporation on Tuesday. You can observe firsthand the thrill of new discoveries in research or interpretations of literature.

If your unit is involved in science, medicine, or engineering, you can *be* in the lab, *see* the instruments, and *talk* with faculty and students doing the work. If your unit involves a social science, law, or business school, you can talk with the faculty about cur-rent events before they hit the five o'clock news. More than in most positions, you can participate in almost the full spectrum of development, from annual-fund mailings to major gifts to deferred gifts to stewardship. You frequently team directly with the faculty to make major solicitations—not a bad experience for the résumé.

The unit also makes significant demands on the unit development officer (UDO) who must deal with budgets and gift accounting plus other unit administrators, central administrators, faculty members, students, volunteers, donors, and prospective donors. Because teaching and research take place within the units, fund raisers can be among the staff closest to the heart of the academic enterprise. Although practices vary among institutions, we will use the title "dean" to represent the unit director and, in the following pages, address five questions related to starting a unit development operation or landing a job in a unit.

- ▶ What is the lay of the land?
- ▶ What would I have to do to succeed?
- ▶ Are there enough resources?
- ▶ What are the pitfalls?
- ▶ If I get (have) the job, how do I keep it going?

What Is the Lay of the Land?

Academic organizations are notoriously opaque. The elegant prose in the handbook that describes schools, departments, and divisions rarely tells those on the outside what is going on. Inside, there are almost always conflicts and issues of territoriality and status—all the rough-and-tumble that makes for good novels. Anyone who sets out to establish a unit fund-raising operation needs to understand how the unit fits into the academic hierarchy. Is the unit permanent? Does it grant degrees? Is it well respected within the community? Or was it established to retain a luminary faculty member so that if the faculty member moves on the unit disappears?

Is the head of the unit esteemed both inside and outside the parent institution? A dean who is at odds with the faculty may survive for years but make fund raising for the unit a nightmare. It is often an excellent idea to request a conference with the department chair during the interview process. The chair's view can be illuminating, and the information offered surprisingly candid. The same goes for a meeting with a fund raiser in another unit who can describe relationships between units and the central development office.

How does the dean view fund raising? As a series of opportunities to make eloquent requests for the unit or as a dreaded burden? How much time is the dean willing to devote to fund raising? If the unit fund raiser is expected to go out alone and bring back a bag of money every Friday, serious problems will soon arise. As a classic example, some years ago a leader of an academic institution became involved in a cause that was close to his heart. He committed himself to it wholeheartedly and, at year's end, almost all the press coverage focused on his cause and reported virtually nothing about the institution's goals and accomplishments. It was a bad year for fund raising.

Do faculty members participate in the fund-raising process? Their opinions may be difficult to determine, but it is usually possible to discern whether they view fund raisers as potentially helpful partners or simply part of the overhead. Involved faculty can be stunningly good members of the fund-raising team. During a campaign at a large university, a seven-figure proposal to fund a building had been sent to a foreign corporation. Word came back that the corporation's vice president for research wanted to visit the campus and meet some key players. The visit began with lunch with the dean, the associate dean for academic affairs, and two department chairs, and it progressed to laboratories where faculty members and graduate students described their research. The afternoon was a huge success. Everyone enjoyed the exchanges, and some lasting friendships resulted. A month later the company pledged its support.

At another university, a faculty member made an appointment with the UDO. He spoke enthusiastically about his research but had never submitted a grant application. As the UDO attempted to get the faculty member to identify potential donors and discuss fund-raising strategies, the faculty member reacted with outrage, saying that this was the UDO's job. By presenting his research to the unit officer, he believed he had done his work.

Beyond establishing where the unit fits into the academic enterprise, unit fund raisers must understand their position in the university-wide development hierarchy. In some universities, salaries and reporting relationships for unit officers flow from the central development office. In others, they come solely from the individual schools. A third model combines both sources. From the outset, UDOs must set clear expectations with the dean and the central development organization. Satisfying both groups is one of the many complex skills that UDOs must master.

What Would I Have to Do to Succeed?

During the interview process, a few skillful questions can produce invaluable information. For instance, why is the unit is hiring a development officer? Because the unit has first-rate leadership and great untapped potential? Or because the dean is a terrible fund raiser and the unit wants to insert you as a stopgap? Or is it because if medicine has a development officer, then arts and sciences has to have one, too? What it will take to succeed will be vastly different in those three cases. Each can be viable as long as expectations are clear and all sides agree on what the UDO should accomplish.

To understand what you are getting into, ask questions about the prospect base; the mix of corporate, foundation, and individual giving; the percentage of alumni participation; and the history of giving. Is a capital campaign in the works? How many volunteers are engaged? How active have they been? How the unit has done fund raising in the past will indicate how open it is to new ideas.

How much of the work is tangential to the boilerplate in the job description? Success may be defined by good fund raising, but gaining the approval of the faculty or alumni, raising the visibility of the unit, and advancing the reputation of an ambitious dean may be equally critical elements. Rarely would deans admit that they wanted to present themselves as spectacular fund raisers so as to land a university presidency somewhere. But that may be what is at play.

Who will perform your performance evaluation? How many people will be involved in preparing it? For instance, a dean might routinely ask department chairs for their opinion of your work, assuming they know what you were doing. You should also ascertain what role the central development office plays in the evaluation process.

What are your possibilities for promotion, and how can you best position yourself? UDOs are sometimes overlooked when the time comes for promotions. Ask questions during the interview process about potential future steps. Ask representatives from the central office how you can effectively remain part of the larger development community while you work in a different location.

What staff members are already on board? What are their roles and expectations? You will need to review the current staff and the way it will be configured if you join the unit. Even before you get the job, however, meet the incumbents and assess whether you would enjoy working with them. If you sense weaknesses or personality conflicts, ask the dean how he or she views the situation.

Regardless of the formal job description or what others may say, your relationship with your dean will determine the actual parameters of the job. If your co-workers have little experience in development, your role might well include a substantial amount of on-the-job training of the dean, department chairs, and relevant staff members. If your dean is knowledgeable about development but likes to delegate that authority, you may need to put effort into mapping a strategy. Conversely, if your dean is knowledgeable and does not like to delegate development responsibilities, your role becomes more akin to an aide. Regardless of your dean's knowledge, skills, or management style, some portion of your job will consist of doing what the dean does not want to do.

Gauge how you would work with the dean. More than in any other area of the university, your success will be tied to this relationship. If it deteriorates, you may be out of a job. Ask questions about style, how much travel the dean anticipates, and how the dean prefers to do fund raising. It is important to begin the job with expectations that match his or her objectives.

Unspoken assessments notwithstanding, there will be an annual accounting of how much money the unit raised and for what purposes. The total needs to meet expectations—that is an absolute. You should definitely know how much is expected and which gifts have the highest priority (e.g., annual, unrestricted, endowment, etc.). How much latitude are you allowed to reach the goal? Solicitations for six- and seven-figure major gifts customarily take 18 months or more to conclude; ratcheting up an annual giving program, both in dollar totals and percent participation, can take enormous effort for little return. Remember, your primary job is to raise money. Do that well amid all the distractions, and your job will be secure and your career will prosper.

At the conclusion of the discussions, with job in hand, you should be confident that at the end of six months you will have clear answers to three questions:

▶ What is expected of me?

▶ How am I doing?

▶ Where can I get help?

A fourth question to keep in mind and to answer in the broadest sense is, What's in it for me? The most effective performers are those who receive personal satisfaction from their surroundings—from functioning on behalf of their institution and from the pleasure of working in an intellectually stimulating environment. As one contented long-time unit fund raiser said, "If I were rich, I would have paid them to let me be here."

Are There Enough Resources?

At this stage you should have a good idea of what is expected. You should know the nature of the unit's academic needs and goals, where fund raising fits in, dollar targets, names of important players, and what gifts will be most useful. Now take an inventory of the available resources, and evaluate them against the goals.

First, whom are you going to ask for money? To function effectively, the UDO must have an identifiable group that can be asked for money. Is there a roster of past and prospective donors? Is there a group with a logical tie to the unit? A medical school development officer might look to alumni, the pharmaceutical industry, healthcare foundations, and grateful patients. A division of humanities might develop a message to persuade alumni and foundations.

If a prospect list exists, who owns it? Who determines when a solicitation can proceed? If the prospects are assigned to the unit, the work is straightforward. If the prospects are held centrally or jointly among units, you will have to coordinate with other development staff members before your work can start. If there is no prospect list, or if the list is outdated or for some reason unusable, you can anticipate investing a significant effort before focused fund raising can take place. What systems are in place to clear and track prospects? How will disagreements be resolved?

What resources are available for actual solicitations at all levels? Is there a corps of volunteers? Will faculty members help? Can you rely on help from the central office, perhaps in calling on prospects in outlying areas, advising on legal questions or tax matters, providing communications or writing support, or involving the university president or provost? Expect donors of large gifts to the unit to want to meet senior officers of the university. What administrative support is available in the unit? A publications specialist? A mailing specialist? An alumni relations officer? Are enough people available to help with the fund raising, or will you be short-handed? Do you have the right staff?

In one instance a new UDO inherited a group that was primarily oriented toward producing a glossy alumni magazine featuring faculty-written articles. The publication was expensive to produce and generated no income. Nevertheless, it took almost two years to discontinue the magazine, reorient the staff, and smooth ruffled feathers of faculty members who viewed the magazine as a vehicle for highlighting their programs. Happily, when more money started coming in, all was forgiven.

Will you have an adequate budget? You must have enough money for the staff you need, routine supplies and expenses, professional training, mailings (if direct mail solicitations are in order), telephone, computers and office equipment, electronic mail, travel, perhaps professional services of various kinds, and a small reserve. Before accepting the task of setting up a unit development office, get your plan approved in writing. Verbal promises made when a dean has a fat contingency fund are quickly forgotten when an academic emergency drains the account.

Finally, there is the thorny question of space. The closer to the dean's office your group is situated, the better. The location identifies you as a valued member of the core staff. You can observe the unit's operation daily without having to set up appointments. You can build personal relationships with key players in the unit. As a result, you will become an able advocate to prospective donors and a well-informed interpreter to the staff in the central development office. If space is limited and your section is exiled to an outlying area, walk around and talk with faculty and students. Be as informed as you can about the inner workings of your unit.

How valuable an inside perspective can be was demonstrated during a particular campaign. Conventional wisdom held that faculty members should help only with solicitations for their own research program. One UDO realized that the faculty generally felt isolated from the development process because they had never been treated as full participants. The fund raiser teamed successfully with them by requesting their help in meeting with a prospective donor, asking them only to describe their work. The officer briefed them fully on the prospect and the purpose of the solicitation (regardless whether it was for their area), and then diligently reported the results, usually including a copy to the department chair. As six- and seven-figure gifts materialized, with the faculty sharing the credit, reluctance evaporated. The central staff had a more difficult task because they tended to showcase the faculty, not treat them as full participants in a solicitation. Many faculty members soon saw that the situation was a waste of time and directed their attention elsewhere.

What Are the Pitfalls?

Although belonging to an academic unit has advantages, drawbacks do exist. Most senior academic administrators are tenured, and their careers are spent in teaching and research. However eminent and articulate those people may be, their appointment may have little to do with management skills. Often they will say—and mean—that their true love is teaching (or research), and that they view moving into administration as a temporary demotion. That kind of attitude can produce poor management practices, limited involvement in fund raising, and low morale within the unit.

Keep in mind that the dean's failures do not absolve UDOs from raising as much money as possible: Creating and maintaining a successful fund-raising operation is your job. There is a risk that the institution's fund-raising community may perceive you as one of the dean's staff and not as a full member of the larger development group. When possibilities for promotion arise, you may not be considered. A corollary to this is that if the dean leaves, the successor may want to bring in his or her own people, jeopardizing your position. Even if the central advancement office pays your salary, you will have little job security if your relationship with the dean sours.

Many academic units have a lean staff. Work accumulates with a survey here, a committee there, and not enough bodies to handle it all. Development gets a series of peripheral tasks, which are embraced as a respite from the hard, sweaty business of raising money. But if dollar totals plummet, so does your career regardless of whether other aspects of your job—publications or alumni relations—are flourishing. You may turn out to be an incompetent juggler. Successful UDOs have countless balls in the air. They keep an eye on central development, negotiate for access to prospects, conduct solicitations, douse fires, deal with faculty, communicate with alumni, plan an event, and take the lumps for the staff or the dean when something goes really wrong.

The dean may not be able to say no, and you can sink under the weight of pet projects. Sooner or later some faculty member or student will ask you for help with a special undertaking. If it is not already on the priority list, refer that person to the dean. The danger is that the dean might say yes to everything—until you become overwhelmed with programs that are mostly unattractive to donors. Quickly, you can be confronted with a growing population that feels ignored.

If I Get (Have) the Job, How Do I Keep It?

First, find out how the boss likes to communicate. Through scheduled meetings? Casual conversations in the hall? E-mail? Written memoranda? Whatever it is, adapt to it, schedule it, stick to it. Identify the people who should know who you are and what you are doing. They may be in the central development office, the alumni association, other academic units, key faculty positions, or the central university administration. Decide how and when to communicate with those individuals. Never waste their time or appear to be blowing your own horn, especially with people who can help you get your job done.

It is essential to be on good terms with the dean's assistant. So is walking around the departments to see what the faculty is doing. Eminent professors can be surprisingly pleasant when someone in the administration takes an interest in their work. At one West Coast institution, the UDO happened to bump into a faculty member who had developed public-key cryptography, a computer-based security system. To the officer's surprise, the professor spent three quarters of an hour describing, in layperson's terms, the significance of the codes and how they worked.

Build a small set of development colleagues who can help you brainstorm and solve problems. Those relationships will reduce the feeling of isolation that can grow within a unit and help in building strategies. Such colleagues can be other UDOs, individuals who share similar regional responsibilities, or even people at other institutions. Many schools (law, business, or engineering) have national affinity groups you can tap into to help build your network.

Find out which development items have highest priority. For instance, a new dean who wants an early success to establish his or her credentials has intimated to the faculty that endowed professorships are the number-one need. That information tells you where to push hardest. Envision what will happen. Avoid surprises.

Identify all prospects and donors assigned to the unit. Obtain a history of overall giving for the past five years, and analyze the patterns. How much has the unit received each year? In what amounts? From what sources? For what purposes? Prepare a graph to project what might be expected next year. Sketch in what changes and improvements you hope to make.

Identify the group of prospects you will be asking for major gifts. Rank them in order, and devise a solicitation plan for each one. Do the same for all other large-gift prospects. Start with the most important; make a realistic schedule for the remainder. Decide which additional tasks need to be completed in the first 12 months. Compile that schedule, share it with the dean, and get agreement on the contents. (If appropriate, share it with central development.)

Carefully manage expectations. An extreme example of the failure to do so occurred some years ago at a well-known private college. A wealthy businessman had given a building to another institution and, hoping that he might do the same for them, the college invited him to join the board. No one asked whether his philanthropic interests extended to the college—and they did not. Assuming that the president wanted his advice on how to run the college, he proceeded to schedule meetings to share his wisdom. Both men had strong opinions, and the outcome was predictably negative.

Make sure you understand exactly what the dean needs to know about the development operation and what you will do every day. This will have two positive outcomes. First, when the dean passes through the office, he or she will have a reasonable idea of what is going on. Second, because you know what is important to share, the dean will never be caught short. For instance, if one of the elements of your plan is to meet with department chairs, clear that activity with the dean, ask for advice, and report on those meetings. Then, when a faculty gathering takes place, the dean will know exactly what happened and be better informed about the department.

Know which decisions are yours to make and which should be referred to the dean. Make internal development decisions—about prospect ranking, solicitation sequence, and ways to ask for gifts—quickly and expeditiously. Make things happen, but do not get caught setting academic priorities. Avoid being the mouse between two elephants: If there is a disagreement between two deans or a dean and one of the chairs, even though the issue pertains to development, do not feel compelled to intervene. The elephants can survive such a rumble, but the mouse cannot afford even a casual bump.

Resist the temptation to speak for the dean. If you misspeak or there is disagreement, especially with the faculty, the matter will wind up on the dean's desk and usually put you in a bad light. However, you do need to master the fine art of borrowed clout, by which you make it clear that, in specific situations, you act with the dean's express authority. The department chair who wants to invite an alumnus to sit on a committee needs to know that the dean wants the chair to wait until after a planned gift solicitation has been made. If you meet resistance, do not push it. (Remember the mouse and elephants!)

Remember that from the onset, at all times in all situations, you are the unit's authority and chief resource on all matters pertaining to development. To plant the seed, establish yourself as the source of development information and conduct minor household chores. Provide your dean and chairs with monthly gift totals. Prepare semiannual reports on various fund balances. Someone needs the database address for an alumnus updated? No problem! Mailing labels for invitations to an event? Glad to oblige! Once your dean and unit heads get used to coming to you for little tasks, they will approach you for big ones as well.

Craft a mission statement that goes to the heart of what you and your staff need to think about every day. One statement that has worked well for others is as follows: "Raise the most money for the highest priority at the least cost in an absolutely ethical manner." Another unit fund raiser created a screen saver that scrolled "Go forth and raise money."

We have described effective techniques for setting up a unit development office and functioning as a UDO. Master the intricacies, and your career will blossom. You will be visible and effective, have a broad range of experiences, and possess a solid understanding of the academic enterprise and the philanthropic world that supports it.

Recommendations for Best Practice

- What is the lay of the land? Explore how the unit fits into the rest of the institution; ascertain the views of the dean and faculty toward development.

- How can I succeed? Use the interview process to determine and clarify expectations in the unit and in central development.

- Are there enough resources? Discuss whether you have a sufficient budget and staff, where you will be housed, and who your prospects will be.

- What are the pitfalls? Figure out how you can stay on a development career path and stay focused on development—and not be diverted by reassignment to other tasks.

- How do I keep the job going? Identify how to best communicate with the dean and others, build a strategic plan, and do not forget that raising money is the highest priority.

CHAPTER 11

Managing a Unit Development Office

John W. Crowe

Vice President for Advancement, Claremont Graduate University

In 1985, when I moved from a small, specialized residential college of 500 students to an urban university of 30,000 students in 22 schools and programs, I knew life would be different. In my first interview with the university vice president, he described the decentralized organization of my new institution as a feudal system. (He was quick to distinguish between "feudal" and "futile," although there were days . . .) He explained that the university had been moving toward decentralization for several years, and that each school was essentially its own kingdom. The budgetary system, modeled after Harvard's, was decentralized and, as a result, so was institutional advancement. I was to be the first development officer whose salary was paid for entirely by an individual school. Until that point, as the university eased into decentralization, salaries had been split.

I took the job as the chief academic development officer for the University of Southern California's (USC's) School of Medicine, a huge independent enterprise 10 miles from the main campus—the model of an academic feudal kingdom if ever there was one. Four years later, I moved to the central office where I became the development "liaison" to 10 small professional schools. My job was to coordinate and advise, and I had very little authority. After another five years and I was back at a school, running the advancement program in the school of business, the university's largest unit and its signature program. With 7,000 students and nearly 60,000 alumni, what is now the Marshall School of Business operates much like a university within a university. During my 16 years at USC, I saw the university evolve into a system not unlike the British Empire. Although we all paid homage to a common flag and single head of state, each school or unit had a different currency, language, and culture. In my case, the Marshall School had the independence of Canada.

If you are a unit development officer (UDO), you have the challenge and the satisfaction of doing it all. You are like the vice president of a small college, but (I would argue) your world is more complex. As a part of a large university, you have allegiances and obligations unfamiliar to the head of a small-college program. We are hired first as development officers. Units want their own fund-raising programs directed to their own constituencies. But to be successful, we have to learn and effectively deploy all of the advancement skills. In this chapter, I lay out some aspects of unit development program and describe some ways to gain personal and professional satisfaction. To do it well, unit programs must do it all.

Staffing

For some UDOs, staffing is a non-issue: You are it. Even if this is your situation now, chances are good that it will change. The combined unit staffs at most universities today greatly outnumber the central staff, and data cited by Hall (see Chapter 2, this volume) indicate that the growth in university advancement today takes place in the units, not the central office. Be that as it may, unit staffs do vary in size, from one person to several dozen.

The UDO of a one-person shop is often seen as the dean or director's person, sometimes even as an alter ego. Moving from the one-person shop to a staff with segmented duties is an important transition. As the staff grows, the team's persona begins to emerge. Instead of one person supporting the dean, the UDO becomes the leader of a team supporting the school.

Growing a staff does not always mean hiring people to fill full-time positions. You can assemble a de facto staff simply by drawing on the services already available from (and paid by) the central advancement office or other parts of the university. In many instances, you are already paying for these services whether you use them or not—they are part the institution's overhead. By bringing together representatives or contacts from these service units in a monthly or quarterly "staff meeting," you can effectively create a staff and harness resources on behalf of your school and your development operation.

By using such de facto staffing, even a one-person unit office with a limited budget can deliver a full-service advancement operation with development, communications, and alumni relations. Inevitably, you will see that some services need to be performed in-house, inasmuch as they characterize your school's personality, and you will be pushed to hire your own staff. The business school at USC, for example, has its own magazine, press relations, alumni association, and corporate relations and development programs. But the school staff also draws heavily on central services such as planned giving, prospect research, and event coordination. In part, this is to keep costs in line and prevent duplication of services. But the main reason we use particular central services is because we trusted the individuals delivering them. (Trust was key, and in those instances where we could not trust central people to do the job as well as us, we did it ourselves.) The rule of thumb: Use central services and thus other people's money to support your unit whenever you can.

Finding good people is always difficult; finding good people to work in a unit adds an additional wrinkle. You need people who understand or who have the potential to understand the discipline or the profession or the mission of the unit and who are comfortable meeting and working with faculty, staff, and alumni in that specialty. In addition, your hires must also have allegiance to and understanding of the university as a whole, as well as command of the big picture of higher education. That is a lot!

As your staff matures and demonstrates its effectiveness, others at the university will raid you. While you go through normal defensive maneuvers, take this for the compliment that it is. Given the all-too-frequent movement of development staff nationwide, it is obviously better for the university to retain talent within the family. Make the time to recruit good people, invest personal time in their development, commit yourself to their careers (and tell them that), provide them a wealth of experiences and challenges—and then let them go when the time comes.

Be aware that within a decentralized university, salary scales can differ considerably. At USC, although we had a common set of position job specifications and salary grades, salaries for the same post could vary as much as 20 percent from unit to unit. Make sure your staff salaries are at least above the mean—and then create a professional environment where money is secondary.

Prospect Management

Any university that plans to decentralize or distribute its development program must commit itself to maintaining a central database and, more important, a uniform procedure of prospect management and assignment. Such a prospect-management system calls for all development officers, central-based or unit-based, to record religiously into a central database open for all to read their contacts with prospects and suspects. In turn, officers must consult this database before they initiate contact with an alumnus or possible donor.

In a large university, the possibility that prospects have overlapping interests is immense—and adds complexity. To cite one case, an alumna and prospective donor took an undergraduate degree in education, but her graduate degree was in philosophy. Her husband had a degree in engineering and their children and their respective spouses held degrees in six other schools. Nonetheless, the alumna has made it clear that, because of her career successes, her real interest was business, whereas her husband wanted to support the library. In addition, both had a strong commitment to the medical school where one son was successfully treated for a life-threatening illness. They made significant gifts to all three units.

A good prospect-management system works to identify and cultivate such individuals toward the largest gift or gifts they can make. Although most decentralized universities let units "own" their alumni, the alumni may wish to support and get involved in different units. In order to be both fair and effective in the management of all donor prospects, both unit and central officers need some forum in which to come together and discuss prospect activity in a professional manner.

Once a prospect is identified and rated, a development officer asks that the prospect be "assigned" to him or her. Respectful of the multiple interests a prospect might manifest, a good system allows the assignment of multiple development officers. Assignments are for cultivation and education only. The units work to move a prospect to solicitation readiness, but they do not have approval to ask for a gift.

The institution's dance with the potential donor has to be carefully choreographed, with relevant development officers alerting each other as to planned contacts. In a centralized office, in theory, the director has the ability to coordinate prospect activity by walking up and down the hall. As the staff moves out to the schools and units, such daily communication is lost, often to the detriment of prospect management and coordination. But no university can afford to have UDOs from different units crashing into each other as they pursue a prospect. It is embarrassing—and bad business practice. In coordinating their moves, development officers must treat each other with the highest level of respect and professionalism. We must come up with methods and mechanisms to communicate—both personally and officially—if for no other reason than we do not want to embarrass the prospects, the university, or ourselves.

Clearance

Cultivation should culminate into a plan to solicit—and there can be only one university solicitation at a time. Who gets to go? In these situations, UDOs must often rise above their natural allegiances and remember that they work for the university—and the people who generously invest in it. As was indicated earlier, most universities operate a trafficking forum where development officers can come together as colleagues to determine who has the best case. Based on the experience of once managing that process at

USC, I can tell you that it is a position of virtually no authority wherein you function less like a judge and more like a labor negotiator mediating compromise between adversaries.

In most situations, after all facts are fully presented, it is obvious which unit should be cleared for solicitation; the prospect, if properly cultivated, will already have indicated what he or she wants to support. Many times, the "debate" helps crystallize strategy as development officers comment and provide new information. Sometimes, however, the preferred area is still unclear, or the prospect appears to have equal interest in multiple areas. In such cases, a neutral party might have to call on the prospect and ask for a decision. This individual is usually a volunteer, peer, and trusted friend—not a staff person. And all parties should clearly understand that this consultation is simply the final step in cultivation—not a solicitation.

It may not always be possible to gain agreement as to solicitation clearance among territorial UDOs at the first level of discussion. In such cases, the deans or the heads of the respective units might be asked to craft a compromise, although they often have difficulties overcoming territorial tendencies. It is not unheard of for the final decision to rise to the level of the president. As awkward and conflicting as such situations might be, someone has to make a decision and grant exclusive clearance.

Clearance is, in fact, the pinnacle of the prospect-management process. Once a prospect is cleared by a particular unit, all other development officers must agree to not talk about a gift in any manner. Clearance means exactly that: One unit has a clear path to solicit the prospect and no one else at the university—not even the president—may interfere. The effectiveness of a clearance system depends on the respect development officers have for one another, for the university, and, ultimately, for the prospect. Any violation of clearance compromises everyone, and that is bad business.

Board Development and Maintenance

Like a small university, your unit may have a board of lay people, usually influential alumni, donors, and people drawn from the profession. Such boards—variously called "advisors," "visitors," or "friends of"— are or should be your best advocates. Having said that, let me make one point quickly and perfectly clear: An advisory board or board of visitors or "friends of" does not constitute a governing board inasmuch as it does not possess the fiduciary or governance responsibility of your institutional board of trustees or regents. Therein lies the rub: How do you involve high-powered people on a board that has no power?

You will hear numerous stories of boards that have failed, deans who have little use for boards, and development officers who consider boards a waste of their precious time. But what is the alternative? A development process without volunteers? A dean and his hired gun cruising the countryside for donors? And what do you do with individuals who have already made substantial gifts? Or donors who can and will make even more such gifts if you can keep them engaged in the ongoing development of your school or unit?

Although we all have had experience with poor volunteers, we know that volunteers expand our reach and provide credibility. They give us access to the people we want to meet, and their gifts are larger than they would be if they were not involved. Service on boards contributes to the cultivation for new giving. In short, we need these boards. Without them, we are not operating on all cylinders and we will not achieve our full fund-raising potential.

The formula for the success of an active board is simple: selective recruitment of the right kind of people, direction and involvement by a dean who believes in the capability of the board, and support by competent staff. Good board prospects have an overriding love for both the university and the unit. Loyalties in small units are the most intense. Board members admire and value the work of the unit and are normally involved in some other aspect of the unit, perhaps lecturing in a course or mentoring students. They admire the dean or director, and they understand the limitations of their role.

Beyond these qualities and affinities, however, members of well-functioning boards also admire one another and enjoy opportunities for fellowship and networking that board membership affords. When selecting a board, in addition to considering what a potential board member might do for or bring to your school, also consider the mix of personalities and personal or professional affinities among potential board members.

At Claremont Graduate University, we use a matrix to ensure that our boards are balanced and diverse and get us where we want to go. We look naturally at age, gender, and ethnicity. But we also look at the number of alumni. Too many or two few? We look at regions, professions, and any other key factors that affect a unit. What types of people or experiences do you need to make your board robust? The matrix or grid, with "qualities" listed along the left and numbers plotted out over a period of years, quickly profiles areas of overabundance and scarcity.

Alumni and Parent Relations

You cannot run a successful development program unless you work with people who are involved in the life of your school or unit. The most logical candidates are alumni and parents—individuals who have already invested greatly in your institution. In addition to paying tuition dollars, they have staked their lives and careers, or the lives and careers of their children, on your program. They certainly were—and may still be—believers. So how do you rekindle or reinforce those beliefs and solicit their continued investment?

At most universities today, the keenest loyalty is directed to smaller entities rather than to the university itself. Despite the outdated beliefs of university alumni directors, most alumni relate to a given school, department, or social organization. Alumni never attended the university as a whole. They know only the part of the large university they experienced, and it is this natural affinity we want to fan into love and lifelong devotion.

Toward that end, units need to provide opportunities to involve alumni and parents. Professional schools in particular have an edge; schools of medicine, law, and business routinely link alumni and perform valuable continuing education for highly defined constituencies. Degree-granting units in general will have an obvious claim on alumni and parental affections, but nonacademic units such as the library, athletics, or student life can also identify people whose first love is their unit. Any school or unit can devise ways to invite people back to help recruit new students, educate current students, and aid in the placement of the graduates.

Your task is to reconnect alumni and parents by means of special programs, networking, and camaraderie. Your job is to remind them of how the unit has benefited their lives. The simplest and probably the best way to go about this process is to consult those in your university alumni relations office. With their advice and often-active participation, you can formulate a plan to attract and engage your specific alumni. More often than not, you can also recruit their help in implementing your plan, or at least allow you to piggyback some of your initiatives onto their ongoing programs, such as homecoming, club meetings, alumni travel tours, and the like. Ask alumni relations staff to sit in on your staff meetings, and see if it does not yield results. You are not in competition. Your assignment is the same, and you need to help one another.

Corporate Relations

Whereas others in this book touch on corporate relations in more depth, I need to at least mention this subject and its importance to unit advancement. For most units, there is a professional tie. In academic units as well as administrative ones, there may be opportunities for research and consulting. Support groups or industrial associates groups could be formed. Some units will be able to develop full research-and-development relationships, whereas others will find consulting roles for students and faculty. Corporate leaders form a source of lecturers and instructors, and student placement is another obvious area of potential corporate involvement. A good corporate relations program is interested in gifts, but also in relationships and resources that help advance the unit and allow it to meet its mission.

International Development

Following the analogy of the British Empire, many units today are trying to develop their own foreign-relations programs. Higher education has become one of America's greatest international commodities, and many of our universities have large numbers of international alumni and parents of international students. Developing a program to reach these alumni and parents, however, is costly and complex—and should not be entered into naively.

To economize (and maybe to control), some decentralized universities have centralized international development. But international alumni, maybe even more than domestic alumni, have allegiances to units. Their contact with the institution while they were students was limited to the school they attended. They bonded only with the faculty and programs within the school. The alumni they know now are people who graduated from the same program.

If you really want to enter into international development, be strategic and think cheap. First, look at your list and see where you have the potential for impact. Which one or two countries make sense? It is not unusual, for example, for alumni from one particular country to graduate from the same degree program. For historical reasons and patterns, USC alumni from one country are almost exclusively business majors, whereas public administration graduates predominately come from another country. Education alumni come primarily from yet another. Examine your migration patterns; they will signal the area(s) to concentrate on. You may even choose to cooperate with another unit and share costs.

Determine whether international alumni will come to you. Most of those who attended our universities are people of means and truly international citizens. When I started an international development program at USC, I was surprised to discover that many of the international alumni and parents I was seeking overseas owned beautiful homes and had business relationships right in my own state. Many were spending large amounts of time close to the campus, and I was busy chasing them as "foreigners." Obviously, these individuals made especially good prospects. They had maintained ties to our region, making it much easier for us to reconnect them to the university. And, as people familiar with our culture, they were more likely to understand the role and importance of philanthropy.

Establishing contact is not that difficult; maintaining contact in a program of cultivation is. You will not be able to get to Asia or Europe as often as you need, so send friends. To save expense and time, involve faculty and other administrators who routinely travel abroad in the cultivation process. Admissions officers, for example, can make great courtesy calls, telling our prospects about news in the unit. Faculty on consulting projects or in faculty exchanges can make great emissaries. Keeping the list of international prospects small, keeping the relationship active, and making sure university representatives contact prospects whenever officers are in their country ensures the best chance of success in developing gifts from international alumni and parents.

Stewardship and Special Events

Once your unit has successfully courted, identified, evaluated, and solicited a distinct group of prospects, you must support this constituency with a program of stewardship and events. The ultimate value of the stewardship process is to bond such donors even closer to the unit, enhancing small-group loyalty to a school. Because UDOs cannot rely on centralized university stewardship to keep donors enthused, you need to dedicate some staff time to the function of creating satisfied donors who believe their gift has bettered the unit—and who soon will be ready for the next ask.

All donors deserve to be thanked and recognized for their support. Special programs should recognize donors of chairs, scholarship endowments, and other projects. At USC, we have had great success with a university-wide support group that provides an umbrella of services and events to donors who support a school or unit. This program makes donors feel a palpable connection to the university. But in order for this connection to extend to a unit, it must have a corresponding "downlink" to the service and a "portal" for the donor to access the service. Toward this end, UDOs and the central stewardship office often devise a matrix of services that can be delivered via a single program or event.

Several years ago USC decided to revamp its traditional President's Associates group to reflect the realities of a decentralized development program and donors who support units. Historically, the Associates had been a support group for donors making unrestricted gifts to support presidential priorities. We recreated it as a giving society with various levels for donors to direct gifts to specific units.

The President's Associates became a way to offer various university courtesies, ranging from library and parking privileges to invitations to special on-campus programs hosted by the president. At the unit level, individual schools sponsored one of more events for their own donors as a way to say thanks and reinforce giving. As a result, instead of fighting the President's Associates, UDOs became its biggest advocates.

Communications and Marketing

Communications and marketing is an important function that must be part of a unit program. The question is, How much can you afford? Bigger units may have the resources to perform marketing and to operate their own news bureaus, magazine, and Web site. They may decide to lend a unifying "corporate" look to publications coming from all parts of the school, including admissions. This can be expensive, but every unit needs to plan for some level of communications.

The first step is to provide donors, alumni, and potential constituents with some type of baseline communication. Historically, this function has been fulfilled by conventional print newsletters or magazines that are expensive and time-consuming to produce. Consequently, many schools are successfully publishing easier-to-produce and more timely e-mailed newsletters that carry the message quickly and directly. At least for now, many people consider this a more personal form of communication than the traditional printed newsletter.

More important than the medium is the frequency and timeliness of publication. If you want to treat your readers as those in the know, give them advance knowledge of news from your unit. Put in front of them news and information they can use. Consistency is important. I would rather mail a three-page letter from the dean four times a year than save up for an annual edition of a color magazine.

Quickly becoming a necessity—as important as the baseline house organ—is your Web site. We are rapidly reaching the point where computers and hypertext messaging are replacing conventional print-based communication. If you do not have a Web site, you simply cannot communicate with a significant segment of the public who have an interest in your school— potential students, parents of potential students, potential faculty, and the like. To those who depend on the Internet and e-mail the way most people used to depend on books, newspapers, letters, and telephones, the absence of a Web site means you essentially do not exist.

The design and maintenance of a Web site can be expensive, but it does not have to be. Again, first look to your institutional resources for assistance. Inasmuch as virtually every university has a Web site, the staff member who maintains it is the most obvious source of assistance. Often, resources also exist within your school—among your staff, faculty, and students.

The key to a good Web site is the architecture, the layout design, and the linkage between its various parts. Although you want your site to be eye-catching and informative, you also want it to be user-friendly and easy to download. When in doubt, opt for the simple and the accessible. A conventional display of information that is quick to load and easy to download beats an innovative site design that takes minutes to load and view.

In designing a Web site, pay attention to its "common look and feel." That is, your Web site, although distinctive in its own right, should nevertheless look and feel like it is a part of the university site. Similarly, sub-units should also look and feel like they are a part of the school Web site. Viewers should be able to tell at a glance that whether they are looking at the Web site for a program, school, or university, they are all are part of the same institution.

Marketing Strategy

Your communications operation should be informed by a marketing strategy, however rudimentary. The first step is to determine your unit's competitive advantage. What makes your unit distinctive if not unique, and how can you best portray that trait over and against other internal or external competitors? A lot is being written about marketing organizations these days, leading UDOs to the perhaps erroneous conclusion that they must have either personal expertise or ready expertise at hand.

Understanding a few key buzzwords can dispel much of the mystery surrounding marketing. The buzzword of the hour is "branding," but all branding essentially means is the effective and consistent communication of a school's or unit's competitive advantage. Another marketing buzzword is "positioning," which refers to the location of your unit in terms of its perceived mission or quality in relation to competitive units. At the unit level, however, positioning is a function of branding or the articulation of your competitive advantage. If you can articulate clearly, consistently, and in a positive light what is unique or different about your unit, you have already done all the branding or positioning necessary to successfully market your unit.

Second, you need to segment your natural constituency into stakeholders—alumni, parents, donors, employers, prospective students, faculty, prospective faculty, and funding sources, among others—and prioritize their importance. Determine how best to communicate to each of these stakeholder groups, and then find a mechanism to indicate whether they are receiving your message. Adjust accordingly. Although it is often difficult to implement, a mechanism to assess the impact of your mission on a targeted constituency is crucial to the success of your marketing process. Indeed, any marketing initiative that does not include such a mechanism is no true marketing effort.

Conclusion

Staffing, prospect management, clearance, board development and maintenance, alumni and parent relations, corporate relations, international development, stewardship and special events, communications and marketing are the essential elements that a UDO needs to manage in addition to the actual cultivation and solicitation of gifts. There are books like this one as well as conferences and workshops on virtually all of these topics. But also look around. Find out who is doing something well, and take that person to lunch to acquire information. There are fellow UDOs managing these elements in an exemplary manner. They can serve as models. From them, you can assemble your own set of management tools and procedures. And then get to it. You will achieve better results and increase your sense of professional satisfaction—not to mention your personal marketability.

Recommendations for Best Practice

- Stay close to your dean. Promote your dean. The dean's success is your success. When you support your alumni, that support is seen as emanating from the dean. Your stewardship efforts are seen as the dean's efforts. A good staff makes a successful dean—and a successful dean has successful advancement people.

- Stay close to faculty. Let them know you are their advocate—which you are. They in turn will be your advocates with the dean, school administration, alumni, and, most important, donors. If they believe you are there to truly help the school (and them), they will convey this to alumni and donors. Most faculty members have been around the school longer than you have. Their rolodexes are better than any database you have. Get to know these people and show respect for their work, and they will show respect for yours.

- Talk about the uniqueness of your alumni and the program you offer. Every university teaches business, but no other university does it with the same people in the same manner and in the same place as you do.

- Stay close to central development. In a truly decentralized university, school development staff is insulated from the harm that may be caused by central development. But this "détente" means little gets done. The central office has experts and expertise. It has prospects, and its staff can help you swing gifts your way. Treat these people as colleagues, not the enemy, and they will find gifts for both of you.

- Keep tabs on the other schools at the university. Learn from their successes and their mistakes. Although they may be dealing with alumni and donors from a different discipline, the culture is much the same for all the schools. Help your colleagues in these schools. They are not your competitors. In a decentralized university, it is hard to maintain clean lines between prospects. You are dealing with dual-degree holders, parents, spouses, and siblings. A little kindness toward competitors in other schools will benefit you in the long run. More important, all of you will do a better job of serving the alumni of your university—alumni who find the pettiness of a decentralized university distasteful.

- Keeps tabs on counterpart schools at competing universities. You will be surprised how much you have in common. I used to consult often with my counterpart at our cross-town rival. The behavior of our deans, our faculty, and our alumni was surprisingly similar. Talking through various issues gave us insight on the problems we both faced—and made solutions jump out in front of us.

- Show donors that you are the signature program of the university. Position yourself as the one program people think of when they think of your university. How do you become the signature program? You tell them. More important, you demonstrate that a gift to your unit is one that will benefit and strengthen the whole university

- Run the whole show—whether you have the people or not. Once you are out in a school or unit, you are advancement—fund raiser, alumni leader, and communications specialist. You cannot can't simply be one and not the other two. Like a stool, your program needs all three legs to stand. Somebody has to tell the story to alumni before they are ready to be solicited. Sitting around waiting for more staff can be a long wait. Create demand by being three talented people in one.

- With your new-found skills, you are the go-to person at the school. You are at the center of it all, in consultation with the dean, administration, faculty, alumni, and various external constituencies. Relish the role and reinforce it.

- Remember that you work for the university as well as the school. Conduct yourself as a university person, and your donors and even your staff will think better of you. You just happen to work at the best unit in the university.

CHAPTER 12

Unit-Based Campaigning

Scott Nichols

Dean for Development, Harvard Law School

"What's all this talk about campaigns, and what in the world does it have to do with my little unit? After all, we're simply struggling to get in a few big gifts now and then." It is a common refrain heard in many a unit development office. But the reality is different. In this era of mega-campaigning, the rampant pace and scope of campaigning influences us more than we may think.

When Stanford University launched the first billion-dollar campaign, few imagined the extraordinary ramifications. Within the next decade, 23 other universities launched campaigns of at least a billion dollars, according to the Grenzebach Glier & Associates *2001 Monthly Planner*. Waiting somewhat breathlessly in the wings, sometimes oblivious to the pacesetters in fund raising, unit development officers (UDOs) have found that their earlier somewhat simple existence has become quite complex relatively quickly.

The history of university education in the United States is characterized by seemingly endless tension between centripetal and centrifugal forces. The autonomy (or lack thereof) of the components continues to be a complicated situation fraught with positives and negatives. From a fund-raising perspective, we can start to sort it out from several vantage points:

▶ Campaigns are proliferating at both the unit and university-wide level.

▶ Fund raising is under increased pressure toward centralization.

▶ Units cherish and protect their historical and natural independence.

▶ Most donors, particularly the biggest ones, focus on the impact of their gifts—not on institutional politics and organization.

▶ Units have become effective fund-raising operations.

Debating and documenting these points could fill most of this book, but the UDO must start from a perspective that reflects broader trends in higher education. By any measure, campaigning is one of the critical strategies all of us must adopt. The savvy reader will quickly conclude that the term "campaigning" describes a variety of methods to raise money. After all, are we not always in campaign mode, even if we don't call it that? And what, if anything, is the difference between focusing on a single project, a group of projects, or a large number of objectives packaged into one? The following are the four most common types of campaigns:

- **Project fund raising.** Throughout most of the history of educational fund raising, it has been common to concentrate on one project at a time. A project could be a building, professorship, scholarship, or research center, but it is a single, designated effort.

- **Mini-campaign.** Although occasionally a single-purpose effort, a mini-campaign is typically an intense, short-term effort to reach one or a small number of goals. Often selective in terms of the prospect pool, the mini-campaign is typically a one- to three-year effort that involves only a few volunteers but requires the full attention of the development operation.

- **Capital campaign.** A term now seldom used, the capital campaign is a major effort to concentrate on fund raising that adds to the permanent value of the institution. By definition, the effort excludes support for operations, something most UDOs now find particularly unhelpful.

- **Comprehensive campaign.** Today's most popular strategy—and the result of serious institutional planning and prioritization—the comprehensive campaign is a multiyear, multipurpose set of objectives that encompasses the entire community and the institution's constituencies. Comprehensive campaigns normally last five years or more.

Planning and Coordinating Comprehensive Campaigns

Why are big (as in huge) comprehensive efforts proliferating? Mainly because we have learned the hard way that multipurpose or comprehensive campaigns raise much more money than do mini-campaigns, capital campaigns, or single-purpose campaigns. Unfortunately, every single-purpose campaign conducted by my current institutional unit throughout the 20th century has fallen short of its goal. At the other end of the spectrum, our most recent massive comprehensive campaign exceeded its goal by 20 percent.

In essence, the modern development shop—if it wishes to maximize gift income for the institution—has no choice but to campaign. We know how to do it, and success rates are up. Our better prospects now expect us to come at them aggressively, occasionally beyond the usual annual giving for capital support. Our role is to not disappoint the institution or its prospects. What should a UDO with campaign instincts do in the complex world of a university? The steps are twofold: planning and coordination.

A UDO who is not currently waging a campaign should be planning one. Several factors demand this. First, all development officers need to clearly define and prioritize institutional goals, unit and otherwise. When we approach capital prospects or they present themselves, all involved have to be aware of leading themes, priorities, and objectives. Too often priorities are determined exclusively by the dean, unit heads, or a small number of individuals—which leads to a less effective "project du jour" approach as opposed to a cohesive, compelling set of objectives. Gone are the days when we answered prospect inquiries with a single option or seemingly limitless menu of institutional activities. The tougher, smarter donor environment today demands that we think through our priorities, precisely define our objectives, and—yes—perform serious long-range planning.

Planning a campaign is an art and science that presents a considerable number of options. For units, the opening question is whether to plan locally or within a larger university effort. To a large extent, the answer is determined from the top down. If a university-wide, formal process exists, find the unit's place within that context. If not, proceed vigorously to create a process. Educational planning has a rhythm, an institutional cycle that reflects the dean, the community, and the moment in history. Very often, needs impel us to begin formal planning. For the UDO, the academic side of the unit must lead and provide sanction. The unit head must be perceived as leader of a community that has envisioned, researched, debated, decided, and unified around common aspirations. Only then can we, the fund raisers, begin to plan a comprehensive campaign.

For UDOs, long-range planning is the driving force behind comprehensive campaigns. Once we accept the reality of living within a larger community, we face myriad coordination issues. Prime among these is whether to confederate or maintain some degree of independence, to the extent that it is possible. Experiments abound throughout higher education. No single model for campaigning exists. Highly centralized university efforts, like decentralized ones, have advantages and disadvantages.

It is logical to conclude that in unity there is strength. A university-wide, centralized effort offers many positives, most notably efficiency. Priorities are clear to all, communications and publications are consistent, and momentum develops evenly and on a schedule that reinforces a master plan. With top volunteers and donors playing on the same team at the same time, special opportunities materialize to build esprit de corps, raise sights, update, and steward. Cross-unit programs are highlighted, the president's time is highly focused, and the institution seems whole—marching in the same direction at the same speed. Centralized prospect clearance, research, special events, and stewardship are not only possible, but also often provide resources to units for activities that would otherwise be impossible or too expensive. Smaller units, in particular, benefit from activities, budget, and staff that are unavailable at any other time. For many, the whole is greater than the sum of the parts.

Advantages and Disadvantages of Centralized Campaigns

The greatest advantage of centralized campaigns is that numerous resources are centralized. These resources include the following:

▶ The president's time and attention

▶ The time and attention of trustees and governing bodies

▶ Additional budget

▶ Increased research capacity

▶ Additional special events and cultivation activities

▶ More-extensive communications vehicles

▶ Greater regional coverage

▶ Efficient, wider stewardship opportunities

The single biggest disadvantage is prospect clearance. Sparks fly over centralization of prospects. Many institutions have implemented such a system, but seldom without some degree of conflict. Stronger units do not appreciate reallocation of existing prospects. Smaller, less affluent units aggressively seek to broaden their prospect base, often at the expense of larger, more affluent units. For many large units, a centralized campaign seems merely a cover for reallocating resources through the redistribution of top prospects.

Also, centralized campaigns often violate the "primacy of degree" principle. In prior, gentler eras, units maintained total control of their alumni constituencies. Centralized campaigns, however, typically operate on the premise that a body beyond the unit will determine how to approach graduates and who will do it. To be precluded from dealing freely with one's own graduates—to be deprived of primacy of degree—is anathema to UDOs and frequently the cause of major conflict.

In addition, it is usually very difficult to coordinate infrastructure in a centralized campaign. Synthesizing databases, gift recording, stewardship activities, a kickoff, annual events, publication schedules, budgets, and joint or shared personnel can be extraordinarily difficult and contentious. The trauma represented by centralizing and shifting existing infrastructure can be severe—one size clearly does not fit all. Consider the difference in alumni activities, corporate/foundation strategies, size of database, annual donor activities, and the role of the dean. At the end of the day, the needs of a medical school development operation simply do not mesh with those of a school of education. One apt historical analogy is D-Day in World War II. Watching an institution launch a centralized campaign reminds me of the challenge Supreme Allied Commander Dwight D. Eisenhower faced when he had to mobilize and coordinate the armies of many countries for the invasion of Europe.

Weighing Campaign Strategies

Before deciding on whether a centralized or decentralized campaign strategy is best for you, you should also consider the following advantages of decentralized campaigns:

▶ Having control over all prospects

▶ Timing that is entirely appropriate to the unit

▶ Quicker ability to cultivate and solicit

▶ Less time spent on negotiating and coordinating with central bureaucracy

▶ Total focus on the unit as opposed to on shared objectives

▶ More targeted use of top volunteers and staff

▶ A more manageable, controllable campaign strategy

▶ Simpler data base and infrastructure requirements

▶ A strong sense of self-reliance

Considering all the pluses and minuses, what campaign strategy works best for you? Before you answer, keep in mind that a UDO's most powerful fund-raising tool is the campaign. Utilizing that tool in concert with the rest of the institution is advisable if the additional resources augment your fund-raising efforts. However, units must continually assess whether the advantages of coordinated campaigns outweigh the disadvantages. For large units, I recommend an independent route separate from an undergraduate college-centric effort. For smaller units, hooking onto the big train as it leaves the station presents the best opportunities for success. As campaigning proliferates, err on the side of doing more, not less. Perhaps the best course of action is simply to jump on the campaign bandwagon as soon as you can—whether you have company or not!

Recommendations for Best Practice

- Attack! The most important step is to conduct vigorous fund raising with comprehensive campaigning—whether as part of a university-wide effort or independently. The centralized/decentralized debate is no excuse for paralysis. The only losing move is not to play.

- Big units do better with independent campaigns. Established fund-raising programs in law, business, and medical schools seldom mesh particularly well with campaigns centered on undergraduate education. With traditional constituencies and overlapping top prospects, large units often end up in wrestling matches over key prospects, winning some but invariably losing some in the process. Philosophically, there is one overarching reason why large units should campaign off-cycle from university-wide efforts: Everyone raises more money! Do not hesitate to ask overlapping top prospects for major capital commitments. Massive efforts that target top prospects once every 10 to 15 years are less effective than two asks during the same period by two separate campaigns. The most successful multiversity development operations (in terms of hard cash) find that leapfrog campaigning maximizes gift income.

- Small units do better with university-wide, centralized campaigns. With fewer resources and less well-established programs, smaller units benefit immensely from the economies of scale of a college-centric or university-wide campaign. Greater resources are available for research, cultivation activities, stewardship, planned giving, and corporate/foundation efforts. The president is more available; communications tools and publications prevail, offering unusual opportunities to get the message out.

- Coordinate principal gift prospects. No institution can afford to allow all units open season all the time on top prospects. Whether waging a campaign or not, units should permit some coordination with the most important prospects. For most, prospect coordination—not to be confused with prospect tracking—works best when it is limited to a small number, perhaps 50 to 100. Do not contemplate university-wide coordination of hundreds, possibly thousands, of moves and asks: That is a recipe for endless debate and massive bureaucracy that hobbles cultivation and solicitation. Draw the line at a level where deans, trustees, and presidents are personally acquainted with prospects. As for any single development officer, usually no more than 100 prospects is manageable.

- Protect and respect primacy of degree. Never prohibit a unit from cultivating or communicating with its degree holders. This does not preclude claims, or even priority, in terms of involvement, cultivation, and solicitation by other units. Yet it is a dreadful mistake for units to relinquish opportunities for cultivating relations, however secondary, with its own graduates.

- Create formal, unit-based, volunteer leadership—and use it liberally. Unit development often resembles the quests of Don Quixote: No matter how just the cause, the dream becomes impossible when one battles alone. It is exceptionally advantageous to invite others, particularly alumni, to join in the effort. Over the past 10 to 15 years, formal leadership groups, such as a dean's advisory council or board, have produced amazing results. Even with no legal or fiduciary responsibilities, these boards can have extensive influence. These leaders—not democratically chosen bodies—can fill vacuums institutions frequently avoid. They tread into waters many of us fastidiously avoid, confronting messy challenging issues like centralization. Seldom do we have better advocates than our loyal, involved, educated alumni leaders. Wielded by a savvy dean and UDO, their wisdom, energy, and articulate voices can be powerful weapons.

- Negotiate. Despite inherent tensions, units and central authorities are not natural enemies. Unit officers and central staff must find ways to campaign effectively, either in concert or not. As in any good marriage, it might take a certain amount of give and take. Both sides have much to offer in pursuit of their respective missions. Atmosphere is vital; if both perspectives are treated respectfully, good-faith negotiating can ensure a mutually productive partnership worthy of the highest standards of professionalism.

- Consult. Even if your institutional setting allows you the luxury, do not let a natural instinct for independence determine whether you will work together or separately in a campaign setting. Defining the campaign relationship requires the consensus of the entire unit community, including alumni/volunteer leadership. No matter how righteous the decision in the development office, problems arise if the unit community is either oblivious or contrarian. The broader the mandate, the greater the chance for campaign success.

References

Grenzebach Glier & Associates, *2001 Monthly Planner.*

CHAPTER 13

Directing a Unit-Based Foundation

Paul Gardner

Executive Director, Dental Foundation of North Carolina, Inc.

A friend who worked for many years in the central development office at the University of North Carolina at Chapel Hill (UNC–CH) recently took a position as assistant dean for advancement at a constituent unit on our campus. One of her responsibilities is to serve as executive director of the school's foundation. Just a few weeks after taking the job, she told a colleague, "I didn't realize how much you constituent development officers were doing. I didn't realize all that was involved with being the executive director of a foundation." Neither did I.

Actually, I knew half of it. Because I had worked for nearly nine years as director of development and then assistant dean for development and alumni affairs with the UNC–CH School of Journalism and Mass Communication (JOMC), I certainly was aware of the workload that constituent development officers carry. After all, I had been doing the same things for several years: making personal visits, directing the annual fund, producing thank-you letters and stewardship reports, editing alumni publications, planning events, writing proposals, attending central development office meetings, managing a board of visitors, and, of course, working with a foundation board of directors.

Still, I did not realize all that a foundation executive director does. When I was hired a little over two years ago at the same university as director of development for the School of Dentistry and executive director of the Dental Foundation of North Carolina, Inc. (DFNC), I assumed that my duties would be roughly equivalent to those at JOMC. And, for the most part, they are. Because our alumni relations office is directed by another individual, I have more time to focus on fund raising. But being executive director of the DFNC adds another layer of responsibility that more than makes up for the lack of alumni association responsibilities.

At JOMC, I worked with a foundation board, but I did not have to worry about preparing the annual budget, dealing with investments, preparing fund-authority reports, or working with outside accountants and auditors (at least not a great deal). Because the dean of JOMC served as executive director of the JOMC Foundation, he developed the budget in consultation with our business manager and internal accountant. No fund-authority reports were generated for department chairs or faculty members, because our dean managed all foundation funds himself.

In my position with the DFNC, I have learned a great deal about what executive directors for constituent foundations do. What might I have told my colleague before she left the central development office to join us in the constituent universe? Simply that an executive director of a foundation functions as a vice chancellor or vice president, albeit on a smaller scale. Or, as another colleague who is executive director of her school's foundation says, we are chief operating officers. People have to know who we are, what we do, and why we do it. Our audiences are varied, as are the ways with which we communicate with them.

Marketing and Communications

Alumni and Friends

I am the executive director of a foundation, but I am first and foremost a development officer. How does any good development professional communicate with alumni and friends? Through personal visits, telephone calls, letters, greeting cards, thank-you letters, stewardship reports, newsletters, email, invitations to speak to classes and meet with students, invitations to events, and membership on your foundation board. We use all these means and others to communicate with alumni and friends who make gifts to our foundations.

Try as we might, however, such communication cannot guarantee that prospective donors will understand why a unit needs its own foundation. One executive director tells the story of an alumnus who served on his foundation board for several years but still did not understand why he should name the foundation, instead of the school, as the beneficiary of a planned gift he was establishing. To add insult to injury, when the executive director finally told the former board member how many millions of dollars in assets the foundation had, the donor said, "Well, you don't need my money."

The founders of our school had the foresight to know that private funding would be critical to ensuring excellence in dental education. Although I can find no specific mention of it in the minutes of those early foundation board meetings, I suspect that those school and foundation founders also knew that a foundation established solely for the school would ensure independence and flexibility for future deans—a flexibility that, quite frankly, is not possible if constituents rely solely on a university foundation.

To help our alumni and friends more strongly identify with our foundation, we marketed the foundation as the gift repository of choice. Instead of saying, "I am director of development for the School of Dentistry," I introduce myself as executive director of the DFNC. Certainly, I always include my association with the School of Dentistry, but the foundation is my first identifier. We had a professional designer create a logo or "corporate identity" for the foundation for use on our letterhead, note cards, nametags, and so forth. We also launched our own Web site, which is linked to the School of Dentistry and university development office sites.

The other chief reason for identifying the foundation as a separate organization involves planned giving. At our university, if bequests or other planned giving vehicles are left to the School of Dentistry, the money goes to the University Foundation. The funds still benefit our school, but we have no control over investment or payout. However, if people name the DFNC as the beneficiary, the funds come to our foundation and we decide where to invest and how much to spend each year.

Students

Most students do not know that our foundation exists, and most of those who know it exists do not know why it exists. It is a known fact that students become alumni, and alumni ignorant of the purpose of the foundation are hard to educate. While they are studying in your school, you have a wonderful opportunity to show students how they benefit from the foundation and, in so doing, cultivate relationships with your future donors.

When our associate director and I talk with first- and second-year students during their first week of orientation, we focus our message on what the foundation does to help them. They really perk up when we tell them about the thousands of dollars in scholarships the foundation offers each year. We also invite the students to work with us as volunteers at events and on several other projects throughout the year.

Each year we work with our alumni association to give new students a nice gift. One year, for instance, each student received a canvas bag embroidered with "Class of 2004" to carry books and a laptop computer. Inside, we inserted a letter signed by the presidents of the alumni association and the foundation explaining the purpose of each organization.

Our foundation hosts an annual dinner where scholarship and fellowship recipients can meet donors and the people for whom various awards are named. Donors often make it possible for us to invite students and their guests to our largest annual event, the Best of Dentistry Dinner, and each month we invite a dozen students to an informal lunch with the dean. We also host an annual graduation dinner for students and their guest or spouse. We give each student a school lapel pin with an attached card explaining the meaning of the logo symbols, the history of the school, and our foundation.

When our school holds its annual White Coat Ceremony, the foundation is a sponsor and active participant. The presentation of the white coat to our students marks the completion of the first year of didactic learning and a rite of passage into the clinical phase of their dental education. We make direct annual grants to student organizations from our golf tournament proceeds. Interested organizations submit a proposal and make a presentation to our foundation board. In order to make a serious presentation, students have to learn more about the foundation and how they benefit directly from the foundation's generosity.

Our first senior class gift effort resulted in an 83 percent participation rate, and we hope successive seniors top that figure. Obviously, when students solicit their classmates, we hope they will learn something about the foundation and remember it when they are making future philanthropic decisions, perhaps as a volunteer solicitor in a future campaign. We do not beat our students over the head with it, but we make a serious effort to help them understand what our foundation does for them and for the school, so that when we call on them in their dental practices they will remember us.

Faculty

Many of our restricted and endowed funds benefit specific departments of the school. We share monthly reports on these funds with the department chairs, who serve as fund managers. Generated by our accountant in the school's financial affairs office, these reports provide the fund manager with information about contributions, expenses, total cash, and total funds invested. Essentially, these are monthly stewardship reports for our faculty members. Of course, we also work with faculty members to identify, cultivate, and solicit prospective donors for their individual departments. Additionally, we help them communicate with their alumni, plan their own fund-raising campaigns, and coordinate mail and personal solicitations. We also work with them to select fellowship and scholarship winners in their departments.

Boards and Deans

As the executive director of a foundation, you work with board members who help you and your dean raise, invest, nurture, and award the funds that your alumni and friends contribute. Your board members may be active or passive, but either way you answer to them. Like the board of a corporation, they want to see that you are producing revenue, investing wisely, and doing good things with the money. I have worked with boards that want only to be spoon-fed information so they can rubber-stamp approval on your requests, and I have worked with boards that are more aggressive and involved.

You and your dean need to determine what kind of board you want and build it accordingly. How many meetings do you want to have? How long do you want meetings to run? Do you want a board that focuses on investments? Or one that focuses on helping your students? It is really up to you and your dean, and, with the right choices, you can build the board you want.

Never forget the importance of your board, and never forget this: Your relationship with your dean is crucial. I am fortunate in that I have worked with two deans who understand the importance of fund raising; working with a foundation board; and the value of endowments, planned giving, and long-term investing. You travel with your dean; cultivate, solicit, and steward donors with your dean; schedule the dean's time with prospective donors; prepare him or her for those meetings with donors; and prepare him or her for board meetings. You do not have to be best buddies with your dean, but you certainly should establish a strong relationship—just as you establish relationships with your donors. And always remember that no matter how good your relationship with a donor might be, donors want to see your dean. They want to know his or her vision for your unit: The dean is the CEO.

The University

Obviously, our primary contact with the university is with the central development office. Central development handles much of our gifts processing and can provide a variety of services such as research, planned giving, legal counsel, special events, tickets for sporting events, corporate and foundation giving, and communications. You need to work with central development to coordinate visits with and solicitation of prospects. Inevitably, too, you will attend countless meetings with central development and other constituent unit colleagues.

You will have a good deal of contact with the undergraduate admissions office as you check on the status of applications submitted by the children of your alumni. And you will deal with your own academic-affairs office, since they make admissions decisions on the children of your graduates and non-alumni donors. If you need to hire an accountant or another major-gifts officer, contact your university's personnel office. And even if you invest your foundation funds with an investment firm outside the university, you will still have to deal with your university investment office because it will want to get your business back.

Managing Finances

Hire a good accountant, and work with him or her to implement systems that well serve both of you. The better the in-house systems, the fewer headaches you will suffer with your annual audit. Create annual budgets for your foundation and stick to them. Besides helping you spend wisely, budgets give you an excellent plan for your year. We divide our budget into two major categories—administrative and fund raising—and each category contains about 15–20 line items ranging from salaries and benefits to foundation board meetings and fund-raising travel and events.

Make sure the expenditure lines on your disbursement requests and on your accountant's expenditure reports match your budget-line items. It will make it easier to pull records, especially at the end of the year when outside accountants work on your audit. You will see your accountant almost daily in the normal course of business, but schedule monthly meetings to ensure that deposits are correctly designated and that expenses are charged to the correct funds and to decide whether cash needs to be moved to the investment pool or vice versa.

Executive directors have two essential responsibilities with investments. The primary one is to determine with whom to invest foundation funds. I prefer to invest ours with the university investment office. Our board, of course, has ultimate authority over where the money is invested and, thankfully, they agree with me. A staff of professionals manages the university investment office's daily operations, and a board of volunteers who manage some of the largest and most successful investment firms in the world meets quarterly to determine investment policies and strategies. The board is happy with the university investment office's management, performance, and customer service. That does not mean that we will invest only with the university's investment office. Other outside investment firms have made presentations to our board, and we will certainly continue to keep our options open.

The second responsibility of an executive director is to ensure that a fund's rate of return is acceptable to the foundation's board. I was a journalism major, so I certainly do not pretend to know whether our investments should be in high-tech small caps or in another area. But a colleague who is executive director of another constituent foundation on campus pays more attention to the market and talks weekly with the outside investment managers of his foundation's funds about market trends, investment vehicles, and so forth. How involved do you want to be in your foundation's investments? That is your decision. We must pay attention, of course, but I prefer to let the professionals worry about the market. I read the quarterly reports the investments office sends me, and I attend most of the quarterly investment meetings, but I think my time is better spent with donors who can make our investment pool grow with their contributions.

Other Responsibilities

Great. You got a lot done when you were in the office from 8 to 5. Now you have to attend donor recognition dinners, alumni receptions, retired faculty luncheons, scholarship dinners—and run a day-long golf tournament. Remember, again, that you are first and foremost a development officer. Get used to attending lots of events.

If your school has an alumni association, it is critical that you work closely with it and its professional staff. We must maintain our separate identities and work toward our individual organizational goals, but we must also work together toward the common goal—improving our school.

Finally, (saving the best for last) be prepared to deal with grants. This is not really miscellaneous, but I wanted to save the best for last. Executive directors get to both see the money come in and see how the money is used—all the good things that are done with the contributions alumni and friends entrust to us.

At one scholarship dinner, we asked a scholarship recipient to speak about what the foundation's scholarship support means to her. Since her parents do not have the means to help her financially, she financed her undergraduate education and is putting herself through dental school with student loans and scholarship support. To reduce her expenses, she completed her undergraduate degree in three years. Near the end of her remarks, she said, "Once you're out in the real world, running your successful private practice, I challenge you to set up your own scholarship or fellowship fund with the Dental Foundation." I could not have scripted her any better—and you can bet I have added her name to my list of prospective foundation board members.

Recommendations for Best Practice

- Be a good development officer. Communicate with your alumni and friends, students, and faculty.
- Determine, with your dean, what type of board you want and build accordingly.
- Cultivate and steward a good relationship with the dean of your unit.
- Cultivate and steward good relationships with all departments of your central development office, the university investment office, and other campus units (such as personnel).

- Hire a good accountant, and implement effective accounting systems.
- Build a good relationship with the investment professionals who manage your foundation's funds. Communicate regularly with them and pay close attention to the reports they provide.
- Work with your unit's alumni association to meet your common goal—improving your school.
- Always remember that donors are the ones who make it possible for your foundation to do the good things it does. And enjoy the role you and the foundation play in making those things happen.

IV

MAKING THE CASE FOR UNIT DEVELOPMENT

CHAPTER 14

Defining the Constituencies of the Unit Development Office

Dottie O'Carroll

Director of Development, Development Consortium,
University of Southern California

Harry Vann

Director of Corporate Relations,
College of Electrical and Computing Engineering, Georgia Institute of Technology

"Know your public" is a credo familiar to all institutions. It is of vital importance to the unit development officer (UDO), whose challenge is to convert members of the public at large into donors to a particular academic program. Discovering just who that public is, defining it as constituency, and formulating an approach to reach it is the key to building and sustaining a program.

An effective first step in this process is a thorough review of the unit's academic mission and its strategic plan. Follow this with a close look at the unit's current program components. The long-range vision and more immediate goals of the unit can be measured against existing funding to determine the focus and level of development efforts necessary. This process can be activated by a strategy session led by the UDO and may include the dean, key faculty members, and board leaders. An academic audit such as this for development purposes is key to the next step of defining both the individual and corporate constituencies from which donor prospects and, finally, donors may eventually emerge.

Defining Individual Constituencies

In an academic institution, program components typically fall into the categories of faculty enhancement, program development, student aid, and capital improvements. What varies between institutions and academic units is the subject matter. It is the subject matter and generally the subject matter alone that defines the constituency. Awareness and involvement in any program is a function of an individual's, corporation's, or foundation's interest in a specific area of knowledge or research. Donors rarely find their way to a unit's need based only on a general interest in the institution.

Where should the UDO look for constituents and what is the process of engaging them in the program? Whereas some constituent groups are readily apparent to the unit, others are more subtle, emerging as a function of a specialized program or a particular faculty member. When defining constituents, the UDO should always ask, How do the individuals see themselves? Do they consider themselves first as alumni? Parents? Patrons? Issues advocates? How do they see their linkage to the program? What appeals to them most?

Basic Types of Individual Constituencies

Most academic units can count on the presence of at least four basic types of individual constituencies:

1. Alumni are the core constituents of any unit-based development program, the first to appreciate the program's tradition and values. UDOs can query alumni about their particular interests and commitments to the program, in this way segmenting alumni into sub-constituencies that address a specific aspect of the unit's overall program. For instance, an alumnus may identify strongly with an experience on the debate squad or with the student newspaper. This kind of affinity may create a separate alumni group that supports one of these programs. Or an alumna with a life sciences or engineering background may identify herself as an entrepreneur and become interested in a business school program in entrepreneurial studies.

2. Parents of students in the unit are naturally linked to the institution and to the unit itself during the course of their son's or daughter's education. As investors in the unit for the education of their child, parents qualify as a constituency. Many units develop communications programs to inform parents of academic initiatives and the general news of the school. Others develop an annual-giving program. The University of Southern California (USC) School of Cinema–Television has developed both a communications program and an annual-giving program. Annually, parents are invited to contribute to a specific initiative that is considered vital to the student's education, perhaps an equipment or program fund. A higher level of giving can result from a parent's commitment as an annual donor to the unit. It is in every unit's best interest to screen parents for major gift potential. An active philanthropist with a family

foundation or a board member of a private foundation may be among the parents of a unit's students.

3. Career professionals in the academic area covered by a unit constitute another constituency not to be overlooked. Although individuals may not be alumni of the program, they often have a strong interest in and commitment to the professional education the unit provides. And, too, they may be geographically removed from their alma mater or have an area of expertise that draws them specifically to research conducted by faculty in the unit. Developing a support group with a leadership board is an effective way to engage this constituency. Such a structure provides the professionals with a context in which they can advance the unit and affords an opportunity for collegiality and communication with one another. They can also engage others in the industry. Major gift opportunities for the unit often come from the professionals themselves or through their association with colleagues, consultants, clients, and grant-making agencies.

4. Patrons, clients, patients, customers and advocates constitute a constituency that may be less apparent but can still be a strong force in furthering the unit's development efforts. Identifying those who already have demonstrated a philanthropic interest as a patron of an arts-based organization, for instance, or who have been a national or community advocate for a cause or issue may lead to a commitment or at least more-focused interest in education and research within an academic area. Often, they are individuals of prominence who have been publicly lauded or who have foundations or corporations whose good work has been recognized in the press. Reviewing lists of supporters of arts organizations or advocacy groups to find alumni matches also can be a productive first step in the identification process. Similarly, key-word research on the priorities of foundations and corporations is a good first step in matching corporate priorities to the unit mission.

In addition to these four basic groups, individual constituencies can also be defined by personal relationships. A program directed by or named for a respected faculty member may draw a unique following of alumni and professionals. Likewise, a faculty endowment or capital fund named for a distinguished alumnus of the school may garner funding from family, professionals, and colleagues who have a close relationship with the alumnus but no prior relationship with the unit. Even an event can create a constituency. For instance, the USC Scripter Award is presented annually to a film writer and producer in recognition of the literary and cinematic excellence of a current film. From the participants in this event, major donors have been identified for the university library.

Finally, a unit's leadership group or advisory board can serve as a vehicle for defining and building constituencies. A board can be created or expanded with the target constituent groups in mind so that each constituency is represented by a board member. This strategy has the added advantage of building the constituency with the board member or his or her designated committee at its head. It takes advantage of the opportunity for further identification of individual constituents as board members become aware of each other's goals for the unit.

UDOs have the advantage of attracting a variety of constituencies and, therefore, a range of interests to their programs. They also face the challenge of managing constituent groups. In this light, volunteer leadership, fund-raising potential, and staff resources must always be evaluated in determining the structure of any constituent group.

Most UDOs find that a program constituency is made up of many overlapping groups of individuals whose interests dovetail in various ways with the academic mission of the program. The successful UDO knows his or her public as a group of distinct constituencies whose specific goals can be combined and managed to advance the unit as a whole. Overall, constituents can be defined through a process that matches the goals of the academic plan to the fund-raising priorities of the unit.

In finding constituencies, the UDO must always be aware of how individuals see themselves in relation to the program—as alumni, parents, professional supporters, patrons, advocates, or people with a special relationship to an individual or program in the unit. As constituencies are defined, volunteer leadership representing that constituency is key to advancing fund-raising initiatives. Defining, developing, and managing constituencies are creative processes that match donors' interests to the academic plan of a unit. When successful, UDOs can extend the reach of the unit into an ever-increasing base of support.

Defining Corporate Constituencies

Two elements distinguish a corporate constituency from an individual constituency. First, an individual constituency, by definition, consists of individuals who are motivated principally by their emotional engagement and commitment to an institution or project. While considering whether to make a gift, an individual prospect might be cognizant of the concerns of a spouse, children, other members of the family, or a select community of friends such as classmates or colleagues. But at the end of the day the decision to make a gift is still within the purview of the individual prospect and must be cultivated accordingly.

In a corporate constituency, however, each corporate member represents a group and thus must be cultivated as a group. This means developing a rational alignment of academic mission with a corporate vision and producing clear evidence of the value added by such an alignment to a corporate prospect's products or services. Corporate prospects are also very aware of other corporations within a constituency group, particularly if they are rivals in business such as Ford and GM. Thus, more than individuals, they can be motivated by what another corporation has or has not given.

Second, individuals and corporations differ greatly in the manner in which they associate with and engage an academic unit. Individual prospects can choose to associate with a college or school from a variety of perspectives—as alumni, parents, patrons, issues advocates, or some combination of perspectives—or they can be cultivated and solicited through a variety of motivations. For corporate prospects, however, the motivation for giving is almost always quid pro quo—to get something of tangible or strategic value to the corporation in exchange for whatever it gives the institution. Depending on the length of their vision, corporate donors see themselves, for the most part, as either sponsors or partners of an institution or academic program.

As sponsors, the relationship between the corporation and the institution is specific and relatively short-term and the exchange very tangible and straightforward. Athletic and cultural events, for example, lend themselves well to corporate sponsorships. As partners, however, the relationship is more general—or rather, specific to a number of projects or programs—and long-term, and the exchange is much more strategic and complex, allowing for more transformational types of giving such as endowed chairs or named programs or buildings. In summary, sponsors look for short-term and tangible returns on their gifts, whereas partners see their giving as an investment and therefore seek largely strategic returns over time and mutual growth and success of both corporation and institution as the ultimate goal.

For either sponsorships or partnerships, local companies are sometimes a harder sell than are national or international corporations. Often local companies, rightly believing that they will naturally receive the benefits in terms of personnel and research of having a major university in the area, do not enter into donative relationships with local institutions. Denying student or research access to companies that are neighbors, in effect, could be extremely problematic, especially for public universities, which frequently make the case for legislative support on the basis of being local "engines of commerce."

In such situations, UDOs should try to leverage the local connection through co-sponsorships of events that feature key lawmakers who sit on or chair legislative committees relevant to their products or services, or that highlight the company as a good corporate citizen or benchmark of community excellence. Ultimately, local companies need to be moved to the point where they can see their giving as an investment that will provide them with additional value above and beyond what they might reasonably expect as the result of proximity or tax revenues.

Basic Types of Corporate Constituencies

Because of the strong quid pro quo nature of corporate relationships, corporate constituencies are best defined in terms of their motivation for giving, of which there are essentially four:

▶ Access to students

▶ Entrée into research, continuing education, or training programs

▶ Ability to capitalize on a close association with an institution or its reputation

▶ Access to suppliers

Most corporations seek to form relationships with specific academic units or colleges because they want access to their best students. To identify these companies, the UDO simply needs to ascertain which corporations come to campus to interview and recruit students, year in and year out, regardless of the state of the economy. These are the corporations that are sold on the institutional product as it were or, more often, on the product of a specific college or sub-unit. Over time, these companies have determined that the graduates of that institution or program consistently add value to their enterprise, and they will continually return to the wellspring for the life of their organizations.

The fortunate college or unit will have several such corporations vying for its graduates. If so, the UDO has a leverage point with them, and that is the privilege of access—or rather denial, of the privilege of access. In public institutions, this most often manifests itself more as the facilitation of access to students as opposed to outright denial. In a competitive marketplace, corporations seek to gain this special access to the best and the brightest students and are usually quite willing to pay for the privilege. Sponsored internships, fellowships, and competitions provide these companies with the opportunity to assess students closely in a workplace setting as well as make their presence an integral and visible part of the college culture. Paid membership in a corporate liaison or associates program can also be rewarded with premiums to special-access events such as sponsored pizza parties or receptions. Even job fairs can be restricted corporate sponsors or donors.

Corporations might be interested in forming donative relationships that support and ensure entrée to research they utilize or continuing education programs or training they depend on. Again, the leverage point is access, but because these corporations are usually already consumers of an educational product, denial of access would be self-defeating. Thus, UDOs of units providing such research or training should take a strictly valued-added approach, offering client companies guaranteed or enhanced access to these products and services through membership in a corporate liaison program that provides a fixed number of free or discounted placements or increased access to the research results in an area of interest in exchange for increased support.

Once moved from client to donor, these corporations can then be cultivated over time to move to the major donor level by increasing the value of their return in exchange for increased capital investment in the infrastructure supporting the programs or research of interest through endowed chairs, building additions or renovations, or other programmatic improvements. For instance, through its foundation, Motorola recently gave the Georgia Institute of Technology (Georgia Tech) an endowed chair in electrical and computer engineering, an academic unit that the company had increasingly invested in for over a decade. Over this period, Georgia Tech UDOs were able to persuade the company to move to the next level by pointing to clear evidence of the value returned to the company as the direct result of its previous investments.

Some corporate donors seek to capitalize on a close association with a college or university or seek to trade on the institution's reputation. Universities with nationally and internationally recognized "brand names" can and do attract national and international corporate donors that find tangible or strategic value to a visible association. However, even institutions with more modest regional or local brand recognition can capitalize on such affiliations at some level. Although most of these donors gravitate to high-profile areas such as athletics, the arts, or business, numerous corporations make gifts in other academic areas to enhance their credibility and reputation so as to gain a competitive edge on their competition or add perceived value to a product or service.

For example, AutoCAD, a company that makes design software for architects, has come to dominate its market niche in part through a policy of donating or substantially discounting its products so as to guarantee a continuing stream of users entering the workforce where they often become customers. Velux, a leading manufacturer of sky lighting, has annually sponsored a design competition at the Georgia Tech College of Architecture in which participating students are required to use sky lighting as part of their design solution. First prize in the competition is the Velux Fellowship, a highly sought-after accolade among Georgia Tech students that the company initially funded on an annual basis but later was willing to endow in perpetuity because of its perceived success in adding value to both the college and the company.

One often-overlooked corporate constituency consists of institutional suppliers. These companies have a vested interest in maintaining a strong and healthy relationship with an institution that is both a major customer and, as is often the case with specialized technologies, an erstwhile demonstrator and trainer of its products to future customers. Currently, the strategy of linking giving to vendor contracts is applied unevenly by universities. Thus, whereas a company such as Hewlett-Packard has a giving policy that provides millions of dollars in amenities each year to universities to which they are suppliers, others such as Dell and Gateway provide only small grants to student-based organizations.

For both private and many public universities, a policy of linking vendor rights to giving should be uncontroversial. Even in states where public universities are forbidden by law to enter into exclusive contracts, lucrative and mutually advantageous sidebar agreements regarding corporate giving can and should be secured between client institutions and suppliers. Although such agreements usually are negotiated at the institutional level, UDOs should be alert to making the case for support of their units part of the package of amenities. And in some cases, such as colleges with a larger or highly sought-after student or alumni base, UDOs can enter into their own agreements with a vendor for unit support.

Although their motivations for giving are essentially the same as those of domestic corporations (and thus do not constitute a separate corporate constituency as defined here), international corporations nevertheless can present unfamiliar organizational structures, visions, and cultures that challenge conventional strategies for developing corporate relations. Companies based in the United States that operate internationally present the fewest difficulties in this regard, inasmuch as their organization is likely to follow conventional American models, and their culture is at least familiar with the concept of corporate giving. What sets these companies apart is their vision: A request to give locally must be viewed in the context of global company giving. As a consequence, proposals to such companies might require more explicit descriptions of the return on a gift, and the decision-making process for a gift may be lengthier and more layered than usual.

International corporations that are based overseas typically present even more challenges to conventional development strategies, in part because of a different organizational structure but more so because of corporate cultures that frequently do not include or recognize the concept of corporate giving per se. In these cases, because UDOs typically do not handle the range or sheer number of corporate relationships that central corporate officers handle, UDOs are ideally suited to put in the extra time and effort needed up front to identify an international corporate constituency and map its peculiar topography and anthropology.

Two other types of corporations present special problems to development officers—the professional corporation (P.C.) and the closely held corporation (S-corporation). In both cases, the problem is not identification or even motivation. Rather, the problem is that both lack a simple and easy method of making a corporate gift, because U.S. tax laws provide no mechanism or incentive for giving except at the individual partner or shareholder level. Although daunting, these barriers, too, can be overcome through diligence and persistence. Here, again, the UDO is ideally positioned to devote the necessary time and effort.

Complex Corporate Relationships

Large companies, and even smaller companies over time, can of course have multiple motivations for giving to a college our academic unit. Such complex partnerships are, in fact, quite desirable. They provide the institution with multiple contact points with which to manage and enrich the relationship as well as multiple means of adding value to itself and the donor corporation. In identifying potential corporate donors, therefore, the UDO should consider not only the initial point of contact with a corporation but also the potential for multiple or secondary contacts that might be developed over time.

In so doing, a UDO must have good research on a potential corporate donor. A large corporation, however, might well comprise more territory than a single officer can fully comprehend, much less develop. Once it has been determined that a corporation has the capacity for a strategic partnership (typically at minimum in the seven-figure range), a team comprising development officers from the central corporate office and those from other relevant units should be assembled to develop a step-by-step process of aligning missions and developing value-added projects across the institution.

Internships, for example, are often a good, low-level gift with which to initiate a relationship with a major corporation. The gift then might be cultivated into scholarship or fellowship support, which in turn might lead to membership in a corporate liaison or support group, thereby both broadening and deepening the relationship. Unlike with individual donors, the concept of an "ultimate gift" does not apply to corporate donors; they can continue to give at high levels as long as concomitant benefits accrue mutually to both institution and donor. Although these initial steps can all be managed by a UDO acting alone, the UDO will ultimately need to work closely with the campus-wide director of corporate relations and other relevant unit officers in order to maximize a corporate relationship with the potential for capital investment in the institution.

In summary, the process of developing a relationship with a giant corporation is not unlike the method by which the diminutive Lilliputians in *Gulliver's Travels* were able to capture and control the giant Gulliver by attaching tiny ropes to every part of his body. By coordinating and cooperating as a team, unit and central development officers can connect a giant corporate donor to myriad programs and projects, securing and directing its resources for the benefit of the entire institution.

Areas of Concern

Some institutions may shy away from cultivating corporate donors because of the risk of having their reputations exploited or tainted by an association with corporate donors. Although such risks do exist, they, too, can be identified, and precautions can be taken to minimize them. To start with, in seeking to connect with a given corporation, it is important for UDOs to look both upstream and downstream from the point of initial contact not only for other potential connection points but also for points of misconnection or friction. To cite a classic example, whereas the Honeywell domestic product line of electronic switch and control mechanisms might align well with the research of a university, its production of military missile and guidance systems has proven to be an issue with many institutional cultures.

Even the reputation of a corporation or of the industry in which the corporation operates can be problematic. Another classic example is Arthur Daniels Midlands. Although it no longer manufactures or sells asbestos products and has changed its corporate mission and identity, negative associations are nevertheless still conjured by many university student bodies and boards of trustees. Oil company stalwarts such as ExxonMobil and Texaco, despite being major, long-time supporters of higher education and the arts, have become of late the targets of environmentalists and anti-global-economy factions whose ranks include many students and faculty members, not to mention alumni.

In reality, corporate relationships that go sour or become an embarrassment to the parties involved can be worse than no relationship at all, because they can poison the well for support from other corporations for years to come. Thus, UDOs need to assess carefully the fit between a corporate donor and their units and to monitor closely the political context of an ongoing relationship, even a longstanding one. Attitudes can turn with a headline, and events in remote places, like the DuPont Bhopal disaster in southern India or the *Exxon Valdez* oil spill in northern Alaska, can have major repercussions in the continental United States.

Mergers and acquisitions of donor corporations can also be a source of concern.

Occasionally, a takeover or buyout of a donor company works to the benefit of an institution, particularly if the company with which the institution has the relationship is the one doing the acquisition or if an alumnus is a major stockholder in a buyout. But more often than not, mergers of any sort occasion new debt, new executives, or new strategic priorities that can negatively affect a preexisting partnership with a university. As a rule of thumb, UDOs should assume that after such a change all bets are off. Once the dust has begun to settle, they need to reassess old contacts and commitments and, if necessary, cultivate new ones with the new management.

Still another area of possible concern might be called the "lost leader" situation. Certainly, identifying well-placed alumni in key corporations is a good way to start the development process, because they can provide not only a portal to a corporation but also guidance through its unique culture and maze of decision making. Indeed, sometimes a unit is fortunate enough to identify an alumnus who is so highly placed within a corporation that he or she is able to control the decision-making process with regard to a major gift. If so, then the UDO might well be able to secure a major gift by focusing its cultivation and solicitation exclusively on the alumnus, almost as if he or she were an individual donor.

However, if the ensuing relationship is essentially between the unit and the individual alumnus and does not include cultivation of the corporation itself, then it will typically prove viable only for as long as the alumnus remains in a power position. And in today's volatile corporate marketplace, the relative status of any one executive within a company can change dramatically overnight. To the extent possible, UDOs should develop parallel relationships with other alumni within the corporation and cultivate other points of contact between the institution and the corporation so that, should the leader become "lost" for any reason, other connections that maintain the company's engagement with the unit remain in place. Often, if a UDO's relationship with the key executive alumnus is strong and candid, the alumnus can be enlisted to guide and facilitate a widening range of connections.

A final area of concern can be the faculty of the academic unit itself. Faculty members make up a vital if not essential part of the corporate development process. In fact, most corporate contacts emerge as a function of the research or specialized training delivered by a particular faculty member, who, as in the case of individual donors, can be initially identified with an academic audit conducted for development purposes. The natural tendency of faculty, however, is to work in silos, largely oblivious to the work and therefore the needs of other faculty or of the institution that supports them.

UDOs can often prevail upon new faculty members to identify and contact new potential donor corporations with whom they have associations and enlist senior faculty to assist in fleshing out and developing a fledgling relationship. Faculty in the middle ranks, however, sometimes feel conflicted and even defensive about cooperating in the identification or cultivation of corporations with which they may have contacts or ties. Because they may not want to risk losing a source of revenue for their own research, they must be coached, coaxed, and even bribed by peers, chairs, and deans (but rarely, if ever, by UDOs) to cooperate in a comprehensive approach, even when these faculty members will be the primary beneficiaries of any increased giving.

In the process of defining corporate constituencies, the development officers of academic units play an essential role. As UDOs, they deal with a smaller spectrum of industries and companies than do central officers. Thus, on the revenue side, they can drill down deeper into the infrastructure and resources of a corporation, setting in the bedrock of a company the foundations for relationships that can be sustained throughout an industry's business cycle. On the supply side, UDOs also are instrumental in preventing or undermining the silo mentality of faculty, thereby opening a range of potential connections and fostering new and mutually rewarding opportunities for collaboration between companies and units. In so doing, UDOs not only add value to the resources of their individual units, they also add relevancy and viability to the entire institution in the marketplace and the world.

Recommendations for Best Practice

- Potential individual donor constituencies are best defined by their personal relationship to a unit or institution—alumni and friends; parents and family; associated professionals or professional associations; and patrons, clients, patients, customers, and advocates.
- The leadership group or advisory board of a unit can be used as a vehicle for defining and building constituencies.
- Each individual constituency has a set of specific goals that can be combined with those of other constituencies and matched with the fund-raising priorities of the unit.
- Individual constituencies must be actively managed; they will not manage themselves.
- An academic audit of the unit for development purposes is key to defining both the individual and corporate constituencies from which donors may emerge.
- Potential corporate donor constituencies are best defined by their motivation for seeking to associate with a unit or institution—access to students for employment, to specialized research training, to a customer base, or to become or continue as a vendor.

- In seeking to connect with a given corporation, UDOs need to look both upstream and downstream from the point of initial contact not only for other potential connection points but also for points of misconnection or friction.
- To avoid the "lost leader" situation, UDOs should cultivate the whole corporation, not just key alumni within the organization.
- Corporations with current or potential multiple relationships—complex corporations—need to be managed centrally and cultivated by a team of relevant UDOs in a coordinated approach.
- Whenever possible, UDOs should attempt to engage faculty in the identification process, bringing to bear the influence of their deans and department heads if necessary.

Case Statement arguments

CHAPTER 15

Making the Case for Development in the Academic Unit

James C. Schroeder

Chair, Department of Development, Mayo Foundation

Academic unit development officers (UDOs) can take many roads less traveled in their professional careers and often take detours into in a variety of institutional settings. I have had an opportunity to assist with the academic planning that shaped the case for support for a college of arts and sciences within a large land-grant university undertaking a mega-campaign. In addition, I have led the process of shaping the case for support of a graduate professional school that is planning a major campaign in a highly decentralized fund-raising environment. My experience in managing unit development programs in large, complex institutions has given me useful insights on the characteristics of successful cases. This chapter highlights the most important elements of making a compelling case for an academic unit.

I assume that unit advancement offices consist of professional staff experienced in annual fund and major gifts fund raising, alumni programs, and communications. I also assume that they enjoy some latitude in the way they reflect the school's history, mission, and profile. Such assumptions are givens in decentralized models for institutional advancement, which further supposes that the UDO is the individual primarily responsible for organizing and managing the development program. But even in centralized or hybrid models, UDOs typically possess the authority to coordinate their unit's fund-raising activities. The perspective that independence provides is essential to crafting the case for and celebrating the special character of a particular unit.

I have limited my discussion in several important ways. First, I have chosen not to discuss the mechanics of case writing, because that subject is discussed with considerable expertise elsewhere. Second, I mention only in passing the important issue of unit constituency. Third, I offer no prototype of an ideal case statement because generic models are readily available elsewhere, and specific models are too indigenous to a university or school context to be transferable. Rather, I focus on the arguments that must be marshaled, organized, deployed, and communicated to make an effective case for support.

The discerning reader will note that I use the term *case* in two specific contexts. *Case for support* refers to the overall concept of purpose that defines a unit and justifies its appeal for private giving. It may or may not appear in a single document, and the unit might use it in a variety of circumstances not always directly related to development. *Case statement*, however, refers to a specific document composed to elicit financial support from a specific donor or group of donors, whether a person, corporation, or institution. Please note that *school* generally refers to any academic sub-unit of a university, including programs, departments, divisions, and colleges. The major issues associated with developing a successful case for support include celebrating the institutional context and performing institutional planning; the major issues regarding the case statement are formulating and communicating the case for support. Each of those issues is described in this chapter, with emphasis on the differences and similarities between the cases for arts and sciences and professional schools.

Institutional Context

Because the major purpose of the case for support is to celebrate the unique character of the school, the issue of whether the unit is part of a public or private university is relevant. Many major public universities trace their roots to the original federal land grant legislation of 1862, a measure that fostered the liberal arts and sciences but also granted equal status to engineering, agriculture, and other vocationally or professionally oriented disciplines. However, in deference to Jeffersonian and Jacksonian dictates that schools provide the education necessary to advance a democracy, even state universities founded in the tradition of the classical liberal arts have since the Civil War housed schools of law, medicine, commerce, and the like. The tradition that strong professional schools contribute to the overall quality and reputation of the university is deeply ingrained in all public institutions of higher learning. To make their case for support today, development officers can lay claim to many of the same historic raisons d'être on which those institutions were originally founded.

Their seminal status, coupled with strong societal demand for their products, often enable professional schools to benefit financially by levying higher tuition and fees, receiving special state assistance, and competing for restricted government and private foundation grants and fellowships. Traditionally, within publicly assisted universities, only graduate programs of science have had greater access to government, corporate, and private foundation financial support. Graduate schools are a relatively recent addition to the American university model, originating in 1861 when Yale awarded the first Ph.D.s. Today, graduate schools are the signature feature of research universities, the foundation of much of the institution's reputation and well-being. Because institutional reputations established by graduate-level research often benefit undergraduate programs as well, UDOs of schools of arts and science emphasize that their schools afford students the opportunity to experience both the liberal education necessary for life and the specialized training necessary for a career.

In contrast to public universities, the reputations of many private universities were founded on the centrality and excellence of their undergraduate colleges of liberal arts, with professional schools later becoming prominent. Consequently, central university development operations have traditionally focused on procuring support for schools of arts and sciences and have left graduate and professional schools to fend for themselves. Over time, the phrase "each tub on its own bottom" came to embody the quasi-independent organizational status of professional schools, particularly within the university. Each school typically delineates its own mission and establishes its own curriculum, admission standards, tuition, and faculty salaries within general guidelines set by the university. Their relative autonomy gives professional schools the opportunity to define themselves and chart a course consistent with their culture and traditions while embracing an entrepreneurial vision. That combination provides the basis for designing exciting and effective cases for support.

Another element that differentiates public and private institutions is their respective funding histories. Traditionally, publicly funded universities have had the advantage of direct subvention from the state of a subsidy based on student headcount (commonly known as full-time equivalencies), number of credit hours taught, or some other quantitative measurement. Such state support has kept tuition costs low, making access to public universities relatively high. Usually, public universities have the advantage of being eligible for state-funded construction of campus facilities and infrastructure. Because endowment income and private gifts historically have played little part in their operating budgets, public universities have perceived little need to seek charitable giving.

Over the past three decades, however, as states have moved to cap the percentage of tax-derived support for higher education, the funding situation for public universities has changed dramatically. The trend is now for public institutions to receive a smaller percentage of their operating budget from the state—on average about 33 percent, but in some cases as little as 10 percent. This compels them to generate additional revenues by increasing student tuition and fees and by soliciting private gifts and income from endowments, government agencies, corporations, and foundations. The financial picture of publicly assisted universities has begun to resemble that of private universities, where high tuition, endowment income, and private gifts have traditionally been major sources of revenue for schools of arts and sciences. As a consequence, schools in public and private institutions now frequently include in their case for support the need for student financial assistance to offset increasing costs and for faculty development and research underwriting to recompense soaring operational expenses. Similarly, those schools often make the case for increasing their endowments and securing annual gifts so that they can ensure their futures and advance their visions by seizing opportunities that require funding beyond current budgets.

Even the school's relationship with the university constitutes an institutional context that can impinge on the case for support. Because of the relative autonomy of graduate and professional schools, students and alumni typically identify with their respective schools, not the university. Students and alumni of the undergraduate arts and sciences school, however, identify primarily with the university and only secondarily to their respective school, department, or program. The case for the graduate or professional school might stress the expertise of its faculty and the success of its graduates. Meanwhile the case for the undergraduate arts and sciences school may emphasize the overall quality of the university and of resources such as the library or athletic facilities that contribute to a broad educational experience.

Institutional Planning

The case for support should reflect needs and priorities that result from a rigorous process of institutional planning. That planning involves self-examination of a school's educational programs and activities. Based on that evaluation, the school articulates a plan of action to leverage its strengths and address its deficiencies.

Conducted regularly, the planning process is usually initiated by a president, chancellor, dean, chair, or director. In some instances, particularly if they wish to address a special problem or opportunity, the governing board or visiting committee members might initiate the process. Institutional planning reflects the mission of the school, although the process might amend or modify the mission. In any event, the process provides an opportunity for the academic leadership to assess the perception of the school with both internal and external constituencies. By measuring the outcomes of activities quantitatively and qualitatively, the planning process determines how well the school is achieving its goals. The procedure also strengthens weaker programs that are considered essential to the school's mission and eliminates others deemed unnecessary. For all

Making the Case for Development in the Academic Unit

academic units, that exercise represents an exciting opportunity to raise programs to the next level.

Such planning often generates recommendations that require additional financial resources to support high quality leading-edge programs. Those resources will come either from internal reallocation of the current budget or new income from private gifts. In the academy, tenure, attitudes of collegiality, academic bylaws, political relationships, and inertia make internal reallocation slow and difficult. To act in a timely and decisive manner, the acquisition of new income from private gifts is frequently preferable. That the school has carried out the planning process substantially legitimizes the case for support and implies full endorsement of school leadership, faculty, staff, and even students. The case is further strengthened when institutional planning also includes selected alumni and potential donors.

Just as deans of schools of arts and sciences and of professional schools must demonstrate leadership in planning, they must also encourage and support the development program. In addition, deans, department chairs, faculty, and administrative staff must enthusiastically embrace the case for support and work closely with the advancement unit. Today, job descriptions for senior university administrators, deans, and even department heads and directors typically include responsibility for fund raising—a strong signal that academic leaders must work closely with UDOs. Indeed, as leaders come to understand, appreciate, and nurture the relationship, academic planning and development have become increasingly linked.

Making the Case

After assessing the implications of the institutional context and evaluating the outcomes of institutional planning, the school must assemble information to construct a convincing and comprehensive case statement. Regardless of mission, the school must make its case on multiple levels that fall within two general categories.

- The statement must be intellectually compelling and include specific outcomes and the strategies.
- To allow potential contributors to feel good about their decision to support the school, the statement must appeal to the targeted external audience on an emotional level.

In addition, a skillful case statement has another important audience—the unit's internal constituency. The statement must excite the school's development staff, faculty, and staff, as well as the school's leadership; it must focus collective attention to the task and guide them through daily development decisions. The development staff must be ruthlessly attentive to the timetables outlined in the case statement.

Most important, the case must rest on a solid intellectual basis grounded in teaching and learning. A school of arts and sciences, for example, can make such a case at the graduate and undergraduate level. At the undergraduate level, an arts and sciences school could argue that it represents the heart of the university's educational mission because it exposes students to a broad, liberal education including the arts, humanities, social and behavioral sciences, chemical, physical, and biological sciences, and mathematics. Studies in those subject areas, often framed and encouraged by distribution requirements, represent the academy's best effort to produce well-rounded, educated individuals. Skills engendered by a liberal educational experience—notably the ability to acquire, interpret, organize, synthesize, and formulate new knowledge and information—help students think independently and communicate effectively. Those basic skills apply to almost anything students choose to undertake in their professional, personal, or social life. What makes the intellectual case distinctive is the school's educational mission, which resonates with alumni who have shared that experience and with professionally trained alumni who regret having missed that learning opportunity. The case for the school of arts and science contrasts sharply with that of undergraduate professional schools primarily valued for preparing students for professional practice or graduate training.

At the graduate level, the school can make a persuasive intellectual case based on the relative strength of its training and research programs and their relationship with private, corporate, and industrial partners. Those programs tend to be in the "hard sciences," but a standalone case for private support can be made for strong programs that exist in or across other disciplines. In addition to their appeal as an important, if not essential, credential for entry into a competitive, licensed, and lucrative profession, graduate professional schools can make a similar case. Those circumstances create the opportunity for multiple cases or mini-campaigns within graduate schools of arts and sciences and larger professional schools.

A school makes its intellectual case by addressing two questions related to its stated mission:

▶ How will increased support allow the school to better carry out existing educational activities?

▶ What new and different educational activities can the school undertake with additional financial support?

enhance living/learning environment

To answer the first question, the case statement must detail how increased support will help the school improve the teaching and learning environment. Examples of remedies include the following:

▶ Increasing the number of well-qualified faculty to achieve a lower student/faculty ratio

▶ Supporting additional graduate students to carry out important teaching and research

▶ Increasing student financial aid to attract a different profile of students and enrich the academic and social environment

▶ Enhancing the living and learning environment by improving infrastructure support for laboratories, classrooms, libraries, information technology, recreational facilities, and grounds

In schools where institutional assessment indicates a need for qualitative improvement, the case for additional resources to make educational programs competitive with those at comparable institutions is relatively straightforward. Because most schools carry out their mission and educational objectives very well and enjoy well-deserved and appropriately recognized reputations for quality, making the case for additional resources is more complicated. For undergraduate schools of arts and sciences, that difficult task requires demonstrating a need to address significant shortfalls or to exploit unforeseen opportunities of compelling magnitude and urgency. For graduate and professional schools facing an explosion in technology and the creation of new knowledge that have made the half-life of graduate and professional education increasingly short, indicating sufficient need and writing a compelling case is somewhat easier. Simply to keep current, those schools could argue for additional resources to test and introduce new classroom techniques and technologies, to refresh and reinvigorate the teaching and learning environment, to acquire and apply state-of-the-art research instrumentation and methodologies, and to build or refurbish physical facilities and infrastructure.

Determining what new and different educational activities to undertake to enhance a school's or unit's teaching, learning, or research environment can prove even more difficult than can improving existing educational activities. The case statement must identify specific new propositions in which the value-added dimension must be virtually transparent to a prospect constituency. Once formulated, however, those proposals can be shaped into effective arguments for the perceived competitiveness and prestige of the school, because professional schools are recognized and ranked largely according to their relative strengths in specific disciplines. Highly partisan potential donors could be pitched a proposal about how the alma mater might finally catch up to external and internal traditional rivals. A proposal to potential donors in prestigious executive positions could promote an innovation that would enhance the school's position of preeminence or expand it to emerging areas.

Whatever the sell, the effective case statement should indicate that the proposals result from a consensual decision-making process by the entire academic leadership and faculty of the school—an argument made all the more convincing by the presence of an institutional plan. This kind of case statement helps prospective donors understand how support for a specific proposal will be a positive force for change. New programs and initiatives will differ from institution to institution, but for arts and sciences schools some common examples are as follows:

▶ Additional "practical" courses that assist the student in areas such as business, information technology, and career planning

▶ Opportunities for internships that are integrated with the curriculum

▶ Opportunities for participation in social-enterprise activities such as social service agencies, schools, and nonprofit agencies

▶ Greater emphasis on global economic, social, and political issues plus more opportunities to study and work overseas

▶ Investment in technological and human resources to enable delivery of distance learning to wider audiences

For graduate and professional schools, making the case for support of new program initiatives often places the school on the horns of a difficult educational and political dilemma. On one hand, targeting a limited number of specific school areas for enhanced private gift support might make rational and strategic sense, but it may also seem that school is judging the relative merit of programs and faculty members and labeling them as winners or losers. On the other hand, if the school targets all major academic and operating areas for support, the case statement might enhance the esprit of the faculty and staff but actually dilute the impact of individual private gift support. To avoid that dilemma, the case statement for both the professional and graduate school should focus on proposed outcomes rather than on the programs themselves. Keep in mind the wisdom of another adage that holds that donors would rather climb onto a bandwagon than bail out a failure. And as always, the statement, accompanied by a budget of estimated costs, should describe exactly what the support will be used for and how that activity accomplishes the mission and goals of the school.

Even though the strength of the case relies on its intellectual basis, its ability to motivate action depends almost entirely on its emotional appeal. For many former arts and sciences students, the changes they experienced during the four or five years of undergraduate education between ages 18 and 22 or 23 were the most dramatic of their lives. That was when they felt a new sense of independence and responsibility, when they explored exciting intellectual horizons, and when they developed essential social and interpersonal skills—experiences that serve as the foundation for the rest of their lives. For most alumni, the college years evoke powerful memories. The effective case triggers those memories and reminds them the school remains true to its basic mission.

Although less apparent, the case statement for a professional school can also make an emotional appeal. It might point out to alumni that preparation for their profession had transformed them from inexperienced youth to competent adult. Because the professional school helped them secure their first job and may have provided continuing placement services, you could say the school has contributed fundamentally to whatever personal success and happiness the alumna or alumnus enjoys.

Regardless of subject major, the emotional case is especially compelling to the many donors and prospects who harbor a sense that, sometime during their lifetime, they would like to give something back to their undergraduate, graduate, or professional school. Prospects must manifest a "donative intent," that is, they must want to support the school because it feels right to do so. However, although the case statement should recognize and nurture that instinct, it should never refer to it explicitly. Under no circumstances should the case state or imply that the prospective donor "owes" support to the school. The school should never impose a moral obligation; the concept should stem from the genuine intellectual and emotional response of the prospect to the case.

Communicating the Case

Ultimately, a case statement is only as effective as the means by which it is communicated to the school's multiple audiences. Each audience requires a different form of the case statement as well as different communication vehicles. The complete statement, with all attendant details of vision, needs, opportunities, strategies, and costs, will serve as a source document for various versions. Consequently, the full text of the case statement will be lengthy, and only the school and university leadership is likely to read it entirely.

Once university and school leadership approves the case statement, a small target audience of the school's strongest supporters should evaluate it. Initially, a draft of the case should be sent to that group, followed up with personal meetings to gauge reactions, seek advice, and verify the level of interest. In testing the case statement, the only essential difference between a school of arts and sciences and a professional school is that the arts and sciences school's target audience must include advocates and supporters of each of the school's important academic disciplines. Although a professional school may choose to do the same, its alumni typically relate to the school as a whole rather than to a specific discipline. It may be more effective, therefore, to include within the target audience representatives of each of the specialized fields within the school's professional community.

That initial contact also generates the feedback necessary to edit the substance or tone of the case statement to make it more convincing. Editing for tone is easier to manage and requires little compromise. Editing for message, however, requires a conscious decision to be flexible about accommodating the individual interests of those important supporters. At that stage, the case statement should also argue in favor of an aggressive fund-raising campaign, pointing out that a campaign is not business-as-usual fund raising. Rather it is an intensely focused, highly coordinated endeavor designed to secure substantially greater support for the school than is possible with ordinary development initiatives. By including that argument in the draft circulated to the target donor group, the communication step itself initiates the nucleus fund or quiet phase of a prospective campaign for private support.

After editing the case to address the target group's responses, the case statement is ready for distribution to different segments of the school's audience. Table 1 summarizes a typical segmentation of the target audience and the different vehicles for communicating with each group. Certainly, all segments of the audience benefit from any communication they receive, but to maximize communication every unit office must find the mix of communication vehicles that marries its case for support to the various segments of its donor base.

There are several ways to reach individual audience segments, each requiring a unique combination of communication methods. The objective is to provide the most personalized communication for the best-qualified prospects. The communication process must leverage the time of the dean and other principals to the greatest extent possible. The entire audience needs to learn as much as possible about the case, depending on its level of interest and engagement in the school and the level of resources the school will commit. To simplify this discussion, here are the five general forms of communication:

One-on-One

The dean, particularly in professional schools, should communicate the case for support on a one-on-one basis to each prospective donor. In a school of arts and sciences, a department head or distinguished faculty member may be the most appropriate

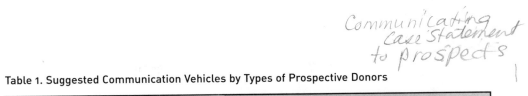

Table 1. Suggested Communication Vehicles by Types of Prospective Donors

Target Audience Segmentation	Communication Vehicles				
	One-on-One	Small Groups	Large Groups	Broad-Based	Mass
Internal constituency University trustees, administration, faculty, staff, and students				●	●
Leadership/principal prospects Top 100–500 highest-qualified prospects (and spouses) who will provide the leadership for increasing financial support and who account for at least 50–70% of the gift total	●				
Major prospects 500–2,000 prospects (and spouses) likely to account for 20–30% of gift total plus future generations of leadership for support	●	●			
High-end annual donors Consistent supporters on annual basis who can be expected to increase giving in context of intensive solicitation effort			●	●	
Donors Other donors or potential donors who can be expected to become annual donors or increase giving in the context of intensive solicitation effort			●	●	
Volunteers Alumni and friends who consistently volunteer assistance in alumni programs, class reunions, peer-driven annual solicitations, and school events who may or may not be current donors but demonstrate longstanding interest in school			●	●	
Alumni and friends Other alumni and stakeholders who currently offer no financial or other types of support				●	●
Community Individuals within the school's city, state, and region, and, in some instances, overseas					●

communicator. Obviously, UDOs may communicate the case as well. Depending on the stage of the relationship, one-on-one communication can be conducted face-to-face, by telephone, by letter or e-mail, or through a third party, such as a volunteer. Written or printed materials, including versions of the case statement, edited to stimulate an emotional response or to profile an area of need or of interest to a specific prospective donor, can facilitate the interchange and be left behind as a reminder.

Small Groups

Small group events hosted by a dean, department head, key faculty member, or volunteer can be used to reach a slightly larger number of special prospective donors and maximize school resources. The format for these activities can be business meetings, meals, or videoconferences; they can be held on campus as free-standing events or in connection with other events. Professional or graduate schools might convene small groups in connection with professional meetings, whereas schools of arts and sciences could use special alumni travel tours to communicate the case. As with one-on-one groups, selected materials can illustrate or elaborate on the case for support and focus the discussion. Campaign leadership can be effective at these events.

Large Groups

Large on- or off-campus group events may be organized specifically to communicate the case for support. Events such as local alumni club meetings or reunions can also provide forums. Again, a dean, department head, key faculty member, or volunteer usually presents the case, although the UDO can be an effective presenter as well. Today, by using distance-learning technology such as satellite or Internet linkage, groups in remote locations hosted by a key volunteer, faculty member, or senior UDO can view or participate.

That concept can be extended to include creative variations. For instance, a school might host a telephone call-in event in which the dean stays in his or her office and discusses the case for support with interested alumni and friends. The telephone service running the event queues questions from the audience, who can hear both the questions and answers. Alternatively, a law or business school might present the case *as* a case. That is, using the case-study method, the dean or a key faculty member presents a hypothetical scenario that presents the central issues of a group discussion and then shapes responses into a case for financial support.

Broad-Based Communication

Many schools use print and electronic media to roll out their cases in stages, with the best potential prospects receiving a case statement before it reaches a broader audience of alumni and friends. Print media vehicles include brochures that are specially mailed or inserted into other mailings, alumni magazines, fund-raising updates, and annual reports. Electronic vehicles include Internet and e-mail technologies.

University Web sites routinely attract a large number of hits from the general public. To take maximum advantage of that interest, the university should create hot links from either the university home page or the development site to individual schools' sites. Links to the school's home page or development site help the school communicate its case to the general public. School Web sites should have a specific development linkage that includes a summary version of the case through which readers can drill down to more levels of detail. A school can also use e-mail "push technology" to deliver updates about information contained in the case.

Mass Communication

Communicating the case to the general public is also important, especially with regard to aspects in which the public has a keen interest. Certainly, one aspect of schools in which alumni, friends, corporations, and foundations all are interested is their ratings and rankings by national publications. A school can use mass-communication vehicles such as newsletters, annual reports, and fact sheets to publicize their rankings as an integral part their case for support. In addition, advertisements for universities, especially when run during radio and television broadcasts of athletic events, can reach broad audiences of alumni and friends. Often donated to the institution as part of the broadcast contract, those ads are normally general and generic in nature. Still, universities sensitive to the needs of individual schools frequently adapt their messages to promote them. You can make the case for support in a more indirect and sophisticated way by sending news releases containing feature articles from national publications such as the *New York Times* and the *Wall Street Journal*, local or regional newspapers and magazines, and selected academic or professional journals.

Conclusion

A thoughtful case for support and a well-crafted case statement are essential to the success of a unit development program and to the future of the school it supports. The cases for support of schools of arts and sciences and of professional schools share many elements. They reflect both the mission of the school and the mission of the university, and they encompass both the institutional vision for the future and the way it will achieve it. For both types of schools, cases must possess intellectual and emotional appeal, and they must get the right information to the right audience at the right time.

But just as arts and sciences differ from professional schools in the fundamental nature of their educational missions, so do their rationales for seeking financial support. Consequently, the intellectual and emotional bases for each case are grounded in key distinctions between broad-based education and professional training. In that regard, their cases celebrate their outstanding characteristics and define the schools in ways that alumni and friends understand and appreciate.

Those similarities and differences manifest themselves throughout the process of making the case for support and the case statement. Care must be taken, therefore, that the case reflects an understanding of the school's institutional context. It must result from a rigorous process of institutional planning that describes fully, accurately, and clearly the school's goals and aspirations. Care, too, must be taken to ensure that the case inspires and compels school administrators, faculty, and supporters to work together. Last, the case must communicate clearly and strategically to many audiences. In summary, the case for support is the foundation for all unit development activities. If the case statement is properly designed and presented, the odds for success improve immeasurably.

Recommendations for Best Practice

- The case should highlight the differences that distinguish the school from other units of the university and from its competition in other institutions.
- The case should be firmly grounded in the mission of the school and reflect leadership's vision for the future.
- The case should incorporate the unit's strategic institutional plan and relate specific proposals for support directly to it.
- The case should describe how the unit, with additional financial support, would either improve existing programs and activities or add programs and activities that enhance existing preeminence or address emerging fields of study.
- The case should have both intellectual and emotional appeal to its target audience.
- The case should be specific enough to show readers how their support will advance the mission and vision of the school.
- The case should use the appropriate vehicles to communicate the message to all segments of the school's constituency.
- The case should carefully match modes of delivering the case statement to the values and interests of the targeted audience.
- The case should never imply that intended readers have a moral obligation to support the school.

CHAPTER 16

Making the Case for Development in Academic Support Units

Timothy L. Seiler

Director, Public Service and The Fund Raising School,
Center on Philanthropy at Indiana University

I began my development career in August 1984 as the unit development officer (UDO) for the University Libraries at Indiana University. Having finished my doctorate in English not too many years before, I believed I had the best possible position in our development system, even though the system was just beginning to test the boundaries of a hybrid (partially centralized, partially decentralized) organization. Why such naïve optimism? First, as a doctoral student I had spent the majority of my hours (both waking and nodding) in the library. I knew firsthand the importance of an up-to-date library with plenty of readily accessible materials. Second, during the years leading up to my collegiate studies, I regularly spent hours in the library—reading, participating in book discussion groups, performing research, and, of course, checking out many books. To me, a library is the preeminent source for information. I cannot imagine a civilized society without libraries. Thus my initial optimism about raising money for libraries—especially university libraries!

Little did I know—but I learned during the next several years—how few people share my enthusiasm. What heightened the shock of this revelation was realizing that my delusions had been sustained by a considerable amount of hype. After all, faculty members regularly described the library as the central support unit for their research work. One of the best-known Indiana faculty members frequently in public called the library the heart of the university. He even led several fund-raising efforts based on that theme. Librarians, too, naturally boasted about their service toward the preservation and transmission of knowledge. Indeed, who was against supporting libraries? What is *not* to love about libraries? Are not libraries the lifeblood of the university? Are not libraries venerated American icons, as sacred and untouchable as apple pie and motherhood?

The astonishing truth about libraries (and especially about fund raising for libraries) is that most people regard them not as icons but as utilities. They are there—and they are expected always to be there—on demand and without fail. Turn on the light switch, and the light goes on. Turn on the faucet, and water comes out. At the library you will find information, knowledge, entertainment—whatever you want whenever you want it. You notice the electricity or the water or the books only when they are *not* there. In short, I learned that most people take libraries for granted and assume that shelves will be continually stocked, books and materials continually acquired and preserved, and staff continually paid, ad infinitum. Given this reality, how do fund raisers make the case for support of libraries or of other similar academic support units such as museums, art galleries, and performance facilities? UDOs for these organizations face the same question: How do you make the case for support of what amounts to an educational utility?

Major Challenges

To make a case for support, the UDO for a library, museum, or arts facility confronts challenges both internal and external. Internally, the challenge is educational. Most library, museum, gallery, and arts facility staffs possess naïve enthusiasm about what they do, and they make equally naïve assumptions about how others perceive them and their organization. They simply do not realize that few people outside the unit share their passion. Sometimes outsiders seem indifferent because they do not understand the unit and its overall role in the institution. The first task, then, is to teach colleagues within the unit how to talk about it in terms that outsiders will understand. Specifically, staff needs to learn that, however helpful to insiders, jargon erects barriers for outsiders. To raise funds from outsiders, they must articulate the arcana of librarianship, curatorship, and production management in everyday language that potential donors can understand.

Altering the way staff members talk about what they do also means altering the way they think about and relate to the unit. The second task of the UDO, then, is to educate staff members as to how their units benefit those who use them. Ask them why anyone outside the unit should care about the museum, the library, or the art gallery. What do users or visitors gain from them? Indeed, what do *non-users* and *non-visitors* gain by the unit's very existence? In other words, what is its cultural, educational, social, and economic impact on the university and its host community? Staff members need to understand that, just as they take for granted the importance of their unit, people outside the unit take for granted its day-to-day utility. Although it can be difficult to educate staff to this humbling and even painful reality, it is nevertheless crucial to writing a compelling case for support.

Having educated internal staff, the UDO can address the second major challenge to making a case for support: educating the external constituency of users, patrons, and visitors. The challenge is twofold: first, to obtain the responses of those stakeholders to the same questions put to the staff regarding the value and perception of the unit; second, to translate responses from insiders and outsiders into words that both can understand. Accomplishing the first task requires focus groups with users or visitors, group tours and open houses, and perhaps the organization of "friends of" groups or advisory boards. The second and more difficult task involves getting insiders and outsiders—providers and clients—to listen to one another and hear what each is saying about the unit.

Defining a Constituency

In carrying out both tasks, UDOs face the difficulty of defining their constituency. Typically, constituencies are defined by their natural affiliation with the organization; in universities, such constituencies normally consist of alumni. Because degrees are awarded by a college of arts and sciences or a professional school, the natural constituencies of the institution belong to development officers in the various academic units. However, museums, arts facilities, and libraries are not degree-granting units so they do not, by definition, have alumni. Does that mean they have no natural constituencies? Certainly not. It means only that, unlike their colleagues in academic units, UDOs in academic support units must build constituencies from the ground up.

Start by defining the stakeholders of your unit. Who exactly are its clients—its users, visitors, and customers? Generally, your constituency of natural affiliation comprises two large categories of stakeholders: *true outsiders*, who have no other affiliation with the unit other than the appeal and utility of its mission, and *alumni*, whose affiliation is based in part on the appeal of its mission and in part upon the unit's association with the university. In either case, building a donor base involves forming strategic alliances with organizations your stakeholders already belong to.

True outsiders might consist of public and independent schools; other arts, performance, or museum organizations; and the various government agencies established to support them. With these groups, highlight how much *their* organizational missions depend on the existence of your unit and how much both the organization and its constituent groups would benefit by collaborating with your unit in distributing and soliciting financial support. Implementing such a strategy usually entails building and sustaining a network of related organizations, plus the formulation, approval, and delivery of joint grant proposals, fund-raising appeals, and special events. Such strategies must be carefully coordinated with the various initiatives described earlier to promote understanding between staff and stakeholders.

With alumni, the best way to build a constituency for university academic support units is to secure institutional support first. When the university designates its arts facilities, museums, and libraries as institutional development priorities, then the entire institution's constituency—the alumni—becomes available to the unit. Without that kind of institutional commitment, academic support units must often be more creative in building a donor base.

The key is to secure the help of your colleagues in the academic units. Typically, they will not share your passionate commitment to your unit, either because they do not understand the role of the academic support unit or because they fear that fund raising for an academic support unit threatens support for their unit. To gain access to *their* alumni, you must form a strategic alliance with the unit based on the advancement of its own case for support.

In the case the Indiana library system, I knew that we operated numerous branch libraries within the system, each dedicated to a specific academic field or discipline—chemistry, geology, psychology, business, public affairs, music, and so on. I began methodically to ask the UDOs of the various schools housing these disciplines to mention the relevant library collection as gift opportunities when soliciting their alumni, arguing that doing so might attract new donors or increase the giving of donors who had resisted previous appeals.

For example, the development officer for the College of Arts and Sciences segmented her alumni by major and separately solicited each segment—alumni of chemistry, biology, English, Spanish, economics, history, and so on. I asked her to make the library collections a gift opportunity for each segment, arguing that her alumni should at least be aware that they could support the library collection in their major. After checking with her dean and department heads (many of whom viewed the library as passionately as I did), she agreed to include library collections in annual gift solicitations. Once donors gave a gift to the library, they became a formal part of my constituency, allowing me to develop the relationship directly on behalf of the library.

Making the Case for Support

Whether they are true outsiders or alumni, few constituents of arts facilities, museums, and libraries understand how these units are funded. Usually, they assume that these units are subsidized by the university or admissions fees (or fines) or a combination of both. To make the case for support to outside constituencies, the UDO must again inform and educate the public about the true nature of unit finances; therefore, it helps to possess good financial data. As UDO for an academic support unit, you must know all the sources of funding for your unit—institutional allocations, other academic support, fees of any kind, gift support, everything. Only by mastering such information can you prove that internal appropriations and fees fall short of the cost of delivering expected programs and services. Once potential grantors or donors understand that internal resources do not fully meet the unit's financial needs, they are generally more responsive to proposals for additional support.

In writing a proposal or case statement, you must also translate internal financial needs into benefits for external grantors and donors. Typically, unit administrators and staff cannot be allowed to state those needs on their own because, left to their own devices, they tend to argue primarily for their own financial needs. As UDO, you must know not only the nature of those needs but also why they must be met. When you understand this, you can craft a case for support based on meeting the needs of the potential donor rather than those of staff or faculty. To prepare the case, you need to ascertain basic information regarding the unit you serve.

Basic Information

▶ **Libraries.** How many people use the library daily, weekly, or monthly? How many books or tapes circulate regularly? How often are other library services—reserve books, archives, electronic database searches—used?

▶ **Museums and galleries.** How many people visit monthly or annually? How many exhibits are mounted during an academic or a calendar year? Does staff prepare traveling exhibits? If so, to what locations? Are materials loaned to other institutions or to local community groups? How do the faculty and students use the exhibits?

▶ **Performing arts.** What kinds of events are produced? Student? Community? Professional? A combination? Who attends performances? How many attend, and how often? Do they pay? How much? Do academic classes meet in the facilities?

Unit Benefits

In addition to curiosity about such fundamentals, potential donors also will have questions regarding the benefits provided by these units.

▶ How do individual users benefit from the facility? How does it inform, enhance, enrich, and empower them?

▶ How is the quality of life in the community enhanced by the presence of those facilities? How extensively do the benefits of the facilities affect the community?

▶ Specifically, do units benefit local service groups, elementary and middle schools, secondary schools, the business community? If so, how? What do these constituencies take away from the facility? Practically, how are they better off?

The WIIFM Factor

Underlying all these questions is the WIIFM factor (an acronym for "What's in it for me?"). This is *the* question that grantors and donors expect you to answer. Why should they fund your unit? Indeed, why should anyone fund an academic support unit? As UDO, your job is to address the WIIFM question persuasively in your proposal or case statement. In addition, the proposal or case statement must also address seminal questions regarding the role and function of academic support units within the university and community. Answering these questions will help you build the case for support necessary to solicit funds for your facility:

▶ How does the community, state, or nation benefit from the library, museum, gallery, theater, or performance facility?

▶ What central need of the university does the facility meet?

▶ What programs or services does the unit offer to meet that need?

▶ Why are those services important to the mission of the university or to that of colleges and schools within the university?

▶ What are the internal markets for those services? How effective is the unit in delivering its services to them?

▶ Does the unit have a strategic plan for improving or expanding those services?

▶ What evidence can the unit cite to demonstrate its competence to carry out this plan?

▶ Who are the people associated with the unit—staff, volunteers, and patrons?

▶ Why does the unit need private gift support? What are its specific financial needs?

▶ Why should members of the university community support the unit financially?

▶ What benefits accrue to internal donors?

The Multiplier Effect

Once you have formulated your case statement, what do you do with it? First and foremost, use it to build *internal* support for your unit. As the UDO, you must remind others throughout the institution that nonacademic units are critical to maintaining the level of excellence expected of the institution as a whole. Moreover, as the UDO, you must remind "insider-outsiders" that true outsiders will care about the facility only when they appreciate how much the entire institution values them.

Be vigilant for opportunities to recruit spokespeople for your facility both within the unit and throughout the institution—and the most effective spokespeople, of course, are the donors themselves. With a little encouragement, internal donors who make gifts to nonacademic units will tell other potential donors and influence them to give as well. If you then make their support visible, you multiply the effect of such giving considerably.

Multiplying the case internally also has an external multiplier effect. As external constituencies become more knowledgeable about the library, for example, and its role in the academic mission of the university, they will want to make sure it maintains its level of excellence. As external donors increasingly recognize units as worthy recipients of their gifts, their giving will catch the attention of university administrators and development officers, establishing the facility as a marketable entity worthy of attention in the university's fund-raising initiatives. As institutional commitment becomes established, academic support units will have opportunities to build and expand internal and external constituencies.

Conclusion

As a result of my experience in advancing academic support units, my initial naïve enthusiasm has come full circle. I now accept the commonly held viewpoint that the university libraries, museums, galleries, and performance facilities are, in truth, utilities. But at the same time, I contend that the utility they most closely resemble is not a water-treatment facility but a nuclear reactor, which generates power with the controlled release of the energy created within its radioactive core. Academic support facilities fuel the university's core disciplines; if they did not exist, universities as we know them would cease to exist. Indeed, the preservation and transfer of knowledge and beauty validate many of the activities that traditionally define the university and justify its privileged place in society. Ultimately, the task of UDOs of academic support units is not to subdue their own enthusiasm but to enlarge it, inform it, and spread it to others. Libraries, museums, galleries, theaters, and concert halls provide the quintessential energy for the life of the mind—and do not let anyone who claims to lead a life of the mind forget it.

Recommendations for Best Practice

- Recognize the fact that most people regard academic support units as utilities.
- Teach colleagues within your academic support unit how to think and talk about the unit in terms that outsiders can understand.

- Educate your staff about how their units benefit those who use, visit, and patronize them.

- Learn how users, patrons, and visitors perceive your unit—and translate the perceptions of insiders and outsiders into terms that both can understand.

- Identify "constituencies of natural affiliation"— true outsiders, who have no affiliation with the unit apart from an interest in its appeal and the utility of its mission, and alumni, whose affiliation may be based partly on the unit's mission and partly on its association with the university.

- Form strategic alliances with the organizations or groups to which your natural affiliates belong. For true outsiders, seek alliances with public and independent schools; with other arts, performance, or museum organizations; and with government agencies established to promote and support them. For alumni, secure institutional priority, if possible, and align your needs with those solicited by units that award degrees. Once alumni become donors, cultivate them directly for additional giving.

- Inform and educate outside constituencies about the true nature of the unit's financial support. Translate the unit's financial needs into benefits for external grantors and donors; address the WIIFM factor (What's in it for me?).

- Build internal support by recruiting spokespeople—preferably donors—both within your unit and throughout the university. Make their support visible.

- Let increased giving to your unit catch the attention of university administrators and development officers, and thereby establish your facility as a marketable entity meriting attention in the university's fund-raising initiatives.

- Increase your enthusiasm for academic support units and spread your enthusiasm to others. Never let anyone in the academic community forget that libraries, museums, galleries, theaters, and concert halls provide the quintessential fuel for their passions and professions.

CHAPTER 17

Making the Case for Development in Dedicated Research and Service Units

Lawrance Bailey

Development Officer, Scripps Institute of Oceanography, University of California, San Diego

E arly in my career, I was recruited to be part of a team responsible for raising money for a new academic hospital. Following a lengthy review process, the university governing board had approved the facility, the plans were in place, and most of the funding had already been secured through financing. The task seemed straightforward. Everyone knows that hospitals provide health care and that raising funds for health care is the easiest kind of fund raising, right? Nothing proved to be further from the truth.

To begin with, significant segments of the community vocally opposed the project. The new hospital had been carefully situated to attract the paying patients needed to secure the economic viability of the university's healthcare system. However, the planners had sited the new building next to a prominent community hospital whose doctors and supporters were adamantly opposed to it—too many hospital beds in the area already. In addition, the new facility had a state-of-the-art design and employed innovative approaches to reduce patients' stress and speed recovery.

What the community saw, however, was a building that did not look like a hospital. Instead, it looked expensive and opulent, and its opponents attacked it as an arrogant extravagance during a time of recession when university employees were being laid off. To make matters worse, when project costs inevitably increased, the university administration, because of its initial assurances to the university governing board that all financing was in hand, decided not publicize the fact that it now needed to raise additional funds. Moreover, the fund-raising goal kept shifting, usually upward, because no one seemed to know exactly how much the project was going to cost.

We never did get a written case statement for the project, because we could never agree on what to publish in the document. What I did not realize was that even though we had numerous good reasons to build a new hospital, we lacked a coherent case for needing the private support to build it. Rather than availing themselves of the easiest kind of fund raising, the unit development officers (UDOs) found themselves trapped in a developmental nightmare—trying to raise money almost on the sly for a project with fuzzy goals that the community did not understand and did not want. Although we ultimately succeeded, the frustrating and painful experience showed me the critical importance of formulating a good case with defined needs and goals. In fact, it showed me that the single most important tool for every development officer is a clear and compelling case for private support.

Those of us who raise money for dedicated units within major research universities have an advantage over colleagues who have broader portfolios. We deal with more focused, less complex organizations and concepts. Preparation of the case statement requires input from fewer participants. The example cited earlier notwithstanding, UDOs find it easier to raise money for health-related causes. But do not be lulled into complacency. Although it is generally easier to develop a case for dedicated units than for the entire university, it still is far from easy.

Case development is one of the most exacting tasks a UDO faces. Writing the statement is not difficult, but creating the elements required to produce it is. The mission, vision, problems, and institutional priorities present the greatest obstacles because the UDO cannot define them for the organization. UDOs can help, but the definitions themselves must come from the organization and its leadership.

In this chapter I address the major points in developing a case for private support for dedicated research and service units such as centers, institutes, laboratories, hospitals, and clinics. I begin by outlining the essential characteristics for a good case. Next, I discuss specific issues that UDOs are likely to encounter. Finally, I explore the practical issues of producing a case. Although much of the chapter emphasizes the nuances of developing cases for dedicated units, it has relevance for all types of case development.

Making a Good Case

The case for support has to answer one fundamental question: Why should anyone care enough to support your organization's priorities now? To answer that difficult question successfully enough to facilitate fund raising, your case statement must possess five critical characteristics.

- It must be clear.
- It must be compelling.
- It must establish the credibility of the unit.

- It must support the unit's mission and vision.
- The unit must own it.

Be Clear

To be effective, a case statement must clear enough to make prospective donors understand what you are saying about the problem your unit is addressing, communicate your vision and priorities, and explain what you want prospects to do. You may understand what your unit does and why it is important, but someone who is not already closely involved with your unit may not. Even if target audience members grasp the basic concept, they are not likely to be aware of your vision or priorities. Do not assume that people understand or appreciate research programs, especially if your unit is in a theoretical or highly technical field. Do you know, for example, what your university's Institute of Geophysics and Planetary Physics does and why it is important?

Follow the basic rules for good communication in preparing the case. Keep language and ideas simple. Research units in particular should avoid jargon and acronyms—scientists are notorious for obfuscation. Also, present the messages in a logical fashion. Ask yourself the following questions:

- What problem are we trying to solve? (establish societal relevance)
- How do we propose to solve it? (establish vision and priorities)
- Why is our organization equipped to solve the problem? (establish credibility)
- What are our priorities, how do they relate to solving the problem, and what do we need to achieve them? (establish fund-raising goals)
- Why do we need the support now? (communicate urgency)

Emphasize what needs to be done to benefit society—not how much money you need. Be clear and specific about the priorities. Relate fund-raising goals to your priorities, priorities to your vision, and vision to societal benefit.

Be Compelling

Federal Reserve Board chairman Alan Greenspan said, "The raison d'être of a research university is to ask questions and to solve problems." From the public's perspective, solving society's problems is the principal value of research universities. That is especially true for dedicated research and service units. Because they do not provide a broad, liberal education, they must focus on something of value. UDOs who want society to support their organizations need to be solving society's problems—or at least working to develop the fundamental knowledge necessary to solve them. To make your case persuasive, be sure it conveys the importance of the problems, the obvious connection between what you are proposing and the solution, and the urgency for contributing to your organization now. The more critical the problems, the more likely it will be that you get the funds you need.

Research programs sometimes focus on goals that are important but not necessarily urgent. For example, the National Aeronautical and Space Administration Center for Exobiology is based at the Scripps Institute of Oceanography (SIO), the organization I currently serve, which is part of the University of California, San Diego (UCSD). Scientists at SIO study the origins of life in the universe. Although perhaps no issue could have greater long-term significance, it lacks the practical urgency of, for example, predicting the collapse of marine fisheries, climatic changes, or El Niño events. For projects that lack urgency, emphasize their importance and long-term relevance to society.

It can be more complicated, although not impossible, to make the case that programs on basic research and theory or on the fine arts address relevant societal problems. Centers in the arts and humanities, for example, can emphasize how they prepare young people for a rapidly changing world by helping them become creative thinkers and problem solvers. Societal relevance is certainly not limited to science, engineering, and medicine.

One of the most common mistakes made in case development is to focus on the needs of the organization rather than on the needs of society. Some case statements are institutional wish lists. Other statements focus entirely on the organization, describing its activities and structure without explaining why it exists. Those approaches may work for promotional brochures, but they do not make good case statements.

Because those of us who raise money for dedicated research and service units can seldom rely on large alumni bases for support, we must be particularly persuasive in seeking private funding. University hospitals and clinics (a possible exception) have the advantage of having a prospect base of grateful patients (although the advantage diminishes if it includes a large number of indigent patients). Regardless of the institutional context, UDOs still need to find interested and concerned friends.

The case for support must, in essence, answer the question every donor asks, "Why should I care?" The most potent way to get endowments is to describe how your project contributes to solving society's problems, whether by developing better ways to communicate, finding new cures for a disease, unveiling the mysteries of an ancient culture, or deciphering the genomes of microbes. Whatever your goals, relate them to issues people care about.

Establish Credibility

You may convince potential donors that you have come up with a good solution to an urgent problem. That does not necessarily mean they will offer you support. You still have to persuade them that your unit is the best choice for implementing the solution. If, for example, your hospital is the only hospital in town, it is a pretty easy sell. But what if there are many hospitals in the city, including other academic medical centers? How do you encourage people on the East Coast to support your West Coast program? Why should they not contribute to a corresponding local program?

To persuade potential donors that you can achieve what you propose, your case statement needs to list your most relevant and outstanding accomplishments, cite honors and awards your unit has received, or describe an exceptional aspect of your unit. Are you larger than your rivals? Do you have specialized equipment? Are you more entrepreneurial? Have your scientists won major awards? What makes you stand out from the crowd? Go with your strengths. If your program is new, play up your potential as opposed to your accomplishments. Distinguish yourself from the competition.

Again, dedicated units are better qualified than are their parent institutions to produce case statements that delineate the unit's special qualities. In many instances, dedicated units really are unique, even if only within their geographic area. Research universities have become so commonplace in America that every state and major community has at least one. Many people do not understand the distinction between a research university and the local college. Why support University X when College Y is in town? One of the frustrations I faced at the UCSD Cancer Center was that, even though it was the only National Cancer Institute-designated clinical cancer center in southern California outside of Los Angeles, it was lumped together with other San Diego community-hospital cancer centers. Only when—through my case statement—I established that my center was the biggest, best, and most innovative of its kind did potential donors focus on my unit.

Support Mission and Vision

Although units of research universities can operate under the university's mission statement, I strongly recommend that units compose their own. Obviously, the mission and vision of the unit should be consistent with those of the university, but you need to distinguish what is special about your program. A clear and concise description or your unit's specific functions, your mission statement is the single most important tool for communicating your unit's special attributes.

At SIO, we spent seven years developing a mission statement. Like most major universities, UCSD, of which SIO is a part, is dedicated to "research, education, and public service," a statement too broad to distinguish it from every other research unit in the university system. One of our biggest hurdles was that people do not understand or fully appreciate what we do—a common problem for many institutes and centers. SIO is a fairly complex unit where more than 300 ongoing research projects cover a broad range of subjects, from climatic change to earthquakes to biomedicine. We obviously had difficulty agreeing on how to describe ourselves to the public. It took some doing, but our mission statement now communicates who we are and what we do.

When I say it took seven years to create a mission statement, I do not mean seven years of constant effort. We made several attempts during that time, but only when we secured the services of an experienced volunteer consultant did we make real progress. After that it took only a year and a half of monthly meetings to formulate our statement. If the development officer writes the mission statement, you are likely to have problems. That official may not take the process seriously, and faculty members (especially those who dislike corporate mumbo jumbo) may view the end product with skepticism. My suggestion is to find an experienced corporate volunteer to shepherd you through the process.

Although the mission statement is important, the vision statement is more critical. The vision statement describes what you are striving to become in 5 or 10 years. It also needs to motivate support. If you have a solid vision, it is easier to develop your case. Effective cases essentially present the institutional vision and outline the priorities.

Preparing our vision statement did not take long because we had already done a lot of homework to develop the mission statement. We had conducted a research review, an academic review, a series of 40 faculty interviews and focus groups, and a campaign-needs assessment. To build an internal consensus about how to describe ourselves to the public, we had developed an institutional positioning paper. Each activity contributed to the development of mission and vision statements.

Do you need to go through such a rigorous effort to develop mission and vision statements? It depends on the complexity of your organization, how much work you have already done, and how difficult it is to get your message to the public. At the minimum, the organization needs to set priorities and establish an internal consensus on its identity and direction.

Create Ownership

Regardless of how you develop mission and vision statements, the unit has to own them to maintain credibility. This is particularly true for the unit leadership. Your director or chief executive has to believe that the statements represent his or her views. To ensure that ownership, leaders need to actively participate in developing and writing those statements. If your unit has a board or advisory group, those people also need to contribute, even if only to comment on potential public reception. UDOs can and often do facilitate the process of creating an institutional vision statement, but the vision itself must derive from the leadership. In practical terms, the mission and vision statements together comprise what I call an "elevator statement"—what you can tell someone about your organization during a short elevator ride.

If viewed as merely a development-office fund-raising gimmick, the case will not receive the necessary support of the leadership, nor from faculty and staff. And sooner or later, potential donors will notice. The case must include the institutional vision and reflect institutional priorities—presuming, of course, that your organization has them. If you are on the university's priority list, chances are that you can enlist your chancellor or president to work on your behalf. Otherwise, you are essentially on your own. But even then, make sure university leaders understand and appreciate your case, because they can still be of significant help.

At the same time, the case for support needs to spring from a societal vision. Your strongest case is one that demonstrates how propelling your institution toward its goals yields a clear benefit to society. By providing a means of testing the case and gaining group ownership, your unit's advisory group can serve as a valuable sounding board. Keep in mind that to effectively present your case to prospective donors, board members need to thoroughly understand and embrace the case. As a rule, in establishing a case for support, the more stakeholders the better.

Although your case is rooted in an institutional and societal vision, its priorities must be tempered by fund-raising realities. Even when the stated priorities reflect the real priorities of the organization, some priorities have more market appeal than do others. Case statements should identify which priorities represent the best candidates for private support. Do not make the mistake, however, of selecting only the easiest targets for fund raising. Such an appeal could elicit substantial funds for marginal activities that do little to fulfill the unit's vision.

Challenges Specific to Dedicated Units

In my experience, three issues present particular challenges in making the case for a dedicated unit. One I have already touched on—institutional context. The other two concern your funding sources and teaching mission. The practical matter of writing and formatting case statements may also present a challenge.

Establishing Institutional Context

Being a unit of a major research university has pluses and minuses. Case statements should emphasize the positive aspects of that relationship, such as access to specialized programs and facilities, a supply of willing and talented students, and a ready pool of experts on a wide range of topics. Show how your plans support the overall mission and vision of the university. If your unit is part of another sub-unit of the institution, such as a research center in a school or college, your statement should acknowledge the relationships and align with the priorities of the organization at each level. You can then capitalize on the favorable image of the university—and the more distinguished the image, the more you should emphasize it. Any center at Harvard, for example, possesses immediate credibility, regardless of its actual quality. Conversely, UDOs of outstanding units at universities with mediocre reputations have to work harder to prove that their unit merits support.

To make an effective and compelling case for support, a unit must also distinguish itself from its host institution. However, doing so without antagonizing the rest of the university can be a delicate balancing act. You must be careful to target only prospective donors who care about your unit and its activities. Frequently, because they may be supporting their own alma mater or their children's university, those donors might not care about the university's overall objectives. If you target donors who are not interested in other schools or are associated with other units of your university, you can broaden the university's donor pool and reduce conflicts with other university development programs.

Clarifying Funding Sources

The public assumes that research universities have resources behind the unit that provide financial support. Although universities often do at least partly subsidize their units—certainly state-supported universities do—the public often mistakenly assumes that all university programs are funded fully by state revenues. For example, SIO receives only 15 percent of its income from the state of California. Moreover, because the University of California system focuses on undergraduate programs, a graduate research institution such as SIO no longer receives state funds for faculty appointments or new buildings. The Birch Aquarium at Scripps is in an even more difficult position. Because the aquarium was built solely with private funds, it receives no state appropriations. Yet because it is a beautiful facility in a spectacular location and part of SIO and UCSD, even some longtime supporters are unaware that it is essentially self-supporting. Although the aquarium has substantial fund-raising needs, few in the community recognize that SIO has to acquire its own funding through private gifts.

align with teaching

If your unit is a private organization, you might not have to overcome such misconceptions about financing—unless your unit is named for a major donor. In that case, the misperception often exists that the donor has fully endowed the unit. Do not compensate by playing up your financial needs so much that you raise questions about your unit's fundamental financial viability. But do not be afraid to admit that you need support. If you commonly encounter the misperception that you have plenty of money, your case statement is the ideal instrument for dispelling it.

Identifying a Teaching Mission

A third challenge arises when teaching is not a formal part of the unit's mission. I have found that a mission to train young people in medicine and science always resonates with donors. If your organization does have formal educational responsibilities, highlight them in your case statement. Rare is the research or clinical unit that does absolutely no training, even informal or ad hoc. Realizing that it adds an extra dimension to your organization that appeals to most donors, highlight whatever teaching you do as well as you can.

Writing the Case Statement

A unit development office must first decide who will actually put fingers to keyboard to write the case statement. The potential expense makes that a tough call. Hiring writers and consultants who specialize in cases can be quite expensive—just the interviews and writing can cost $20,000 or more, not including the cost of producing the document. What can you afford? When cost is not an issue, bring in a specialist. Even if your chief executive is a strong writer, a specialist can polish and substantially improve a case.

If hiring a specialist is not an option, consider the unit head, who is usually most familiar with the issues in the case statement. However, that person probably has the least amount of time to devote to the project and may not possess the requisite writing skills. In that case, either tackle the job yourself or find a capable writer on your staff.

If you lack a writer on staff, investigate resources in your college or university. If the university has already gone through the case-development process, you may be able to piggyback on that work. Alternatively, you might consider your college or university communications or public relations office. In my experience, however, those writers typically lack experience producing the kind of promotional and persuasive material required for a good case statement. Proposal writers can be helpful, but their writing style can be somewhat dry. Ideally, you want the prose to sparkle. Of all the positions in a university and its units, the person most likely to make a good case writer is the person who writes speeches. If you cannot afford a specialist, find a good speechwriter.

Formatting the Case Statement

Cases can range from simple typed white papers to elaborate productions that rival corporate public relations pieces. I prefer simplicity. A few pages of clear, compelling text can be more effective than a glossy magnum opus. I suppose the rationale for creating a high-priced case statement is to make people feel too guilty to throw it away.

Such elaborate productions raise the question of why an organization would spend so much of the money it needs for programs on a development publication. Somewhere in my bookcase I have a case statement for a $25 million campaign for a laboratory that must have cost at least $100,000 to produce. The lab is very distinguished; it did not need full-page four-color photos to impress people. I do not remember the content of the document, but I do remember how expensive it looked.

Although a plain, simple statement on white paper can be adequate, images can be more striking than words in communicating technical concepts or emotional messages. Diagrams, too, can quickly illustrate relationships that might be difficult to concisely describe. At SIO, we like to use photographs of our scientists at work on ships, lowering a piece of equipment into the raging ocean as waves crash over the stern. Hackneyed as it sounds, that picture is indeed worth a thousand words.

In regard to format I recommend moderation—not too many words or too many images. Tailor your case to match your organization. The larger and more complicated your unit, the more complicated the case. Nevertheless, keep the number of messages and elements manageable. As a rule of thumb, I recommend setting no more than six major goals (others advocate no more than three). Try different formats before settling on one. Can you limit the case statement to a four-page foldout and still keep the font size readable? If so, you are doing yourself a favor.

Conclusion

As a unit development officer, you are expected to develop the case for private support for your unit—no simple task or one to undertake lightly. It is a process that involves a number of steps and many participants outside the area of development. Whenever possible, enlist others in the process, and take advantage of resources available from the university. Especially helpful are good planning documents, such as mission and vision statements and a strategic plan or at least a list of organizational priorities. Most important is the presence of competent organizational leadership that understands and appreciates the development process.

If the required planning documents do not exist, start creating them immediately. That task can be very time-consuming, especially if it involves reaching an internal consensus with a large group of scientists or doctors. But the effort you spend in planning the case for support will pay dividends. Having those elements in hand will simplify and expedite the rest of the process and give you the single most important tool you need to develop private support for your unit—a clear and compelling case statement.

Recommendations for Best Practice

- A strong case statement clearly communicates the societal problem your unit is addressing, your vision, your priorities, and what you want prospects to do.

- The most compelling way to get people to contribute is to describe how your unit contributes to solving society's problems. An effective case conveys the importance of the problem, the obvious connection between the activity you propose and the solution, and the urgent need to support your organization.

- Winning case statements distinguish the unit from the competition by listing important and relevant accomplishments, citing honors and awards received by the unit and its members, and describing singular aspects that demonstrate the unit's ability to accomplish what it proposes.

- Although it should support the mission and vision of the university, the unit should have its own mission and vision statements. A mission statement establishes the unit's uniqueness by describing what it does and for whom it does it. A vision statement describes what a unit is striving to become. Along with defining the direction of the institution, it inspires and motivates support. If your unit lacks those documents, find an experienced corporate volunteer to help you write them.

- The strongest case statements demonstrate how moving a unit toward its goals yields unequivocal benefits to society. The unit's personnel, leadership, and principal supporters must own the statement, and the statement must reflect their personal visions for the unit tempered by fund-raising appeal.

- Effective case statements capitalize on the favorable image of the university by aligning with the plans and priorities of the organization at every level. The statement also targets constituencies not already claimed by the institution or its other divisions.

- A case statement should clarify assumptions about unit support. If your unit is part of a state-supported institution, the statement should specify which aspects are subsidized by state revenues and which are not. If your unit is a private organization, the case should admit the need for public support, especially if the public thinks it has plenty of money when it does not. However, do not play up financial need to the point at which it raises questions about the unit's fundamental financial viability.

- Training young people resonates well with donors. Highlight whatever teaching you do, whether or not it is a formal part of your mission.

- Ideally, you should hire a specialist to write your case statement. If you cannot, write it yourself or find someone who can do it on staff or within the university, preferably someone with speechwriting experience.

- Keep the format simple. Keep it short, and remember that photos and diagrams often convey information more efficiently than words. As a rule of thumb, set forth no more than three to six messages or goals. Try different formats before settling on one. Even if the unit is large and complex, attempt to limit your case statement to a four-page brochure with a readable font size. Above all, do not let case statement production values undermine your message.

V

Unit Development in Canada and the United Kingdom

CHAPTER 18

Unit Development: A Canadian Perspective

Guy Mallabone

Vice President, External Relations, Southern Alberta Institute of Technology, Calgary

The term *unit development office* is a rarely used in Canadian post-secondary educational institutions. Few Canadian faculty members or institutional administrative staff would recognize it, let alone understand what critical institutional functions it refers to. This does not mean that development functionality does not exist within Canadian institutions. Quite the contrary, strong development activity exists at most Canadian post-secondary educational institutions and within the various institutional units, called "faculties" or "departments" in Canada.

A Common History

Historically, Canadian and U.S. history have much in common in terms of the origin of philanthropy and the roots of private and public support of higher education. When comparing the roles of development offices in U.S. and Canadian institutions, it is helpful to recognize the evolutionary similarities and differences.

The legal traditions and similarities in societal standards date from the enactment of England's early charitable statutes. Three key Elizabethan laws in particular—one enacted in 1572 with the unfortunate title of An Act for the Punishment of Vagabonds and for Relief of the Poor and Impotent (14 Eliz.I c.5), a 1576 statute with an equally unfortunate title of An Act for Setting of the Poor on Work, and for the Avoiding of Idleness (18 Eliz.I c.3), and the 1601 statute An Act for the Relief of the Poor (39 Eliz. I c.30)—form the core of the entire social legislation at the time and had significant impact on the development of a societal culture predisposed to supporting charitable organizations in both countries. They also had great bearing on modern-day philanthropy and support of U.S. and Canadian public institutions in that they legally encouraged charitably disposed individuals to leave property in trust for establishing stocks of materials for the poor. Over centuries, this common beginning has been considerably augmented by subsequent legislation regarding charitable bequests. In both countries, this legislation has served as a foundation for the evolution of a culture for supporting higher education, and it remains a common precedent for interpreting societal responsibilities to its institutions of higher education.

From this common legal and cultural background, Canada and the United States have evolved independent points of view on the role of the state and, subsequently, the role of private development activity in post-secondary education. Whereas private, sectarian U.S. institutions were driven to fund raising very early on, Canadian universities, following the lead of universities in Great Britain and the Continent, functioned entirely as public entities funded entirely through public resources. Only in the 1980s did some Canadian universities such as the University of Toronto look to private giving as a means of supplementing state funding. But with the restructuring of government priorities in the early 1990s, funding formulas for post-secondary educational institutions significantly changed.

In the case of my own institution, the Southern Alberta Institute of Technology in Calgary, 85 percent of fiscal 1983 operational funding came from the provincial government. In fiscal 1990, government support had dropped to 74 percent, and today it stands at just 46 percent of the total C$140 million budget. As a result, all Canadian universities have been forced to locate alternative funding sources. Whereas, in the past, many institutions considered fund development and alumni relations optional and secondary, today they are core activities critical to institutional survival.

Inasmuch as no private nonprofit degree-granting organizations exist in Canada, Canadian universities, in terms of both history and sophistication, are similar to publicly funded American higher education institutions. Against this common heritage, however, several characteristics of Canadian institutions also differentiate the role of the unit development officer (UDO) from those of U.S. institutions.

Similarities and Differences

Today, almost every Canadian post-secondary educational institution allocates significant resources to key development responsibilities. Consequently, few major differences exist in advancement activity between Canadian and American institutions. All Canadian institutions assign resources to public affairs and communications; most institutions understand the need to focus on fund development and alumni relations. The differences that do exist are more evolutionary than cultural. Having evolved in a somewhat different political system and, as a consequence, getting a late start in the game,

Canadian institutional development is both more rudimentary and smaller in terms of goals and staff.

Just as unit offices in U.S. public institutions evolved fairly recently, only now are Canadian post-secondary educational institutions creating organized *unit* positions. As institutions mature and acquire development expertise, faculties and departments have begun to hire specialists for their units. What has remained significantly different from American institutions, however, is that Canadian institutions rarely group the various development functions under a single position.

Faculty and department units within Canadian institutions usually initiate development activity by hiring a public relations or communications specialist and then hiring fund-raising and alumni relations staff. In almost all cases, unit development staff report directly to the dean of the faculty or unit, but some establish a matrix reporting structure in which they report to the dean by line and to central management by function. Typical titles for development officers at the unit level include "coordinator" or "manager" for both public relations and alumni activities. Many fund-raising people at the unit level are primarily referred to as "faculty development officers" (e.g., at McMaster University in Hamilton, Ontario). Only a few institutions roll up all functions into a single title. In almost every Canadian institution, individuals responsible for development activity at the unit level interact freely and directly with faculty members and staff.

Canadian Terminology

A few significant differences exist between the vocabulary of professional development of U.S. and Canadian institutions. Although it is not uncommon to find the word *advancement* used within Canadian institutions, it usually refers to services such as database, accounting, and research services that support the fund development, alumni relations, and communications units. Although there is evidence that this is changing, *advancement* seldom refers to the unit tasked with establishing and maintaining key institutional relationships. The Schulich School of Business at York University in Toronto calls the position responsible for fund raising, alumni relations, and public relations "chief advancement officer." An increasing number of Canadian chief advancement officers have *advancement* in their titles. For example, Assiniboine Community College in Brandon, Manitoba, has a "director, college advancement and external relations"; Queen's University in Kingston, Ontario, has a "vice president, advancement"; and Concordia University in Montreal has an "executive director of advancement."

College refers to distinctively Canadian institutions that provide one-year certificates, two-year diplomas, and some four-year applied degrees; *college* rarely refers to a separate school within a university. *University* is reserved for four-year degree-granting research-focused institutions. The units within a university or college are usually called faculties (academic units such as "Faculty of Medicine" or "Faculty of Gradate Studies") and departments (nonacademic units). Academic staff members are commonly referred to as faculty members, nonacademic employees simply as staff.

The term *school*, although not uncommon within Canadian institutions, seldom refers to a specific unit. More often it denotes a special unit within the institution. An increasing number of Canadian business and management faculties have re-branded themselves as schools. For example, the University of Alberta Faculty of Business was recently renamed the School of Business. Other prominent Canadian schools have also recently made the change. *School* also commonly refers to independent high schools. The term *post-secondary educational institution* is used instead of *higher education institution* to universally refer to post-high school educational institutions.

Centralization Versus Decentralization

Whereas U.S. institutions have long debated centralized versus decentralized development structures, many Canadian post-secondary educational institutions have become aware of the issue only recently. Whereas the trend in the United States is generally toward decentralization, the jury is still out on how Canadian institutions will evolve. Canadian institutions in which unit-development activity has grown remain strongly centralized in structure, maintaining control over issues of planning, prioritization, and support.

Some institutions, in search of the perfect structure for their organizational culture, devise imaginative innovations. The University of British Columbia, after searching for the perfect solution and reviewing models from around North America, decided on a centralized approach. The final structure chosen placed the development units into different portfolios centrally, rather than keeping them together under a traditional external-relations or external-affairs portfolio. The responsibility for fund development belongs to the vice president of finance; public affairs and alumni relations offers report to different vice presidents.

In reality, institutions often settle the issue of centralized versus decentralized structure through natural evolution, sometimes by inertia and outside market forces, but rarely through a proactive central plan. A case in point is the University of Alberta in Edmonton. It began its development work with strong centralized alumni and communications departments, adding fund development into the mix when it began to prepare a large integrated fund-raising campaign. Over the course of the campaign, the institution evolved into a "best practice" hybrid model, incorporating strong central offices for alumni, public relations, and development, while it encouraged the building of strong unit offices. This hybrid model adequately addressed issues of traffic control and coordination of messages and relationships, and unit deans saw firsthand the advantages to investing in development functionality. Today, the University of Alberta is evolving into a decentralized model, whereby the faculties are increasing their investment to build on the success of the past campaign while the central administration is decreasing its investment.

In terms of trends for the coordination and structure of development staff, Canadian institutions have come up with various solutions. Some institutions have maintained strong central control (University of Toronto), others have evolved into decentralized models (University of Alberta), and still others have considered hybrid models (University of Western Ontario and University of Calgary). The concept of matrix management among Canadian institutions is still relatively uncommon, with funds development a rare exception.

Government Relations

Government relations has become a standard element within the development portfolio in Canadian institutions. Although significantly less important today than 10 years ago, government remains a significant funder to Canadian institutions. In Canadian institutions, the management of the government relationship is part of the central advancement portfolio and rarely the responsibility of unit development. UDOs are aware of the advantages to their faculties and departments of interrelating their unit strengths to the agendas of local, provincial, and federal governments. Oftentimes alumni events, fund development events, and communications messages include government as a key audience. By and large, however, Canadian institutions manage this relationship centrally, and the typical title for the person responsible is "director of government relations." One final note on government relations: Although having someone on staff responsible for managing government relations and advocacy is appropriate in the Canadian context, that person would never be called a "lobbyist."

Alumni Relations

Because alumni relations activity is a central part of every development operation, most Canadian institutions maintain central responsibility for it and assign a liaison role to individual academic and support units. Recently, however, the professional faculties (usually led by business and engineering) began to hire dedicated alumni unit officers to support central office activities. The University of Western Ontario, for example, has two central positions—"director, alumni relations and development" and "associate director alumni programs"—to coordinate alumni activity among unit officers with alumni relations responsibilities (e.g., "alumni relations officer, School of Business" and "alumni and development officer, Faculty of Medicine and Dentistry"). The hiring of unit-specific staff for alumni activity often happens when the activity level and sophistication in alumni relationship-building increase dramatically. It is not unusual for Canadian institutions approaching their second century of existence to have been involved in alumni relations activity for only 15 years or so. As recently as the early 1990s, community colleges were known to have thrown out old alumni addresses and records because they failed to understand their importance to the institution.

Most Canadian institutions have structured alumni support groups as independent alumni associations with elected governance structures. Canadian institutions, like their American counterparts, are not immune to the politics and the challenges that an independent alumni board of directors presents to efficiently delivering alumni relations programs. Many institutions are examining alternative alumni relations governing structures. The University of Calgary is a recent example of a large institution that has replaced an independent and autonomous board with an appointed institutional advisory alumni council.

President's Office

Although nearly every major Canadian college or university president understands that institutional development needs to be part of his or her administration, not all of them view it as a priority. Even so, more professional search descriptions for presidents seek candidates with a solid understanding and appreciation of institutional advancement. "Institutional advancement has become a priority for presidential search descriptions," says Brent Shervey, Canadian executive search consultant for Korn/Ferry International. "I've certainly seen it from my perspective. More and more Canadian institutions recognize that the president is the most important advancement ambassador, and are willing to recognize this reality in their position descriptions."

Fund Development

Of the major development functions within Canadian institutions, fund development is the best understood and most well established. Most Canadian institutions recognized the limitations of "light-switch fund raising"—gearing up operations for major campaigns and disbanding them several years later after raising the money. Consequently, they migrated to mission-based fund-raising programs and ongoing major gift campaigns. Since the mid-1980s, Canadian campuses have awakened to the need for integrating ongoing development activities into the mainstream life of the institution. With this growing awareness has come growing ambition: Canada has yet to complete its first billion-dollar campaign, although the University of Toronto has raised more than $800 million toward its ongoing "shifting" target.

UDOs in many Canadian institutions play a key role by attending and participating in the centrally run development functions, the most important of which is prospect management. Although protocols and procedures for prospect management vary among institutions, in most Canadian universities all constituencies (both central and faculty-based) participate on an equal footing, often including the formal representation of the alumni relations and communications departments as well as the president's office. Even in areas such as management of the annual fund—which most Canadian institutions locate centrally to streamline approaches and maximize efficiencies—care is taken not to lose or water down unit messages, but rather to personalize them while integrating them into the overall institutional message.

Communications

Although most Canadian institutions possess centralized communications agencies, the functions are typically no more evolved than are their fund development operations. The mission of communications departments is to take care of central messaging responsibilities and image management. In most Canadian institutions, communications with government is managed separately, oftentimes out of the president's office.

Here as elsewhere, Canadian universities have manifest increased appreciation for the responsibilities of UDOs and particularly of the critical role that communications plays in their success. Thus, just as alumni and development activities have begun to decentralize, institutions are also considering decentralizing some elements of the central communications office. Many institutions are actively pursuing matrix management of certain marketing and public relations functions.

Advancement Services

Advancement services generally include the key support functions of gift processing, prospect research, database management, and finance. Because the logic and efficiency of centralizing them is long established, few Canadian UDOs are responsible for these core functions. Having said this, however, many UDOs augment the core support provided by the central office in areas such as supplementary gift acknowledgment and unit-based prospect research. The creation of additional databases, though, is considered counter-efficient to the institution.

Conclusion

Canadian development professionals, like their American counterparts, believe that people give their love, support, and money to the causes they feel closest to. In this light, they understand that their primary role is to bring people closer to the institutions they serve. Whether they are involved in fund development, alumni relations, communications, government relations, or another development-related role, Canadian development professionals understand the need to seamlessly integrate development activities, whether they are located centrally or in faculties and departments.

The golden age of development at Canada's post-secondary educational institutions is well underway. As development matures and develops, we can expect to see institutions and specific units direct more resources to and prioritize core institutional activities. Fund development is emulating best practice associated with managing relationships, and we have already seen the launching of Canada's first billion-dollar campaign. Having grown beyond simple promotional activity, public relations is providing the critical leadership for key institutional strategies such as branding, marketing, and image management. Alumni relations has been firmly established; recognized as the professional stewards of one of the institution's greatest assets, it is successfully engaging graduates in all aspects of institutional life.

Although the future is bright, Canada's development professionals face the challenges of both doing more of what they are doing now, and doing it better in an ever-changing environment. The challenges facing Canada's growing post-secondary development profession include stabilizing the role of government funding, emphasizing the importance of private philanthropic support, accommodating new societal policy issues such as protection of privacy and freedom to information, and managing the growing previously nonexistent political presence of groups such as organized alumni and donor groups. Canadian UDOs serve on the front line in dealing with these important opportunities and challenges—no other professional provides a clearer perspective on future opportunities. Because of their unique institutional perspective, their ability to steward key assets—including money, alumni, and image—and the reduced role of government in post-secondary education, the importance of Canadian UDOs will continue to rise and expand.

CHAPTER 19

Unit Development in the United Kingdom

Tania Jane Rawlinson
Development Director, University College Oxford

To understand an English unit development officer (UDO), you need to be aware of a unique development setting—one that defines itself as young, growing, and evolving, yet grounded in traditions that date back hundreds of years. The tensions and opportunities created by this unusual setting can take North Americans by surprise. It certainly surprised me, an American returning to England after a few years of fund raising in the States—this in spite of my initial grounding during the early 1990s as a graduate student assistant in a pioneering Oxford college fund-raising office.

In this book, others have covered the range of models under which UDOs may operate. They have examined the creation and implementation of cases and campaigns, described the latest thinking about training, professional development, and best practice. In the United Kingdom, we operate under similarly diverse conditions, face similar challenges as well as others of our own, and are reaching similar conclusions as are our North American counterparts. In this chapter, therefore, I first draw a general sketch of the historical, educational, and structural settings within which UK development models are built. Next, I outline the opportunities and pressures that affect unit development structures. Finally, I describe several models whereby unit development most successfully takes place in the United Kingdom.

Comparisons to North America

It is important to note from the outset that many of my UK colleagues balk when we are described as following a North American lead. Some say that our potential funders—particularly alumni—have a different approach toward philanthropy. Indeed, statistics demonstrate markedly different British and North American giving levels and patterns. Many believe that the application of North American models to UK universities is unfair both in terms of expected results and to our alumni and other potential supporters themselves. The true development pioneers in the United Kingdom, however, are those who believe that because of our differences, we must—and can—adopt innovative approaches to institutional development.

First, it is crucial to recognize that, in relative terms, the United Kingdom has very few "development" offices (as they are almost universally still known here). CASE has only approximately 82 four-year university member institutions in the United Kingdom, a country with a population of 60 million. Many UK offices are only a few months or a few years old, and offices more than a decade old are described as longstanding. Iain More, managing partner of the Iain More Associates consulting business, recalls that only six people (including himself) attended the first gathering of UK development professionals, held in the United States in 1984, and that CASE itself was not established formally in England until 1994.

It is fair to say that, even a decade ago, only a handful of UK universities had made even a minimal investment in development. Many did not retain alumni records, let alone disseminate news or hold events. Fund raising was the province of the few (and of the rich) universities. Since World War II, government funding had been largely sufficient to make universities complacent about how they would make ends meet. It was not until Prime Minister Margaret Thatcher's era, when a fixed amount of government funding was divided not just among traditional universities but also with the old polytechnics (the equivalent of North American community colleges) that institutions of higher education became concerned with private funding.

But need does not instantly produce a culture conducive to fund raising—either from the perspective of the institution or of the alumni. Many UK universities continue to be governed by academics alone, without the guidance (or financial support) of a body of trustees or governors typical of American institutions. Until recently, the job description for the post of chancellor or vice chancellor, rough equivalents of North American university presidents, seldom referred to fund raising.

Investment in development offices—where fund raising is undertaken—is made cautiously, with a careful eye on rate of return. Some universities still consider their development offices as experimental and are prepared to cut back or cease development activity altogether if results are not good enough. Many others have not established development offices at all. For example, the University of Bradford, a comfortable institution with 10,000 students and a solid reputation—including as one of the United Kingdom's highest rates of graduate employment—has only a small alumni office and no fund-raising office at all.

Within this context, it is understandable that development staff levels seldom represent even a quarter of their North American counterparts. The central development office of Cambridge University, one of the better-staffed offices, currently employs 11 fund-raising staff members along with another 35 or so college-level fund raisers (many of whom also bear alumni relations responsibilities). Yet Cambridge competes transatlantically with Harvard and Yale, which have literally hundreds of fund-raising staff spread across units and the central development office.

In contrast, Nottingham University, with 15,000 students, has been running a successful development program over the past seven years—including a £35 million capital campaign—with no more than eight development professionals at any time. The University of York, a young and dynamic institution with a student body of 8,000, is in the process of setting up a development office with four staff members (including the director). As Anthony Hilton wrote in an op ed piece on ThisIsLondon.co.uk in July 2001, "The structures and experience within the [UK] academic community to tap into [prospects' good will to give] are still in their infancy. Fund raising in America is big business. Here it is done on a shoestring."

Now consider the alumni themselves. Those from traditional universities grew up under a post-World War II system, rather similar to those of North American public universities in the 1960s and 1970s, where funding came largely from the government. Neither parents nor students paid higher-education fees, and government "student grants" covered living expenses. At the universities themselves, buildings and small book prizes and professorships were named for either the great and good or for historical college benefactors—not for recent, living donors. After graduation, alumni contact from their university was sporadic at best, in most cases nonexistent.

Polytechnic students, who were similarly funded by the government, typically regarded their institutions as a means to an end (vocational qualifications) rather than as an alma mater. Some argue that, as they became universities in 1993 and consequently began to resemble more traditional universities, alumni felt increasingly distanced from their institutions. At the same time, the polytechnics did little to encourage good alumni relations, in many cases not even maintaining alumni address lists.

Taking this background of low institutional investment in development, little cultivation of alumni expectations, and a general sense among alumni and other prospective funders that universities are well-funded by tax money, it is hardly surprising that in the UK philanthropic inclinations seldom include higher education. North American alumni assume that one's university will stay in touch, ask for funds annually, and run periodic capital campaigns. A North American industry based in a city with a major university will expect to cultivate a relationship with that university. The UK versions of these potential funders—both alumni and corporate—are often initially surprised by friend- and fund-raising approaches from universities. In 1999 Paul J. Summerfield wrote in *The Chronicle of Philanthropy*, "the British generally adopt an attitude that the government, not the community of charity, should provide specific services for society. People who are poor, homeless, or ill, most Brits believe, should receive support from the state. The same applies for educational, arts, and social institutions."

Of course, the irony of positing that fund raising is new to the United Kingdom is that the very roots of a philanthropic tradition for higher education are to be found in England, Scotland, and Wales. Philanthropy at my University College, known as "Univ" within Oxford, goes back 750 years to its foundation when a legacy of 300 marks endowed 12 scholars and Univ was born. Read the history of any Oxbridge college, or of British universities as a whole and—although the academics do not like to think of it this way, and even archivists are surprised when it is pointed out—you will find more pages devoted to descriptions of gifts and their stewardship than to scholars and their teachings. Perhaps it is safest to say that the development profession is being rediscovered and reestablished in the UK higher education sector. Almost in spite of our longstanding historical traditions, UK development officers can and must show a pioneering spirit to conquer prejudices and raise funds.

Structure of Unit Development

Innovative thinkers in UK fund raising have recognized that the new-found novelty of fund raising—that is, the absence of recent institutional/funder experience of educational development—works to our advantage because we are operating in an environment with few expectations. By starting from scratch, we can tailor our development efforts to our institutions. Within this context, British UDOs have found a unique justification for their specialized work. As this book makes clear, central university development professionals must work hard to change prospects' perceptions of higher education. They are working tirelessly to raise prospects' sights about the institution as a whole, including its mission and its function within a wider community. They must persuade funders not to think of universities as constrained by—or, indeed, able to depend on—government support.

Many in the United Kingdom operate such small development offices that they are effectively UDOs. They are hired by visionary vice chancellors or secretaries and asked to create a fund-raising strategy and program. They must be multiskilled individuals capable of covering all bases with a small team—from alumni and community relations through publications and events to fund raising at every level. Their messages must be broad yet targeted, and they tend to focus on higher net-worth prospects likely to deliver the biggest return on investment. They must identify and then appeal to funders and audiences who are most likely to be sympathetic to and interested in their aims.

In the larger UK development offices, UDOs are the norm precisely because they can follow a similar pattern. Because no department in the UK has even a tenth of the staff of Harvard Business School, individual UDOs are multi-taskers again. They are now almost always (the same was not true five years ago) based at the central development office. And they have strong ties to their units either because they are alumni themselves, they are being paid in part or full by the unit, or the head of the unit is committed to fund-raising objectives.

Success Stories and Lessons Learned

Bristol University is a traditional university widely acknowledged to enjoy strong fund-raising success. With more than 12,000 students and 64,000 contactable alumni, Bristol has recently achieved its £85 million goal raised over an ongoing 10-year campaign mixing annual and capital targets. At Bristol, a central office with 17 staff members manages development functions and ensures that all prospects are appropriately tracked. The university decides on fund-raising focal points both centrally and in individual departments. Resources are then invested in the development office on a project basis, increasing staffing levels for some projects and reallocating others when goals change.

Some departments (and in two cases, individual donors) have chosen to invest in permanent fund raising, allowing UDOs to focus on specific units while maintaining direct links with the centralized office. Prospect management is undertaken centrally—but because the departments that have chosen to invest in fund raising are relatively few, the pressures of prospect allocation are not as yet strong. Bristol's greatest strength is its flexibility: As one project reaches a conclusion, the UDO moves across to new project(s), sometimes bringing his or her prospect relationships along.

At University College London, with 17,000 students and 75,000 contactable alumni, and about £50 million raised since the development office was established seven years ago, the structure is a bit more organic. The annual fund is managed separately from major gifts; otherwise, the office operates within the context of a university-driven development plan. Growing out of the more general corporate plan of the university, this plan is driven by the provost (president). It involves a general case statement and underlying theme that encompasses the entire university, but its aim is to come up with broad fund-raising themes that can be tailored to an individual prospect's wishes and funding opportunities. When individual units at the college ask for fund-raising support, they are asked to produce not just wish lists but prospect lists as well. Consequently, the academics themselves are integrally involved with development work from the very first step.

In the development office, fund raisers meet fortnightly to discuss and allocate prospects and to review the status of projects across the university. Although individual fund raisers are no longer specifically assigned to any one unit or project (they once were), as prospects are allocated,some fund raisers find themselves focusing on particular areas. However, Development Director Simon Pennington says, "None of our fund raisers are specialists, which means we can be truly prospect-driven rather than project-driven at all times." The interrelation of prospects, the broad skills base of all fund raisers, and the project-driven environment may all be familiar to North Americans, but the intimate interweaving of academic units' and individual donors' goals is a uniquely British approach.

Catrin Tilley arrived at the University of Edinburgh (20,000 students and about 80,000 contactable alumni) about five years ago to find a central office that had once been an innovative development office but that had, over time, lost its fund-raising focus. A handful of dissatisfied unit heads had even hired their own UDOs to do their fund-raising work, an arrangement Tilley felt was unfair to those UDOs, particularly in a country where fund raising can be a misunderstood profession. Tilley believes that "without being in a fund-raising work environment on a daily basis, development professionals are isolated. Under our old structure, there was overwhelming pressure for those staff members to become academic administrators."

Like University College London, Edinburgh has since moved toward a centralized development program that operates within a hybrid model. Although a forthcoming capital campaign is likely to involve a number of unit- and project-based objectives, the development office will remain centralized, and prospect (as well as project) allocation will be based on regular review. Prospects themselves, as well as departmental needs or desires, are likely to drive the angles and approaches adopted for particular projects. Tilley says that prospect allocation has not been too tricky thus far because they have been managing relatively few major prospects. When clashes do arise in the future, they will be solved not just by internal politics but by reference to the desires of donors themselves. "The management of relationships at Edinburgh will be cooperative," Tilley states, "but based on the principle of involving donors more closely in the university. Our motivation is to maximize the bottom line in fund raising terms from individuals. We will only be successful at that if we build donors' interests into the heart of our operation."

The Oxford and Cambridge models are perhaps the most distinctive in the United

Kingdom and, insofar as the tensions of prospect-sharing go, they are also probably most similar to U.S. models. As was noted earlier, because Oxbridge has been fund raising longer and has invested more in its development effort than have most other UK models, the sophistication and frequency of higher-level approaches is well honed. Oxford and Cambridge are both complex universities with hybrid development offices—centralized offices with individual UDOs supporting particular departments, faculties, and projects—but they also have an added dimension. Each university is composed of individual tutorial "colleges," each self-governing yet integrally linked to the university. Most Oxbridge alumni describe themselves by their college, saying, "I am an alumnus of Exeter College, Oxford" rather than, "I was at Oxford." But their degrees come from the university, and, particularly with major initiatives that change the nature of the institution, only the university can realize particular donor objectives.

When Oxbridge began taking development seriously in the late 1980s, both the universities and many of their colleges invested in development offices. For the most part, these were not coordinated; each college made its own decision as to whether and how much to invest in a development office. Therefore, both Oxford and Cambridge have, in addition to central offices and UDOs who undertake project work for departments and faculties (although in every case these answer primarily to the central offices), a number of college development offices with entirely separate agendas and aims. Some have as many as five or six full-time staff members operating a development agenda almost independently of the university itself.

Because both universities and all their colleges are self-governing, independent (yet interdependent) entities, each must be proactive about fund raising. In either case, development officers work to further the institution that pays them, be it a college or university or even a department within a university. Oxford and Cambridge have coped with this multidimensional arrangement in slightly different ways, and both continue to evolve. However, joint approaches to major donors are becoming more typical: The integrated approach seems to work better than independent or even managed relations do.

In Cambridge, if both a college and the university have set their sights on an alumnus, company, or trust, there is no formal procedure to determine who gets to make the first approach (one Cambridge fund raiser described it as "a friendly bunfight"). Oxford has a loosely defined formal arrangement for prospects worth more than £100,000, but there is regular dissent about how to interpret those guidelines and no real governance over those who interpret them in an unpopular way. "Friendly bunfight" might serve as a good description here, too.

However, Oxbridge does sometimes find university and college working hand-in-hand when particular donors (especially those with deep pockets) are involved. In these cases, relationships are with increasing frequency developed jointly by collegiate and university development officers working closely with proactive academics at both college and university levels. They are by their nature driven by the interests of the prospective donor. For example, Oxford University offers one of the United Kingdom's more generous bursary packages for students. It can do this because of the initiative of a central university-based donor who offered half the required funds. Individual colleges will contribute further funds—most of which will be raised by individual college development professionals from our own alumni—to make the bursaries a reality.

In general, Oxford and Cambridge's central development offices, the faculties, and the colleges have of necessity evolved a donor- and academically driven approach to prospect allocation and, even more crucially, to the creation of fund-raising objectives. In this, they are very much like most other major UK universities that possess the resources to hire UDOs.

Conclusion

Clearly, in the United Kingdom fund raisers are *not* considered a necessary part of the fabric of each university department, faculty, college, or even institution. We are still the exception rather than the norm. It takes a visionary dean or head of department to perceive the value of a fund raiser and to commit either the time or the salary needed to support a UDO. Because this institutional investment is almost always voluntary, there is usually a commitment on the part of the dean to maximize the output of his or her UDO. In this case, the UDO is, indeed, in and of the college or department rather than merely a tolerated presence. Many academics have also had to become de facto fund raisers themselves. In these situations, UDOs typically see themselves as simply guiding and assisting the development activity undertaken by academics in their units.

In effect, the United Kingdom is re-learning its fund-raising practice by creating a range of models where—assuming enough resources are devoted to the development office—the UDO and the small-office, multi-skilled development professional is at the heart and center of university development. Because of a perception that our prospects are less naturally inclined to support higher education, we must start immediately with focused, targeted development initiatives. Prospects and public perception must be identified, considered, and brought on board before projects are undertaken, so the most creative and innovative among us work from a position of participation in institutional decision-making.

Perhaps because we are relative newcomers, we in the United Kingdom are experiencing evolution from a different perspective. Indeed, many development professionals are catapulted into the development world because of specific interests in the items for which they are fund raising. Even those at the top of the profession have usually been in the field for no more than 5 to 10 years.

The hybrid UDO model is becoming the norm at the better-resourced British development offices, and the efforts of the most successful amongst us are integral to the planning and execution of institutional development in the purest sense of the term. As Hilenski points out in Chapter 1, the UDO's authority and charge derive from the intrinsic mission of the college. Here in the United Kingdom, we are discovering that the intrinsic mission of the college is often integrally related to the resources our efforts uncover. The dynamic this creates can be magical in development terms. What could we accomplish if we had the staff and resources of our North American colleagues? Harvard might like to mind its step!

CONCLUSION

Charting the Future of Unit Development

F. A. Hilenski

U nit development officers (UDOs) in American universities serve their institutions by applying the concepts and practice of the modern professional fund raiser to the ancient function of fund raising in the academy. Accordingly, this Handbook describes the UDO position in terms of its distinct (if not unique) functionality within the organizational context of college or unit that it serves, rather than on the basis of any distinct or unique form of fund-raising practice.

UDOs typically employ the same model of best practice utilized by other major-gift fund raisers. They use the five *I*s—identification, information, interest, involvement, and investment—(or some variation thereof) as a template for developing a prospect into a donor. They use the moves management system (or some variation thereof) to direct and track the players and activities through this cycle. And they build long-term sustainable relationships between institutions and donors sufficient to impel donors from their first annual gift through their first special gift and on to a culminating, once-in-a-lifetime ultimate gift (see Dunlop 1993, 97–108).

As I outlined in the Introduction, this model of professional practice originated in the for-profit consulting world outside of the university, deriving directly from the methods pioneered by early modern fund raisers such as Bishop William Lawrence, Charles Sumner Ward, Lyman L. Pierce, and John Price Jones. The model links contemporary development officers with the itinerant professional fund raisers of the pre-1960s-era who were hired on periodically and temporarily to conduct their capital campaigns. Before them, the model links with 18th- and 19th-century "paid solicitors," independent agents—often clergy—who were commissioned to raise money for sectarian liberal arts colleges along with other Christian charities. Still earlier antecedents were the commissioned agents sent to England in the 17th century to solicit support for fledgling colonial colleges.

The struggle to bring these part-time, extraneous operators first into the university hierarchy and finally onto the executive cabinet—a movement generally referred to as centralization—has indeed been, as Hall observes in Chapter 2, a long and difficult one. Nevertheless, centralization has succeeded in large part by employing this legacy of professional knowledge and experience to acquire a remarkable amount of tangible assets on behalf of American colleges and universities. But this success has come at a price. In addition to dealing with the misperception, misunderstanding, and mistrust of other programs and offices that have seen their suns set or at least cloud over in the dawn of development, development officers of all stripes also have had to contend with disrespect, suspicion, and even outright hostility on the part of some faculty and administrators even as they are about the business of obtaining support for them. I, personally, will never forget the moment when a seemingly sunny conversation with a former academic colleague suddenly turned dark, as he baldly accused me of being "an agent of the marketplace" and a "corrupting influence within the academy."

This Handbook takes a different tack. It portrays the UDO as an extension of the line of masters, deans, bursars, and faculty members—the historic "benefaction-chasers" of academe—who have linked the academy with donors since the origins of the university college. In other words, it defines the position not in terms of its practice, but rather in terms of its organizational context and inherent functionality within the institution, drawing on the knowledge and experience of UDOs themselves to articulate this ontogeny. This Handbook effectively updates the functions of these historic benefaction-chasers and vests them in the position of the modern UDO, disclosing in the process the roles UDOs play as educators and negotiators in addition to being fund raisers. Only in this light, I contend, can the position of the UDO be seen for what it is, and, therefore, understood and appreciated for what it does. As educators, negotiators, and fund raisers, modern UDOs effectively perform three functions:

1. They maintain a close professional relationship with their dean or unit head and with unit-affiliated constituencies inside and outside the university;

2. They manage the innate organizational complexity of their positions; and

3. They make the case for their college or unit.

In this book, current and former UDOs from all over the United States and from the United Kingdom and Canada testify both to the commonality of these tasks and the common nature of their approach. Their experience and perceptions provide rich soil in which to plant new careers or to grow new understanding in careers that are not so new. In addition, the book may also evoke new appreciation of what UDOs have and will continue to provide. Although this book certainly contains much practical and applied knowledge, it primarily offers commentary on various facets of the UDO position. Having now mapped the present coastline of the position, can these charts help UDOs navigate its future parameters, or at the very least keep them from piling onto the rocks? I think so, insofar as they coincide with what Colin Lucas, vice chancellor of Oxford University, has termed as the "banners" of contemporary university education that institutions ignore at their peril—cultural inclusiveness, technological and scientific innovation, and international awareness and presence.

Dealing with Diversity

During the past 30 years, America's colleges and universities have had to adapt to and adopt—awkwardly at times, incompletely even now—new and different cohorts of faculty, students, and alumni. As these new alumni now enter into the period of their maximum earning power, university development offices in general and unit development offices in particular will need to adapt and adopt new and different techniques and best practices in order to build and maintain relationships with them.

For almost two decades now, women have constituted more than half of the students enrolled in all American higher educational institutions and are becoming an increasingly significant part of the demographic mix of alumni as well. At the same time, the number and "market share" of students of color have increased within both academic and alumni demographics. In addition, categories of so-called new students—returning adults and students with disabilities—have grown to the point where they constitute a substantial part of the student community and alumni base. And as institutions have become more global, they also have produced an increasingly significant international alumni base, in terms of both local leadership and size. In fact, the throw-weight of their international alumni cohorts together with their substantial investment in overseas programs and facilities have given some American institutions a political and economic impact in relevant host countries comparable to that at home.

Over this period, as development officers have become more aware of the growing diversity in their alumni and donor base, they also have become more aware of what this diversity means in terms of alumni participation and giving. For the most part, however, this awareness has not as yet translated into the development of new or different fundraising techniques and practices designed to engage these cohorts—and understandably so. Given the crushing weight of ever-higher goals and bigger campaigns, few development offices can spare the time and effort it takes to develop such new methodologies, much less to coach officers in their use. For many institutions, the cold facts are that the potential of these new cohorts of alumni and potential donors does not as yet justify subtracting time and effort from conventional cohorts of alumni and donors, many of whom are still under-participating or relatively untapped.

Fund raising with regard to these new cohorts therefore seemingly stands at a crossroads. Either fund raisers can continue to simply follow the money and plow old but still rich donor ground over and over again, or they can take the time away from current cohorts to develop the cases for support and best practice necessary to succeed with the demographics of a new era still just over the horizon. Which road to take? The answer, of course, is that university fund raising needs to travel both roads simultaneously, with UDOs taking the lead in developing cases for support and best practice for new donor cohorts out of necessity as much as by design.

Why do UDOs in particular need to take the lead in this initiative? Because they are frequently the first point of contact for these new cohorts, whose members typically relate to those parts of the university with which they most closely identify, that is, their majors, departments, and schools. In so doing, they are acting no differently than virtually any alumnus does in seeking initially to reconnect and engage with an alma mater. It is what new alumni do after their initial contact that sets them apart from the norm.

Because members of these cohorts often encountered barriers, bias, and even outright discrimination as students, as alumni they frequently harbor suspicion and even hostility toward the institution and its conventional motives, methods, and procedures, including—one is tempted to say, especially—those regarding fund raising. Thus, although they might initially reconnect with the university through their home unit, as it were, new alumni often seek to link to segments of the current student body or faculty who look, think, and act like themselves, regardless of where these cohorts might be located within the institution.

The donative interests of these alumni can spread quickly to an interdisciplinary level or to another unit entirely, because, first and foremost, they want to influence positively the lives of like students and faculty. Moreover, given their history and experience, these prospects often believe they can do so better than can the host institution. Consequently, when these prospects become donors, they frequently want more direct control of the management of their gifts and more hands-on involvement in the delivery of the benefits they have sponsored. Similarly, their perception of the mission of the institution—and of the terms of their social contract with it—also is likely to differ from that of conventional donor cohorts, as will their patterns of institutional involvement.

Although UDOs are becoming increasingly adept at making the case for unit support with such cohorts, they for the most part remain less adept at integrating within it a case for interdisciplinary or multidisciplinary support of like cohorts of students and faculty, much less handling the unconventional needs and demands of an intense and inquisitive donor base. Given that many of the difficulties in making such a case or accommodating such donor involvement are institutional in nature, UDOs alone cannot develop the programs, policies, and procedures necessary to address the needs and demands of these cohorts of new alumni. They can, however, use their offices as "street-level" educators and negotiators to affect the internal adjustments that must be made if these alumni are ever to be fully integrated and engaged in the institution, and so establish the social contract between institution and constituent that is the essential foundation for giving.

And just as the faces of university donors are changing, so are the faces of university faculty and administrators. In my 20-plus years as a UDO, it has been my privilege to serve five deans, two of the last three of whom have been women. Given student demographic trends for the past two or three decades, it is inevitable that women, who presently predominate the student ranks, should have an increasing presence in the faculty and leadership of the university as well. And as they and others of the new cohorts begin to make their presence felt within the university, they will serve as role models and mentors to a new generation of students whose diversity is now an accepted, if not still fully accommodated, norm. In building donative relationships with these most recently enfranchised members of the university community, UDOs thus should be particularly alert to the special utility such faculty and administrators can provide as role models and mentors to alumni as well as students.

Managing Technology

As a UDO of a technological university, I am especially attuned to "the question concerning technology," as Heidegger (1977) put it. Be that as it may, most thinking human beings would agree, I believe, that we currently are living in an age of technology wherein the question concerning technology—that is, the nature and implications of human interaction with sophisticated electronic tools—has become one of the defining issues of society and culture worldwide.

In the realm of philanthropy, the human encounter with technology has manifested at least two discernable results. In the first case, technology has reinforced the developmental-services dimension of our field, and in so doing reshaped the field itself. When I entered the profession some 20 years ago, data entry still largely involved file cards and donor tracking was essentially a matter of an individual officer's personal memory. Not only has the computerization of data and reporting transformed our record keeping, but the computerization of all record keeping enables us to research donors to an unprecedented and heretofore inconceivable depth and degree.

In fact, electronic data gathering and networking have reached a point where only our ethics and integrity as professionals prevent us from employing the kind of psycho-demographic profiling used routinely in commercial marketing and security. Even without such profiling, however, when development officers call on potential donors, they may well do so knowing more about their prospects' interests and capacities than the prospects may know themselves. Moreover, officers can now coordinate a range of activities and "moves" not only across vast space but also over great timeframes and among a large team of volunteers and professionals—all courtesy of technology.

The second discernable impact of technology on fund raising is only now beginning to manifest itself and may ultimately prove to be more an aberration than a full-fledged alteration. Nevertheless, some fund-raising circles are beginning to make the case that technology—specifically the Internet—has created a new breed of "cyber-donors," who respond more positively to interactive electronic appeals than to conventional person-to-person cultivation approaches. Whole new consulting firms and new divisions of old consulting firms, in fact, have been founded on the basis of this theory, which has yet to demonstrate conclusive—much less compelling—proof of concept. These enterprises may yet go the way of the dot-coms—but they may equally be harbingers of an entirely new dimension of fund raising.

For UDOs, these machinations of philanthropic technology mean that their world, already sufficiently complex, is about to become more complex still. Like other development officers functioning at multiple levels inside and outside the university, UDOs have had to master the basic technologies of databases, search engines, and e-mail. Now, it appears that they will have to integrate into their tradecraft not only these interactive technologies but also the ethos these technologies portend if they are to affect the giving of this new class of cyber-donor.

Recently, Microsoft ran a series of ads in which a member of a corporate information technology team pronounces a particularly complex problem impossible to solve. Although the problems differ from ad to ad, the tag line always reads the same: "The software disagrees." This Hal-like notion that computer software has some form of independent existence, and that this existence is superior to human existence, although understandable when expressed in the context of marketing computer software, also has begun to creep into our popular culture and thinking as well, with some troubling implications.

How far will such thinking go? As Heidegger (1977) also pointed out, the power of technology is never neutral, but rather it is always reaching out aggressively to transform phenomenon in its own terms. So, as we embrace technology to help us in our fund raising, how, then, is technology transforming our fund raising in turn? For example, where does the cyber-donor believe donative intent lies? Is it still a human element, driving human giving with the assistance of technology? Or is it now a function of the software, as it were, with humans being merely instruments logging into some form of technological gratuity?

If the latter, then what are the terms of the social contract this ethos signifies? What are the university's obligations to a constituency composed essentially of computers or, more precisely, computer users who think like Microsoft advertisements? What case can be made to such a constituency for support of the very professors, disciplines, and programs that—lest we forget—developed and educated both the computer and its most ardent and proficient users? On the flip side, what are the philanthropic obligations of constituent members who see themselves not as independent moral agents but as walking financial reserves for an institution? Stay tuned for more such questions . . . the answers to which we do not have a clue.

Making a New Case

During 1992–1993, the Pew Charitable Trusts sponsored a transatlantic dialogue among 24 educational leaders and scholars from central and western Europe and the United States. The participants were charged with assessing "the challenges and opportunities now facing the university on both sides of the Atlantic." Reporting on the dialogue, the interlocutors stated, "We came collectively to see that a single, fundamental proposition and its principal corollary describe the world of the modern university:

- ▶ *Proposition:* The changes most important to the university are those that are external to it. What is new is the use of societal demand—in the American context, market forces—to reshape the university.

- ▶ *Principal Corollary:* The failure to understand these changes puts the university at risk. The danger is that the university has become less relevant to society precisely because it has not fully understood the new demands being placed on it" (*Policy Perspectives* 1993, p. 1A).

Heretofore, societies in both Europe and America funneled their collective demands through designated public agencies—ministries, legislatures, governorships, and the like—that became powerful levers of political and financial support. However, the Pew discussants argued that, at least since the end of the Cold War, universities worldwide have had to cope with an increasingly more diffuse state of affairs. Today, power and money are no longer concentrated in public agencies, but rather are being progressively distributed among an ever-widening circle of nongovernment organizations and private individuals throughout all sectors of society in all parts of the world, each imposing its particular societal demand or "market forces" on the agenda of the university.

The Pew Report authors contended that it is these new sets of societal demands or market forces that universities by and large have failed to grasp. Consequently, they have placed themselves at risk of being perceived as "less relevant" to their host societies and thus less worthy of financial support. The authors believe that only by renegotiating the "social contract" with their relevant constituent communities can universities refocus on this new paradigm of diffused societal demand and so regain their social relevance and support. This critique provides a useful context for understanding the evolution of American colleges and universities over the last generation with regard to their social contract with the nation.

When I entered graduate school in 1969, the nation and the world were still operating within the framework of the Cold War. To maintain their relevance in American society—and to retain their basis of support—colleges and universities therefore made substantial scientific, technological, and ideological contributions to national security, which was largely defined in terms of the containment of Communism worldwide with a particular focus on Vietnam. The need to demonstrate such relevance was palpable, at times almost to the point of absurdity. I still wonder about the logic that enabled me, a graduate student in 18th-century English literature, to complete a master's degree and a Ph.D. on a fully paid federal fellowship established ostensibly to bolster the national defense. But whether splitting atoms or infinitives, everyone in higher education at that time—right down to students in the most arcane of disciplines—knew that, to obtain or retain financial support, one must demonstrate relevance, or at least obeisance, to the societal need for national defense.

During the late 1980s, however, the terms of the social contract between American society and its universities underwent a major shift. With the end of the Cold War, national security, at least in terms of national defense, no longer represented the premier societal demand. With the implosion of the Soviet Union and the collapse of Marxist economies worldwide, capitalism ruled as the New World Order. To retain its leadership position as the world's leading capitalist country, it was incumbent upon the United States not just to maintain but also to enhance its status as such. Not surprisingly, therefore, President Clinton, soon after his election in 1992, announced that, in the post-Cold war era, economic success and global predominance would be synonymous with national security. In this light, it quickly became clear that, in order to retain financial support, American institutions of higher education would have to demonstrate their relevance not so much to the nation's military defense as to its economic defense.

Accordingly, America's colleges and universities rapidly began converting from quasi-defense industries to engines of commerce, capable of both producing the necessary human capital to drive a global economy and functioning as profit centers in and of themselves. Thus was launched an era of "technology transfer," of "entrepreneurial" universities and faculty members, and—not inconsequentially—of billion-dollar capital campaigns and multibillion-dollar university endowments. In fact, the steep escalation in the sheer number of campaigns and the volume of their goals mirrored more than the unprecedented economic growth of the period. It also signaled an unprecedented redistribution of financial and political power from public agencies to corporations, foundations, and private individuals, a process of diffusion in which these campaigns themselves played a major role.

Among American colleges and universities, "economic impact" became a hallmark of excellence and the arbitrage of societal esteem and support. Over the course of the 1990s, the societal demand for economic security was increasingly perceived as a need for American economic hegemony, and "globalization" became a codeword for the spread of American power and wealth worldwide through international capitalism. As one of the principal transmitters of American social and political influence, American universities therefore deserve considerable credit (or blame) for the remarkable success of global capitalism and its attendant policies of democratization—prima facie evidence of their relevance and obeisance to the revised post-Cold War definition of national security.

Throughout these three decades, tens of thousands of development officers (including me) wrote millions of case statements and proposals that, implicitly or explicitly, drew successfully on the terms of this social contract as manifested in the mission statements of our host institutions. Indeed, as Panas famously documented in his pioneering study *Mega Gifts: Who Gives Them, Who Gets Them* (1984), the number-one reason by far that major donors give to a school or college is "belief in the mission of the institution." Stated Panas:

> The mission of the organization is of primary, overriding, and paramount significance. Nothing else is as important. Everything else pales in importance. No matter how appealing the specific program or project may seem, nothing is as powerful an incentive as an abiding and impelling belief in the mission of the institution. Don't discuss the program, the campaign, the need. First, sell the mission.

Reasons two, three, and four on Panas's list make clear how institutions can instill and make manifest this belief by involving supporters through an official governing body of the institution, the organization of a campaign, or a personal history of engagement with the institution as an adult. But, as Panas also made clear, what turns supporters into donors is not the conventional tripartite mission statement of a college or university to teach, to perform research, and to provide public service. Rather, it is how well the university can convince them that its teaching, researching, and service are addressing societal demands in terms of the social contract between the institution and its constituent community. Over the past 30 years, educational development officers of all stripes have done exactly that—incrementally sold the mission of their institutions in terms of societal demand through countless individual discussions with donors, tens of millions of asks, and millions of gifts.

Reason number five on Panas's list—"Great interest in a specific program"—particularly drives home the special role of the UDO in this process. According to Panas, "Donors wish to give to something that makes a difference, a cause of consequential proportions, a program that has the potential for creating a significant change for good"—that is, something that fulfills the social contract of the institution. "Even a new roof or the replacement of a boiler should be transformed into a selling point of significance. It must be for more than just filling a need. Odds of getting a mega gift are far better if the new roof can be shown to be a reordering of social and human services. The new roof is the steak; serving mankind is the sizzle. Serve the sizzle, not the steak" (1984, 190–191). Looking after the academy's "roofs and boilers"—intellectual disciplines, fields, and programs—is, in fact, the special responsibility of UDOs. Switching metaphors, it is our stock in trade to cook up and serve the sizzle (the points of social relevance) that makes the steak (the disciplines, fields, and programs) so appetizing.

UDOs like me make this case day in and day out in personal terms, tailoring the whole cloth of the institutional social contract to fit the profile of individual donor interest. And as societal power and financial resources become more diffuse, such individual constituent commitment to the social contract at the collegiate and institutional levels becomes more important. Indeed, as the ancient colleges at Oxford and Cambridge especially attest, such constituent commitment incrementally and collectively creates and cements into place an essential bond that can sustain a university for centuries regardless of the political, social, or economic vicissitudes of a given period.

Creating and cementing this bond, this sustaining social contract between individual constituents and the quintessential core of the university—its intellectual and professional disciplines, fields, and programs—is the principal distinguishing function of the UDO. It is a functionality that both aligns the position in terms of the history of western colleges and universities and sets it apart from other forms of development or advancement activity.

As I write these remarks, not long after the tragic events of September 11, 2001, it is already clear that the era in which national security equated simply with economic hegemony is ending and a new era is dawning. The rough beast now slouching toward Bethlehem to be born has not as yet fully revealed itself, but evidence of its presence can already be discerned. The meaning of national security is once again undergoing redefinition, with a redefinition of the terms of the social contract between American society and its colleges and universities certain to follow.

Americans at all levels do not seem to be pressing for more military defense per se (although certainly that need is present) or more economic defense per se (although that need is present as well). Instead, what appears to be called for is some manner of principled and perhaps even spiritual defense of the United States, its democratic institutions, values, and its lifestyle—what columnist George F. Will has described as a patriotic "summons to normalcy." Toward this end, I believe that, in the post 9/11 era, the nation must learn to "wage peace"—to dust off a 1970s buzzword—as competently as it wages war, and perhaps even more so.

By waging peace, I mean attacking the root causes of war, most prominently poverty, ill health, and injustice. Perhaps no institution in American society knows more about these causes and their solutions than do its universities. Waging peace is therefore something American universities understand and at which they can eventually become proficient. Indeed, its traditional tripartite societal mission together with its largely self-generated mission to educate the leadership of the world arguably locate the American university at the forefront of institutions already waging peace against global ignorance, hatred, and evil.

Consequently, it is more than reasonable for Americans to demand that their institutions of higher education demonstrate relevance and obeisance to a concept of national security defined in terms of the elimination of the root cases of terrorism. But implicit in this concept of national security is a need not only for greater international awareness on the part of American universities, but also a greater presence on the global scene. Most institutions are, in fact, already "internationalized," to the extent that they are already dealing with international students, research, and curricula. The need now is for American institutions to be more self-conscious of their international roles, and more proactive in demonstrating their relevance, in the context of contemporary terms of national security, to the social demands of the world, which are essentially identical to the root causes of terrorism—that is, to eliminate ignorance, poverty, and injustice. Indeed, not to recognize and address this need puts not only the institution in peril but the nation as well.

And it will be the unique responsibility of UDOs to educate potential donors at the street level to this new mission and to the vital role that their units play in fulfilling this mission. It will also be their special if not unique responsibility to negotiate with each and every donor individually a new set of personal terms for the social contract that will build and cement the essential bond between their universities and the new generation of donors—in all of its diversity—already within their gates.

The Decentralization Debate

Dealing with diversity, managing technology, and making a new case—these three changes to the worldview of the UDO are all driven by forces external to the university. But the UDO position must also contend with changes driven by internal forces as well, specifically those bound up in the dynamics of the continuing decentralization of university development operations. In 1993, when Hall first documented the terms and scope of the gap in perception between central development office vice presidents and UDOs, she characterized the dialectic at work as a "debate." Today, the debate is essentially over, and, for the most part, the forces promoting decentralization in one form or another have won. In *The Dean's Role in Fund Raising*, Hall hazarded the judgment (based on admittedly slight data) that a decentralized or distributed development strategy did in fact provide a university with a small but significant competitive advantage in terms of dollars raised. Although no one has subsequently determined whether this advantage has held up or even widened, individual institutions nevertheless have voted with their feet overwhelmingly in favor of the decentralized development model.

Moreover, as a result of its perceived success, many universities have extended this model by placing UDOs in interdisciplinary units (such as research labs or program centers) and academic support units (such as libraries or fine arts centers) where donor pools are murky and the potential for conflicting interests among donors is high. Thus far, universities have largely avoided such conflicts, mainly by virtue of the fact that the direct constituencies for interdisciplinary or support units are relatively small and that such units, because of the interdependence of their organizational missions, have made common cause with relevant academic units.

But what happens to this delicate balance of interests when UDOs get assigned to nonacademic units, such as housing or student services? Such positions already exist and in all likelihood will increase. The direct constituencies of such units are vast and can easily overwhelm fragile academic or disciplinary borders, creating the potential for enormous conflicts of interest for donors. It is already too late to just say no to these developments; at any rate, the history of decentralization in the academy suggests that expansion of this type will stop only when it reaches a point of negative returns—and we are a long way from there. Thus, we may have to go further down this path before we all can see that, ultimately, radical decentralization enervates rather than enlarges "the uses of the multiversity," in Kerr's (1982) memorable phrase, atomizing it to the point where overall institutional relevance, if not coherence, no longer effectively exists.

This day of reckoning may be closer than we think, however. What gives me hope is the attention being paid now to integrated marketing, a concept that began appearing in CURRENTS and other trade publications in the late 1990s (see Ahles 1998; Ferrari and Lauer 2000; Lauer 1999; Lawlor 1998; Moore 2000; Pollack 2000; Simpson 1998; VandenBerg 2000). Quite apart from the new techniques and practices it brings to bear, integrated marketing starts with the idea that, in the case of institutions of higher education, there is a core mission and a prescribed set of activities that need to be marketed to customers. "To market" means, fundamentally, to offer for sale. Thus, when we say we are going "to market the university to the customer," we mean that we are going to sell the "products" of the university—its teaching, research, and service—to end-users or purchasers, principally students, employers, clients, funding agencies, and the public.

How do we sell these products to these customers? By convincing them that the product will add value to their lives and careers, to their companies, to their communities, or to the polity as a whole. How do we convince customers that the products of a university add value to their lives and livelihoods? By bringing together and coordinating—integrating—the various mechanisms the university uses to make this sale, including advancement, recruiting, public relations, and programmatic marketing per se. How does integrating these mechanisms affect the dialectics of decentralization? By giving it a comprehensive strategic overview to focus and direct collectively the techniques each mechanism employs. Although it is impossible to see the ultimate outcome of all of these developments from here, the short-term result is clear: more relationships for UDOs to foster, more organizational complexity for UDOs to manage, and more cases for support for UDOs to develop.

And what of the UDO position itself? Now that we have won the decentralization debate, what (if any) are the rewards? In reviewing the status of UDOs today, I am reminded of the ancient Chinese proverb that counsels care in the selection of wishes—because you just might get what you ask for. Doubtless, UDOs over the past three decades have proven their value not just to their units but to their host institutions as well. Their now near ubiquity throughout not just American universities but increasingly within British and Canadian institutions further testifies to their versatility, utility, and success.

But having won the war for their place within the university, UDOs may have lost the battle for the hearts and minds of at least the current generation of central development office vice presidents. Many vice presidents who have been forced down (in their minds) the slippery slope of decentralization by the sheer necessity of meeting increasingly enormous campaign goals nonetheless yet harbor doubts about the wisdom of this course. Their concern centers on whether decentralized development will wind up making the institution less capable of organizing itself to raise the increasing amounts of funds necessary to maintain the momentum of growth and improvement. A number of presidents also fear that decentralized fund raising can affect negatively their ability to control and direct the university's mission and agenda. Such concerns may explain, at least in part, why it is that, even after a generation of existence and proven worth, so few UDOs have graduated to vice presidential ranks. No doubt this too shall pass, but for the moment at least, the UDO career path beyond the level of the unit is a roadbed still under construction.

The Question of Place

An issue that does need to be addressed immediately is the ongoing question of the UDO's rightful place within the university firmament. Whether by virtue of a simple duck test—if it walks like a duck, swims like a duck, and quacks like a duck, it is a duck—or by analysis of the historical functionality of fund raising in the university college presented in this Handbook, the conclusion is the same: UDOs are, or should be, members of the management of the college or unity in which they serve. The only rational argument against this position centers on the issue of control—how can a vice president for development or a university president control and direct resources to institutional needs and priorities without direct supervision of all of the officers responsible for resource generation?

The issue of control of resource development is a very real and vexing one, but to my mind, the solutions we apply, such as hybrid development appointments or dual reporting lines, work only to obscure and confuse the real problem facing the modern university—its collective failure to understand the new demands or market forces being placed on it. Universities in both the United States and Europe have put themselves in danger of becoming less relevant to society, and thus less worthy of societal support.

The solution to this problem does not lie simply in the garnering of more and more resources, but rather in clarifying and communicating institutional missions. Concentrating on the supply side of the equation instead of the demand side, in fact, will only deepen the danger these institutions face, allowing an illusion of relevance to take the place of real reform and change. Rather than focus on issues of control, universities instead need to review, revise, and reinstate the terms of the social contract with their host societies. Once they can demonstrate that their missions are aligned with the demands of society, the resources necessary to support these missions will be forthcoming.

In this process of mission redefinition and alignment, no unit is more critical than that of the university college. When all is said and done, it is the faculty and staff of the university college that must deliver the teaching, research, and service that fulfill the promise of the institutional mission. And the key to empowering the faculty and staff to deliver as promised is the dean.

Good management, whether in corporations or universities, is all about putting decision making and resources at the level where the problem solving must take place. In the modern university, as in the colleges of antiquity, that means putting them at the disposal of the dean. The function of fund raising, like the functions of admissions, curriculum development, or research administration, is one of the management tools that should be at the disposal of the dean, which means that, like these other functions, it needs to be controlled and directed by the dean.

Why, one must ask, is fund raising the one management function to require a separate or dual reporting line to a university-level officer? Is it because it is more complex than enrollment management or more critical than curriculum development? Does it require more coordination between the college and university-level management than does grant administration? Although one could quibble about any one of these questions, by and large the answer in every case clearly is no.

So why do we perpetuate this aberration? Certainly institutional culture and historic precedent and even simple inertia are partial reasons, but the main reason that universities have not relinquished full control of the fund-raising function to deans is because it involves the control of money—or more precisely, the control of money that can be orchestrated and directed by university managers. None of the other management functions conducted by collegiate managers comprise the control of so useful and thus prized a commodity. It is, in fact, as much the utility as the sheer amount of the money garnered by fund raising that makes it so difficult to place the decision making regarding its acquisition at the logical level of problem solving, that is, the university college deanship. And so, by and large, universities make do with hybrid solutions or, in some instances, retain control of fund raising at the institutional level entirely.

But maintaining even partial institutional control also means that the institution must continue to focus on resource acquisition rather concentrating on clarifying the institutional mission and aligning its teaching, research, and service with the demands of its constituent society. In this instance, the tactical advantages provided by private gift donations appear to blind many universities to the strategic advantages of a relevant mission and viable social contract.

Until and unless universities can sort out the relative tactical and strategic advantages of fund raising versus mission management, UDOs will continue to be mere agents of their constituent units rather than full members of their management, perpetually in but never of the college, their line of authority obscured and hence their effectiveness curbed. In the perpetuation of this condition there is, of course, a deep irony, for as the example of the university colleges of Oxbridge have demonstrated for centuries, fund raising at the collegiate level can, in fact, work to define at the street level the social demands by which the mission of the university is made relevant and its social contract kept viable and healthy.

The thread that runs through all these topics is the need for more strategic awareness on the part of UDOs now and in the future. This awareness should be grounded in a thorough working knowledge not only of best practice and tradecraft but also of the historic functionality of fund raising in the academy in general and the university college in particular. Only in this light are all the roles a UDO plays—fund raiser, educator, negotiator—fully revealed. Strategic awareness is further required to fulfill these roles that, collectively and incrementally, build and cement the essential bond between a university and its constituency from generation to generation. Specifically, such awareness enables UDOs to address proactively the position's three fundamental areas of responsibility:

- Establish and maintain a close professional relationship with the dean or unit head and a set of key relationships with unit-affiliated constituencies both inside and outside the college and university;
- Manage the organizational complexity the position inherently entails; and
- Make the case for support of academic and professional disciplines, fields, and programs.

At the end of the day, what it takes to master the role of UDO is the same as what it takes to master any practicing profession—to be a "reflective practitioner," to borrow a phrase coined by Schon (1987). In *Educating the Reflective Practitioner*, Schon argued that skillful professional practice often depends less on factual knowledge or rigid decision-making models than on the capacity to reflect before taking action in cases where established theories do not apply. This ability to perform what he later termed "reflection-in-action"—to learn by doing and to continue to learn by doing through reflection on the "core of artistry" at the heart of any profession—is the key to mastering a profession. It is especially helpful in the case of what Glazer (1974), a sociologist, called the "minor professions" such as fund raising, where defining the competencies and the methods to teach them are still open-ended questions.

With regard to the UDO position, each chapter in this book is an exercise in such reflection-in-action. Each chapter offers hard-won knowledge learned by doing and useful refection on some portion of the core of artistry demonstrated by extraordinary practitioners, each of whom has gone to great pains to disclose candidly and lucidly the knowledge and insight they possess for the benefit of their professional colleagues. To the extent that such case studies of reflection-in-action inspire like reflection in readers, this Handbook will have achieved its intended purpose.

References

Ahles, Catherine B. "Red-Hot Research." CURRENTS, October 1998.

Cohen, David. "Is 'Modern Oxford' a Sign of the Times or an Oxymoron?" *The Chronicle of Higher Education*, January 25, 2002.

Dunlop, D. "Major Gift Programs" in Worth, Michael J., Ed., *Educational Fund Raising: Principles and Practices*. Oryx Press, 1993.

Ferrari, Michael R. & Lauer, Larry D. "Vision of the Future." CURRENTS, April 2000.

Glazer, Nathan. "The Schools of the Minor Professions." *Minerva*, 12(3), 1974.

Hall, Margarete Rooney. *The Dean's Role in Fund Raising*. The Johns Hopkins Press, 1993.

Heidegger, Martin; Lovitt, William, translator. *The Question Concerning Technology and Other Essays*. Harper Books, 1977.

Kerr, Clark. *The Uses of the University*. Harvard University Press, 1982.

Lauer, Larry D. "Marketing Across the Board." CURRENTS, January 1999.

Lawlor, J. "Brand Identity." CURRENTS, October 1998.

Moore, Robert H. "Putting More into Marketing." CURRENTS, April 2000.

Panas, J. *Mega Gifts: Who Gives Them, Who Gets Them*. Bonus Books, 1984.

Pollack, Rachel H. "Signs Point to Yes." CURRENTS, April 2000.

Schon, Donald A. *Educating the Reflective Practitioner*. Jossey-Bass, 1987.

Simpson, Christopher. "The Day We Closed the News Bureau: How Indiana University Survived the Switch from Promotions-Oriented PR to Integrated Marketing." CURRENTS, January 1998.

"Summary of Transatlantic Discussions." *Policy Perspectives*, June 1993.

VandenBerg, Patricia R. "Singular Sensation." CURRENTS, April 2000.

Bibliography

Academic Health Care Fund Raising: Planning and Operating a Successful Development Program. Association for Healthcare Philanthropy, 1996.

Barden, Dennis M. "Two for the Money: Make the Dean Your Partner in Fund Raising," CURRENTS, June 1988.

Buchanan, Peter McE., Ed. *Handbook of Institutional Advancement.* Council for Advancement and Support of Education, 2000.

Burlingame, Dwight, Ed. *Library Fundraising: Models for Success.* American Library Association, 1995.

Carnie, Christopher. "Fund-Raising Renaissance: After Years of Public Funding, European Institutions Are Once Again Seeking Private Support. But What Will They Find?" CURRENTS, October 1999.

Collins, Mary Ellen. "Orchestrating a Harmonious Campaign: Flexibility, Trust, and a Positive Attitude Helped UVA Complete a Unified Campaign at a Decentralized Institution," CURRENTS, April 2001.

Corson-Finnerty, Adam and Laura Blanchard. *Fundraising and Friend-Raising on the Web.* American Library Association, 1998.

Dewey, Barbara. *Raising Money for Academic and Research Libraries: How-to-Do-It Manual for Librarians.* Neal-Schuman Publishers, 1991.

Eckert, Gerald, and Rachel H. Pollack. "Sowing the Seeds of Philanthropy: Deans and Faculty Members Have a Crucial Role to Play in Developing Private Institutional Support," CURRENTS, September 2000.

Estey, Gretta P. and Steve Wilkerson. "Harmonious Arrangements: Your Institution's Character May Set the Tone for a Centralized Ensemble—Or a Decentralized Collection of Soloists," CURRENTS, June 1994.

Hall, Margarete Rooney. *The Dean's Role in Fund Raising.* Johns Hopkins University Press, 1993.

Hall, Margarete Rooney. "The Decentralization of Development: Impact on Power, Priorities, Faculty Perceptions," *Teachers College Record*, Spring 1992.

Hayter, Scott. "Stranger in a Strange Land: A North American Learns Advancement in the UK," CURRENTS, October 2000.

Hillman, Lucille. *Fund Raising and Law Library Development.* Glanville Publishers Inc., 1998.

Hogan, Lynn K. "Fund Raising at Academic Medical Centers," in *Handbook of Institutional Advancement*. Council for Advancement and Support of Education, 2000.

Kelly, John. "From a Sprinkle to a Shower: Once Rare, Education Fund Raising Has Taken Off in Continental Europe," CURRENTS, October 2000.

Kelly, Thomas F. "Organization of the Development Program," in *Handbook of Institutional Advancement*, Peter McE. Buchanan, Ed. Council for Advancement and Support of Education, 2000.

Kerber, Beth-Ann. *How to Raise More Money for Your Healthcare Organization*. Health Resources Publishing, 1996.

Lowenstein, Ralph L. *Pragmatic Fund-Raising for College Administrators and Development Officers*. University Press of Florida, 1997.

Mercer, Joye. "Fund Raising Has Become a Job Requirement for Many Deans: Officials Who Used to Focus on Academic Issues Find Themselves Courting Potential Donors," *Chronicle of Higher Education*, July 18, 1997.

Murphy, Mary Kay, Ed. *Building Bridges: Fund Raising for Deans, Faculty, and Development Officers*. Council for Advancement and Support of Education, 1992.

Murphy, Mary Kay. "Multiply and Be Fruitful: Making the Most of Deans and Faculty in Development," CURRENTS, September 1993.

Murphy, Mary Kay. "The Role of Academic Leaders in Advancement," in *Handbook of Institutional Advancement*, Peter McE. Buchanan, Ed. Council for Advancement and Support of Education, 2000.

Netherton, Robin Goldman. "First-Rate Findings: Two Award-Winning Studies Explore Decentralized Fund Raising and the Uses of Alumni Research," CURRENTS, November/December 1990.

Phelan, Joseph F., Ed. *College and University Foundations: Serving America's Public Higher Education*. Association of Governing Boards of Universities and Colleges, 1997.

Rhodes, Frank H. T., Ed. *Successful Fund Raising for Higher Education: The Advancement of Learning*. ACE/Oryx Press, October 1997.

Sabo, Sandra R. "A Fertile Climate: Essential Elements for Raising the Green," CURRENTS, June 1994.

Sabo, Sandra R. "Hybrids in Bloom: Taking One Cutting from the Centralized Model and Another from the Decentralized Has Blossomed into Fund-Raising Success for Some Institutions," CURRENTS, June 1994.

Sandberg, J. Robert. "Organizing Your Operation: Which Model Will Help You Attract the Most Gifts from Doctors, Lawyers, Indian Chiefs?," CURRENTS, March 1985.

Sevier, Robert A. *Strategic Planning in Higher Education: Theory and Practice*. Council for Advancement and Support of Education, 2000.

Steele, Victoria and Stephen D. Elder. *Becoming a Fundraiser: The Principles and Practices of Library Development*. American Library Association, 1992.

Taylor, Martha A. "Making Beautiful Music: To Involve Deans and Activate Donors, Consider a Centralized Yet Coordinated Approach," CURRENTS, March 1985.

Toy, Laura L. and Kathleen E. Loehr. "Shifting Gears: A Project-Team Approach to Major Gift Fund Raising Offers Flexibility, Efficiency, and Results—Without a Campaign," CURRENTS, November/December 2000.

Wentworth, Eric B. "A Primer on Institutionally Related Foundations," in *Handbook of Institutional Advancement*, Peter McE. Buchanan, Ed. Council for Advancement and Support of Education, 2000.

Worth, Michael J., Ed. *Educational Fund Raising: Principles and Practice*. ACE/Oryx Press, 1993.

Worth, Michael J. "Positioning the Institution for Successful Fund Raising," in *Handbook of Institutional Advancement*, Peter McE. Buchanan, Ed. Council for Advancement and Support of Education, 2000.

Worth, Michael J. and James W. Asp II. *The Development Officer in Higher Education: Toward an Understanding of the Role*. ASHE-ERIC Higher Education Report No. 4, 1994.

Contributors

F. A. Hilenski

Hilenski entered the advancement field in 1974 when, fresh out of graduate school, he became director of external relations in the College of Liberal Arts at the University of Tennessee, Knoxville. He has since served as associate dean for grants and development in the College of Liberal Arts at the University of South Carolina and as director of development for the College of Architecture at the Georgia Institute of Technology (Georgia Tech). Hilenski is currently director of development and communication for Ivan Allen College at Georgia Tech.

Hilenski received his Ph.D. in English Literature in 1974 from the University of Tennessee, Knoxville. In 1983–1984 he was a Fund for the Improvement of Postsecondary Education Mina Shaughnessy Post-doctoral Fellow at the Harvard School of Education, where his studies were directed by Nathan Glazer and David Reisman. In 1993 he received the so-called CASE Fulbright Fellowship for research in the United Kingdom, becoming the first-ever Fulbright scholar in residence at the University of Hull to study the impact of European Union research and educational policy on British universities. In 1999 Hilenski was accredited as an Advanced Certified Fund Raising Executive by the Association of Fundraising Professionals (AFP), and he is also a member of the AFP International Committee. The author of several articles and reviews on advancement, this is his first publication for CASE Books.

James W. Asp II

Asp is executive director of development at Memorial Sloan-Kettering Cancer Center in New York City. Prior to joining Memorial Sloan-Kettering, Asp spent more than 20 years in development positions at several colleges and universities, including the George Washington University; the University of California, Irvine; and, most recently, Sarah Lawrence College, as vice president for college resources. He is the author of a number of chapters and articles and co-author of *The Development Officer in Higher Education: Toward an Understanding of the Role* (ASHE-ERIC Higher Education Report No. 4, 1994). Asp holds degrees from the University of Minnesota and the George Washington University.

Lawrance Bailey

Bailey is senior director of development for the Scripps Institution of Oceanography at the University of California, San Diego (UCSD). In his early life, he was a writer/researcher for the ABC television game show *Split Second*. His career with the University of California spans more than 20 years—seven years in film and television at UCLA Extension, five years in community affairs and development with the College of Medicine at UC Irvine, three years as associate director of development with UCSD Health Sciences, and, since 1994, development director at Scripps.

Pamela Cook

With 20 years' experience in corporate community relations and nonprofit fund raising, Cook has since 2000 consulted with nonprofit organizations in capital campaign planning and executive search. As community relations manager for the Clorox Company, she oversaw its foundation and disaster relief efforts. For 10 years she worked in higher education fund raising as associate dean of development for the University of Virginia College of Arts and Sciences and as director of individual giving for the Stanford University School of Engineering. She was director of development for the California Academy of Sciences and campaign division director for United Way of Santa Clara County. She was president of the board of the Golden Gate Chapter of the Association of Fundraising Professionals. Cook is a graduate of Duke University (B.A.), University of Virginia (M.A.), and she was a Fulbright Scholar at the Australian National University.

Molly Ford Croft

Croft is the director of development for the Wallace H. Coulter Department of Biomedical Engineering at the Georgia Institute of Technology (Georgia Tech) and Emory University, a partnership between a public and a private university that is the first of its kind in the United States. Croft previously served as director of development for the College of Computing at Georgia Tech, another interdisciplinary program. Croft's first position in higher education was as program director with CASE in Washington, DC. Croft has served on a number of boards, including the Atlanta chapter of the Association of Fundraising Professionals.

Amy Doonan Cronin

Currently chief of staff and special assistant to the president at the University of Virginia, Cronin has worked in the advancement field for 20 years. Prior to joining the president's staff, she was director of individual gifts for the University of Virginia College and Graduate School of Arts and Sciences. Cronin's earlier development experience includes stints as director of annual support at Hobart and William Smith Colleges, and director of annual programs and assistant to the campaign director at the University System of Maryland. Cronin holds a master's degree in public relations from the University of Maryland and is accredited in public relations. Early in her career, she was sports information director at her undergraduate alma mater, Ithaca College, and at Hobart and William Smith Colleges.

John W. Crowe

Currently serving as vice president for advancement at Claremont Graduate University, Crowe has 30 years of experience in higher education working in press relations, publications, alumni, admissions, and development. Before coming to Claremont in 2001, Crowe spent 16 years at the University of Southern California where his various positions included executive director of development at the Keck School of Medicine and senior associate dean for external affairs at the Marshall School of Business. Crowe has also served as a manager at California State University, Dominguez Hills, and at Harvey Mudd College. Crowe is a frequent CASE faculty member specializing in topics such as major gifts, campaign planning, and board development. He is a member of the CASE District VII board.

Dwain N. Fullerton

Fullerton is senior associate dean emeritus at the School of Engineering, Stanford University. During his career he served as vice president for institute relations at the California Institute of Technology and worked on three Stanford capital campaigns. He has experience in almost all phases of educational fund raising, ranging from annual fund activities to solicitation of million-dollar-plus gifts. During the Stanford Centennial Campaign, Fullerton was the engineering school's lead development officer in solicitations for the Paul Allen Center for Integrated Systems Building, the William Gates Computer Science Building, and more than 20 endowed professorships, two of which came from Japan. He holds B.A. and M.A. degrees from Stanford, and he was a Fulbright Scholar.

Marta Garcia

Like many development professionals, Garcia came to the field serendipitously. After completing their educations at Indiana University, she and her husband moved to Lima, Peru, where her fund-raising activities remained at the volunteer level. When the family moved to New York, Garcia joined the Vassar College Development Office, ultimately becoming regional director of development and major gifts. In 1996 Garcia joined the Georgia Institute of Technology as director of development for the College of Engineering. In 1999 she assumed the position of assistant vice president of development, where she now supervises all development activities in the six Georgia Tech colleges, including the nine schools in the College of Engineering and the Ferst Center for the Arts. In addition receiving a degree in Russian and graduate studies at Indiana University, Garcia has studied at several universities in Central and South America, and she has attended professional seminars and programs throughout her career.

Paul Gardner

In 1998 Gardner was named director of development at the School of Dentistry of the University of North Carolina-Chapel Hill and executive director of the Dental Foundation of North Carolina, Inc. In 1986 Gardner graduated from the UNC-Chapel Hill School of Journalism and Mass Communication and from 1989 to 1998 was responsible for directing the school's development and alumni affairs program. Gardner served as an assistant sports information director at the Georgia Institute of Technology (Georgia Tech) 1986–1987, assistant director of development at Georgia Tech in 1987–1988, and assistant director of development at the University of Chicago 1988–1989. In 1989, at the age of 25, Gardner returned to the UNC-Chapel Hill School of Journalism and Mass Communication to become the university's youngest director of development. Later, he was named assistant to the dean for development and alumni affairs and was subsequently promoted to assistant dean for development and alumni affairs.

Margarete Rooney Hall

Hall has been in university advancement for more than 20 years. She is currently a professor in the Department of Public Relations at the University of Florida, teaching graduate-level courses in philanthropy and fund raising and undergraduate-level courses in public relations strategy. Serving as vice president for institutional advancement at Gallaudet University for almost a decade before beginning her professorial adventures, she was also vice president for advancement at Mount Saint Mary's College (Maryland)

and director of development at the University of Maryland Business School. Hall's doctoral research on the decentralization of development in research universities received the Grenzebach Award and resulted in a widely acclaimed book, *The Dean's Role in Fund Raising* (Johns Hopkins University Press, 1993). A frequent speaker at academic and professional conferences, Hall is now doing research on measuring the outcomes of community relations and corporate giving programs as well as on the role of fund raisers in establishing mutually beneficial relationships between organizations and their donors.

John C. Halton III

Halton, assistant dean for college relations in the College of Engineering at the University of Texas at Austin (UT-Austin), is a fine example of someone who has a very comprehensive liberal arts background, yet who is able to function in the "black magic world" of science and technology. His bachelor's degrees are in political science and English. He has master's degrees in theology and journalism, the latter from UT-Austin. Halton has been with the University of Texas more than 25 years. He has worked in the College of Engineering in fund raising for the last 14 years and previously served in the central development office.

Scott Hayter

A graduate of the Royal Military College in Canada, Hayter started his career in the Canadian military in 1976. He moved to the private-school sector in 1988 as deputy head of a boy's boarding school in Niagara, Ontario, where he was responsible for, among many other things, fund raising and alumni affairs. In 1995 he became an associate director of external relations, with primary responsibility for fund raising, at Brock University, Ontario, where he also completed a master's degree in Educational Administration. Hayter joined the University of Durham, England, in 1997 to lead the Development and Alumni Relations Office, which functions as part of a larger integrated-income generation team at the university. Hayter is a frequent speaker on higher-education development issues in the United Kingdom, Europe, and North America, and he has consulted to a number of universities and independent schools.

Guy Mallabone

Mallabone's career in the nonprofit sector spans 22 years and has included senior fundraising positions in the arts, social services, and higher education. He currently serves as the vice president of external relations for the Southern Alberta Institute of Technology in Calgary. He sits on the international board of directors for the Association of

Fundraising Professionals and on the newly independent board of directors for Certified Fund Raising Executive International. A master's graduate in philanthropy and development from St. Mary's University in Minnesota, Mallabone serves as the vice chair of the province of Alberta's charitable advisory committee, is a board member of the Canadian Centre for Social Entrepreneurship, and is an adjunct professor at Grant MacEwan College in Edmonton, Alberta.

Bayley Mason

Mason has more than 40 years' experience in academic fund raising. He retired from Harvard in 1995, but he continues to teach a course in fund raising that he created a dozen years ago at Harvard University Extension School. Mason began his development career at Harvard in 1960, at the Harvard Medical School, and in 1965 he became its first full-time assistant dean for development. From 1971 to 1974 he served as administrative vice president of Oberlin College and then returned east as vice president for development at Boston University. Mason returned to Harvard in 1980 to serve for a decade as associate dean for resources at the John F. Kennedy School of Government. He completed his formal development duties in the central development office, retiring as director of corporate and foundation relations. Mason has been a faculty member for CASE and a founding director of the Investor Responsibility Research Center.

Scott Nichols

Since 1986, Nichols has served as dean for development, alumni affairs, and communications for Harvard Law School. Previously, he worked in advancement at DePaul, Northwestern, and Bucknell universities. He is the chair emeritus of the Section on Institutional Advancement of the American Association of Law Schools, an Executive Committee member of the American Bar Association, and an involved member of CASE, where he currently serves as trustee and as chair of the International Committee of the Board. Nichols has co-authored several books, was a contributing author for the *Handbook of Institutional Advancement* (CASE 1986), and frequently lectures on development. He teaches an annual fund-raising course at the Harvard University Extension School and the module on philanthropy at the Harvard Institute for Educational Management. Nichols holds a doctorate in educational administration from the University of Pennsylvania.

Dottie O'Carroll

With a background in the media, corporate, and nonprofit communications at the *Los Angeles Times*, Moshe Safdie and Associates, and the International Design Conference in Aspen, O'Carroll launched a professional career in university development at the University of Southern California (USC). She is currently director of development for the USC Development Consortium, a department within the Office of University Advancement that manages fund-raising campaigns for multiple units on campus. In that capacity, she has developed strategies for integrating public relations programs into the development plans for units new to the campaign process. She is currently leading the USC Building on Excellence Campaign for the School of Architecture and its two historic houses.

Tania Jane Rawlinson

Since 1998 Rawlinson has been development director at University College, Oxford, covering a full range of advancement activities. She also serves as a consultant to Magdalen and Somerville Colleges (Oxford) on fund raising and strategic planning, is a CASE volunteer, and is a member of the PotWeb Development Committee at Oxford's Ashmolean Museum. Prior to her work in Oxford, Rawlinson was the head of development operations at the English National Opera, and she also worked in major gifts at the State University of New York at Albany. Rawlinson holds degrees from Dartmouth College and Oxford University.

James C. Schroeder

Appointed chair of the Mayo Foundation Department of Development in 2001, Schroeder manages the fund-raising program for all three Mayo Clinic locations: Rochester, MN; Jacksonville, FL; and Scottsdale, AZ. Schroeder previously served as executive director of external relations at the Harvard Business School and as associate dean for development in the College of Arts and Sciences at the University of Illinois at Urbana-Champaign. At the same institution, he served as associate dean for planning and budget, and as assistant dean for administration. Schroeder earned a B.A. degree in Political Science and History at Miami University (Ohio). He earned an M.A. degree in Political Science and a Ph.D. degree in Higher Education Administration from the University of Toledo.

Timothy L. Seiler

Seiler is director of Public Service and the Fund Raising School and assistant professor of philanthropic studies for the Center on Philanthropy at Indiana University. Formerly vice president of the Indiana University Foundation, Seiler was a major gifts officer for university development. An alumnus of the Fund Raising School, Seiler has been a faculty member since 1986 and director since 1994. He teaches customized contract programs as well as core curriculum courses and frequently makes conference and seminar presentations nationally and internationally. Seiler has authored and edited numerous fund-raising publications and is currently co-editor of the quarterly journal *New Directions for Philanthropic Fundraising*. He is editor-in-chief of the new Excellence in Fundraising Workbook Series and author of the series workbook *Developing Your Case for Support* (Jossey-Bass 2000). Seiler serves on the board of the Indiana Youth Institute and the University Faculty Club and is a member of the Wallace Chair Advisory Committee of the American College, PA.

Peter Slee

Since 1993 Slee has been director of marketing and corporate communications at the University of Durham, England, where he is responsible for developing and implementing policies for research, income generation, regional outreach, development and alumni relations, student recruitment, and public relations. His public relations team has won eight major design awards, and he has pioneered the idea of "integrated income generation" in the United Kingdom. Slee, who earned his Ph.D. at the University of Cambridge, began his career as an historian at the universities of Manchester and Durham, writing the prize-winning book, *Learning and a Liberal Education* (Manchester University Press) in 1986. He left higher education in 1989 to work as a policy adviser at the Confederation of British Industry in London before returning to Durham to develop its links with business and industry. In 1991 he became director of university relations at Aston University.

Harry Vann

Vann has been successfully involved with corporate relations in the School of Electrical and Computer Engineering at the Georgia Institute of Technology (Georgia Tech) since 1995, first as the manager of the school's industry partnership program and then as director of corporate relations. He led Georgia Tech's effort to establish a process for valuing large software gifts and was heavily involved in finalizing the institute's first gift of corporate intellectual property. He has presented at the Engineering Development

Forum on the establishment of industrial affiliate programs and on intellectual property issues for corporate development officers, and he was an invited co-speaker on the latter issue at Morgan State University's Conference 2000.

Index

Abrams, Deborah Blackmore, 3
Academic development officer (ADO), vii.
    See also Development offices; Unit
    development officer (UDO)
Academic support units, 199–206
        benefits of, 203–204
        challenges for development, 200–201
        defining constituencies for, 201–202
        making the case for supporting,
            202–203
        multiplier effect, 204–205
        WIIFM (What's in it for me?) factor,
            204
Academic units, 185–198
        case statements for development,
            189–193
        institutional planning, 188–189
        supporting development in support
            units, 202
An Act for Setting of the Poor on Work and
    for the Avoiding of Idleness, 221
An Act for the Punishment of Vagabonds and
    for Relief of the Poor and Impotent, 221
An Act for the Relief of the Poor, 221
Advancement offices, 83, 105, 223. *See also*
    Development offices
Alumni, 78
        and academic support units, 201, 202
        affairs offices, 82–83
        among corporations, 181
        in Canada, 225–226

communicating case statements to,
    194, 195
as core constituents of universities, 172
diversity amongst, 241–243
focusing on, 81
foundations, 167
managing relations with, 144–145
as the most prominent donors, 98
as prospective donors, 141–142
relationship with faculty, 88
social contracts with, 35–36
in the United Kingdom, 230, 231–232
as volunteers, 159
working with current students, 163
American College Public Relations
    Association (ACPRA), 21, 39
Angell, James B., 11
Anticipating future needs, 65–68. *See also*
    Future course of unit development
Arthur Daniels Midlands, 180
Ashton, R., 45
Asp, James W., II, x, 49
Assessment of aptitude of for development,
    58–61. *See also* Evaluation
Assiniboine Community College, Brandon,
    Manitoba, 223
AutoCAD, 177

Balliol College, A History: 1263-1939
    (Jones), 1
Balliol College, Oxford, 1–3

Baltimore Federated Charities, 20
Best practice recommendations
    academic support units, 205–206
    campaigns, 158–159
    campus relationships, 74
    case statements for development, 198
    corporations, 182–183
    creating a unit development office, 138
    dedicated research and service units,
        217–218
    foundations, 167–168
    hiring, training and evaluation, 115
    interdisciplinary programs and consor-
        tia of universities, 94–95
    management, 150–151
    professional contacts, 101
    relationships with development offices,
        84–85
    synergy for development, 125
Board of directors, 143–144, 164–165, 180
Borrowed clout, 70–71
Boston University, 76
Branding, 149
Bristol University, UK, 233
British universities, 7, 8
Brittingham, Barbara E., x, 6
Bureaucracy, faculty dealing with, 71
Butler, Nicholas Murray, 10

Cambridge University, 7, 231, 234–236
Campaign management, 19–20, 107, 153–159
    planning and coordinating, 154–156
    public relations, 15–16, 18, 21
    strategies for, 157
The Campus Green: Fund Raising in Higher
    Education (Brittingham and Pezzullo), x
Campus relationships, 65–74
    deans of colleges, 68–69. See also Deans
        of colleges
    department heads, 69–71
    faculty, 71–72
    signs of trouble in, 74
Canada, 221–228
    advancement services, 227–228
    alumni relations, 225–226

centralized vs. decentralized
    development offices, 224–225
differences between development
    programs, 222–223
English law, 221–222
fund raising campaigns in, 226–227
government relations, 225
terminology, 223–224
Capital campaigns, 154
Career professionals, 173
Carnegie, Andrew, 11–12
Carson, Barrett, 92
CASE Fulbright Fellowships, 1
Case statements, 186, 189–193
    academic support units, 203
    best practice recommendations,
        217–218
    communicating, 193–197
    emphasizing institutional relationships,
        214
    for research and service units, 208–210,
        215–216
Catalysts, 50–51, 56
Centralized unit development offices, 33,
    75–84
    in Canada, 224–225
    compared to unit development
        officers, 110
    compared with decentralized units,
        41–42
    controlling access to presidents, 80
    evolution of unit development officers,
        39–40
    foundations, 165–166
    fund raising campaigns, 156–157
    hiring individuals from, 108
    knowledge of institution, 104
    operational issues of, 42–43
    relationship with unit development
        officers, 76–77, 105
    research on, 44–46
    tensions between public relations and
        alumni affairs, 82–83
    at the University of Edinburgh, UK,
        234

Chairs of departments, 69–71
Charity, 4
Chief advancement officers, 45
The Chronicle of Philanthropy (Summerfield), 232
Church Pension Fund Campaign, 15–16
Clap, Thomas, 8
Claremont Graduate University, 144
Clients, 97–98, 173
Clinton, Bill, 246
Closely held corporations, 179
Cold War, 246
College presidents, 8
    in Canada, 226
    centralized development offices, 39–40
    controlling access to, 80
    hiring campaign managers, 19–20
    in the Industrial Age, 12
Colleges in Canada, 223–224
Colonial era of fund-raising, 6–8
Communications, 82, 84
    in Canada, 227
    case statements for development, 193–197, 209–210
    foundations, 162–163
    international agencies, 101
    management, 148
Competitiveness, 91
Concordia University, Montreal, 223
Consortia of universities, 87, 92–94
Constituencies, 171–183. *See also* Alumni
    defining, 171–174
    defining corporate, 174–180
Contracts
    with administration, 70
    with donors, 3
    with faculty, 72
Cook, Pamela, 129
Cooperation between departments, 91
Cooperation between universities, 99
Cornell University, 11
Corporations, 19, 174–180
    areas of concern, 180–182
    complex relationships, 179–180
    as donors, 98

managing relations with, 145–146
types of motivation for giving, 176–179
Council for Advancement and Support of Education (CASE), 99, 230
Council of Colleges of Arts and Sciences, 99
Creation of a unit development office, 129–138
    keys to success, 136–138
    pitfalls of, 135–136
    resources for, 133–135
    succeeding at, 131–133
Credibility, 211
Croft, Molly Ford, 87, 99
Crossover giving, 104
Crowe, John W., 139
Cutlip, Scott M., 12, 13
    on Harvard University's 1919-20 fund-raising, 17
    on the Washington YMCA campaign, 14

Deadlines, 67
Deans of colleges, 25–26, 68–69
    anticipating needs of, 65
    assessment of unit's needs, 60–61
    case statements for development, 194, 196
    completed staff work to, 66–67
    foundations, 164–165
    fund raising expertise, 42
    future course of development, 254
    at Harvard University, 79–80
    institutional planning, 189
    relationship with unit development officers, 31–33, 43–44, 94, 131
    reputation of, 130
    signaling the importance of development, 110
    signs of trouble in relationships with, 74
    working with faculty, 89
The Dean's Role in Fund Raising (Rooney), vii, x
    history of fund-raising, 5

promotion of decentralization, 250
relationship between unit development
  officers and deans, 31
Decentralized development offices. *See*
  Centralized unit development offices; Unit
  development officer (UDO)
Dedicated research and service units,
  207–218
    case statements for development,
      215–216
    challenges for development, 213
    clarifying funding sources, 214–215
    creating a case for development,
      207–213
    creating ownership for development,
      212–213
    establishing credibility, 211
    establishing institutional context, 214
Dell, 178
Dental Foundation of North Carolina, 161,
  162
Department heads, 69–71
*Design for Giving: The Story of the National
  War Fund, Inc.* (Seymour), x, 18
*Designs for Fund Raising: Principles, Patterns,
  Techniques* (Seymour), x, 18
*The Development Officer in Higher Education:
  Toward an Understanding of the Role*
  (Worth and Asp), x
*The Development Officer's Role in Higher
  Education* (Worth and Asp), 50
Development offices, 21–23
    centralized, 24–25. *See also* Centralized
      unit development offices
    compared with unit development
      offices, 37
Disciplinary focus, 33–34
Distance education, 196
Diversity in universities, 241–243
Donors to institutions, 42–43
    academic support units, 201–202
    alumni as, 98. *See also* Alumni
    case statements to, 194
    communication of case statements, 195

diversity amongst, 243
foundations, 162
likely candidates as, 60
meeting students, 163–164
partisan, 192
solicitations to, 134
Drafts of work, 67
Duncan, Robert F., 17
Dunlop, David, x
DuPont, 180
Durham Integrated Income Generation
  Model for Fund Raising, 117–125
    Ogden Centre for Fundamental
      Physics, 121–123
    synergy for development, 119–121
    Wolfson Research Institute, 123–124
Duronio, M. A., 45

Eaton, Nathaniel, 7
Educating the Reflective Practitioner (Schon),
  254
Education of development officers, 103–104
*Educational Fund Raising: Principles and
  Practice* (Worth, Ed.), x
*Educational Fund Raising: Principles and
  Practice* (Worth, Ed.), 82
Eisenhower, Dwight D., 157
Eliot, Charles W., 11, 12
Elizabethan laws, 221–222
Emerson, Guy, 17
Emory University, 87, 92–93
Engineering Development Forum, 99
English law, 221–222
Episcopal Church, 15–16
Erfahrung (knowledge), viii
Estey, Gretta P., 44
European Regional Development Fund
  (ERDF), 124
European universities, 99, 117–118. *See also*
  United Kingdom of Great Britain
Evaluation, 114
    aptitude of for development, 58–61
    of unit development officer's
      performance, 132

Events, 175, 203
Evolution of the unit development officer, 39–46
    decentralization vs. centralization, 41–42, 44–46. *See also* Centralized unit development offices
    operational issues of, 42–43
External vectors, 54–55
Exxon Valdez, 181
ExxonMobil, 180

Faculty, 71–72
    corporate relations with, 181–182
    development in Canada, 223
    diversity amongst, 243
    and foundations, 164
    fund raising, 130–131
    interdisciplinary programs, 88–90
    protocol for dealing with, 94, 136
    to student ratio, 191
Financial aid to students, 191
Fischer, Terry, ix
Five I's of fund raising, 91, 109, 239
Foundations, 161–168
    centralized development offices, 165–166
    deans of colleges, 164–165
    faculty, 164
    management of finances, 166–167
    marketing and communications, 162–163
    other responsibilities, 167
    students, 163–164
Fullerton, Dwain N., 129
Fund raising
    amongst diverse groups of people, 242
    campaigns, 153–159. See also Campaign management
    in Canada, 226–227
    case statements for, 194. *See also* Case statements
    centralized development office campaigns, 156–157
    with corporations, 98
    Durham Integrated Income

Generation Model, 117–125
    projects, 154
    in the United Kingdom, 230, 232, 233–236
    University of Alberta, Edmonton, 224–225
Funding sources, 214–215. *See also* Donors to institutions; Prospect research
Future course of unit development, 239–255
    decentralization vs. centralization, 250–252
    diversity in universities, 241–243
    Pew Report, 245–246
    place within universities, 252–255
    technology, 243–245

Galleries, 203. *See also* Academic support units
Galzer, Nathan, x
Garcia, Marta, 103
Gardner, Paul, 161
Gateway, 178
Georgia Institute of Technology, 35, 87
    contacts per month, 113
    faculty in fund-raising, 89
    and Motorola company, 177
    program with Emory University, 92–93
    skills of development officers, 103
    unit development officer at, 108
    vice president of development, 92
German universities, 11
Gifts to institutions, 3, 42–43. *See also* Donors to institutions
Ginger, Mina C., 21
Government, Canadian, 225
Graduate schools, 187, 190, 191
Grady, Henry, 92
Grants, 167
Great Awakening, 8, 20
Great Britain, 229–237. *See also* United Kingdom of Great Britain
Greenbrier Report, 22, 23, 25, 41
Greenspan, Alan, 209
Grenzebach Glier & Associates, 153
Grunig, S. D., 44
Gulliver's Travels (Swift), 180

Hall, Margaret Rooney, vii, x, 5, 39
    on centralized development offices, 25
    on college presidents, 7
    on decentralized development offices, 250
    on research universities, 33
Halton, John C., III, 65
Handbook, viii
Harvard, John, 7
Harvard University, 6, 11
    adding central support services, 80
    centralized development campaign of, 42
    credibility of, 214
    fund campaign of 1919-1920, 16
    fund raising in the 1960's, 77
    hiring John Price Jones, 17
    memorandum on decentralized fund-raising at, 75
    university-wide campaign in the 1990's, 79–80
    William Lawrence working with, 18
Hayter, Scott, 117
Heidegger, Martin, 244
Hewlett-Packard, 178
Hilenski, F. A., 1, 31, 239
Hilton, Anthony, 231
Hiring campaign managers and unit development officers, 60, 107–109. *See also* Unit development officer (UDO)
History of university fund-raising, 1–27
    early American colleges, 6–11
    emergence of unit development officers, 23–26
    modern American universities, 11–19
    role of fund raisers, 19–23
Honeywell, 180
Hospitals, 207–208
Hybrid development offices, 41

Identification, 91, 109, 239
Indiana University, 199
Industrial Revolution, 11
Information, 91, 109, 239
Interdisciplinary programs, 87–92, 104

differences between programs, 108
faculty for, 88–90
schools and colleges within universities, 90–92
Interest, 91, 109, 239
Internal vectors, 53–54
International relationships, 100–101
    corporations, 178–179
    management of, 145–146
Internships, 179–180
Investment, 91, 109, 230, 239
Investments, 166. *See also* Foundations
Involvement, 91, 109, 239

Joint Infrastructure Fund (JIF), 122, 123
Joint Research Equipment Initiative (JREI), 122, 123
Jones, John, 1, 2
Jones, John Price, 16–17, 18, 239

Kelly, Thomas F., 44–45
Kerr, Clark, 26
Ketchum, Marts and Lundy, 18
Key relationships. *See* Relationships of the unit development officer
Kissinger, Henry, 83

Lauglo, Jon, 46
Lawrence, William, 12, 15–16, 18, 19, 239
Leaders, 51–52, 57
Lee, Ivey, 15–16
Legislative support, 175
Liberal arts education, 190
Liberty Loan campaign, 17
Libraries, 199–200, 203. *See also* Academic support units
Loessin, B. A., 45
Lucas, Colin, 241

Management, 139–151
    alumni and parent relations, 144–145
    board of directors, 143–144
    campaigns, 153–159. See also Campaign management
    communications, 148–149

corporate relations, 145–146
at different universities, 93
of foundations, 166–167
marketing, 148–149
of prospects, 141–142
solicitation clearances to donors,
142–143. *See also* Solicitations
special events, 147
staffing, 140–141
styles of, 73
Managers, 51, 56–57
Mann, Horace, 18
Marketing, 148–149, 162–163
Marshall School of Business, 139
Mason, Bayley, 23–24, 75
Mass communications, 197. *See also*
Communications
McCormack, Samuel Black, 15
Meetings, 110–111
Mega Gifts: Who Gives Them, Who Gets Them
(Panas), 247
Mergers among corporations, 181
Michigan University, 11
Microsoft, 244
Military defenses, 246, 249
Mission statements, 138, 211–212
donors to institutions, 247
for teaching, 215
Motivation for unit development officers, 113
Motorola, 177
Museums, 203. *See also* Academic support
units

National Aeronautical and Space
Administration (NASA), 210
Nichols, Scott, 83, 153
Nietzsche, Friedrich Wilhelm, viii
North American Review, 11
Nottingham University, 231

O'Carroll, Dottie, 171
Ogden Centre for Fundamental Physics,
121–123
Orlansky, D., 46
Overlapping vectors, 55–56

Oxford University, 232, 234–236, 241

Paid solicitors, 20, 21, 239
Panas, J., 247
Parents, 172–173
Particle Physics and Economic Support
Services (PPARC), 122, 123
Patients, 173
Patrons, 97–98, 173
Paustenbaugh, J., 45
Pennington, Simon, 234
Performance evaluations, 132
Performing arts, 203
Pew Charitable Trusts, 245–246
Pezzullo, Thomas R., x, 6
Philanthropy, 4
in America, 6
Elizabethan laws, 221–222
identifying donor interest, 173
objectives for gifts, 84
and technology, 244
in the United Kingdom, 121, 229–230
Pierce, Lyman L., 13, 14, 239
Planning campaigns, 154–156. *See also*
Campaign management
Polytechnic students, 231
Positioning, 149
Princeton University, 40
Print media, 197
Private universities, 186–188
Professional contacts, 97–102
international agencies, 100–101
patrons and clients, 97–98
peer institutions, 99
trade and professional associations,
100
Professional corporations, 179. *See also*
Corporations
Professional schools, 186, 191, 193, 196
Project fund raising, 154
Proposals, 215
Prospect research, 81, 84, 133–134
case statements for development, 193
communication of case statements, 195
coordination of, 158

identifying, 137
management of, 141–142
Public relations, 20, 21
    changing the American university, 18
    Church Pension Fund Campaign,
      15–16
    tensions with unit development offices,
      82–83
Public universities, 186–188, 222
Puritans, 8
Pusey, Nathan, 77

Quality, 68
Queen's University, Kingston, Ontario, 223

Rawlinson, Tania Jane, 229
Recruitment of unit development officers,
    107–109
Regional officers for development, 79
Relationships of the unit development officer,
    65–102
    campus, 65–74. *See also* Campus
      relationships
    centralized development offices, 75–84.
      See also Centralized unit
      development offices
    corporations, 179–180
    to deans, 31–32, 68–69. *See also* Deans
      of colleges
    with interdisciplinary programs and
      university consortia, 87–95. *See also*
      Interdisciplinary programs
    professional contacts, 97–102. *See also*
      Professional contacts
    tensions between different unit offices,
      79–80
Religious affiliations, 8–9
Reports for unit development officers,
    111–113
Research
    and corporations, 177
    dedicated units for, 207–218. *See also*
      Dedicated research and service
      units

of prospects, 81. *See also* Prospect
    research
universities, 209
Reunions, 196
Rockefeller, John D., 12, 15
Role models, 113
Role of fund raisers, 19–23. *See also* Fund
    raising
Role of unit development officers, 31–38
    complexity of organization, 33
    disciplinary focus of, 33–34
    social contracts, 35–37
Rudolph, Frederick J., 9–10
Ryan, Ellen, 44, 45

Sabo, Sandra R., 44
Salespeople, 50, 56
Santayana, George, 1
Schon, Donald A., 254
Schools in Canada, 224
Schroeder, James C., 185
Scripps Institute of Oceanography (SIO),
    210, 212, 214, 216
Sectarianism, 8–9
Seiler, Timothy L., 199
Service units, 207–218
Seymour, Harold J., x, 18
Skills for development, 49–61, 103–107
    evaluation of, 58–61
    types of development officers, 50–52
    vector models for, 52–58
Slee, Peter, 117
Social contracts, 35–37
Solicitations, 142–143, 156, 158. *See also*
    Prospect research
Southern Alberta Institute of Technology in
    Calgary, 222
Special events, 147
Speechwriters, 215
Staff, 134
    completing work, 66–67
    educating for development, 200–201
    management of, 140–141
    working with, 72–73

Stanford University, 153
State universities, 9–10
Strategic integration, 119–121
Students, 90, 94. *See also* Alumni
    corporation access to graduates,
        176–178
    foundations, 163–164
Summerfield, Paul J., 232
Supervisors of unit development officers, 110
Synergy for development, 119–121

Tax laws, 179, 187
Taylor, T. U., 68
Technology, 243–245
Telemarketers, 54
Texaco, 180
Thatcher, Margaret, 230
Tilley, Catrin, 234
Titles for unit development officers, 36–37
Trade associations, 100
Training unit development officers, 109–114
Travers, Linus, 3
Trojahn, L., 45
Trust, 77
    between institutions, 94
    professional contacts, 101
    schools and colleges within
        universities, 90–92
2001 Monthly Planner (Grenzebach Glier &
    Associates), 153

Ufford, Walter S., 20
Unit development officer (UDO), vii–viii,
    23–26
    academic units, 185–198. *See also*
        Academic units
    Canadian terminology, 221
    characteristics of successful, 49–61.
        See also Skills for development
    relationships of, 65–102. *See also*
        Relationships of the unit
        development officer
    titles of, 36–37
    in the United Kingdom, 232–233

United Kingdom of Great Britain, 117–118,
    229–237
    comparisons to North America,
        229–232
    English law, 221–222
    lessons learned in, 233–236
    structure of unit development in,
        232–233
Universities, 33, 34
    in Canada, 224
    consortia of, 87, 92–94
    diversity in, 241–243
    schools and colleges within
        universities, 90–92
    unit development's place in, 252–255
University College London, UK, 233–234
University of Alberta, Edmonton, 224–225
University of Bradford, UK, 230
University of British Colombia, 224
University of Calgary, 225, 226
University of California, 210
University of Durham, England, 117. *See also*
    Durham Integrated Income Generation
    Model for Fund Raising
University of Edinburgh, UK, 234
University of North Carolina, 93, 161–162
University of Pittsburgh, 15
University of Southern California, 139, 172
University of Tennessee, 24
University of Texas, 65, 68
University of Toronto, 225
University of Virginia, 93
University of Western Ontario, 225
University of York, UK, 231

Vann, Harry, 171
Vector models for development officers' role,
    52–58
Velux, 177–178
Vendors of products, 177–178
Veysey, Laurence R., 10, 12, 25
Vision statements, 212
Volunteers, 56, 159
    as board of directors, 144

on development committees, 80
managers, 54

Ward, Charles Sumner, 13, 14–15
Web sites, 148–149, 197
Weld-Peter, 6
Wellesley College, 15
White, Andrew D., 11
Whitfield, George, 8, 20
WIIFM (What's in it for me?) factor, 204
Wilkerson, Steve, 44
Wilson, Woodrow, 16
Witherspoon, John, 40
Wolfson Research Institute, 123–124
Woodson, H. H., 65
Workshop for Development Officers in
    Collegiate Schools of Design, 99
Worth, Michael J., x, 50, 52
Writing style, 215–216

Yale University, 187
YMCA, 13, 14
York University, Toronto, 223